New Casebooks

WILLIAM BLAKE

New Casebooks

New Casebooks

WILLIAM BLAKE

EDITED BY DAVID PUNTER

Macmillan 1996
London

First published 1996 by
MACMILLAN PRESS LTD
Houndmills, Basingstoke, Hampshire RG21 6XS
and London
Companies and representatives
throughout the world

ISBN 0-333-54596–6 hardcover
ISBN 0-333-54597–4 paperback

A catalogue record for this book is available
from the British Library.

10   9   8   7   6   5   4   3   2   1
05   04   03   02   01   00   99   98   97   96

Printed in Hong Kong

Contents

v

Acknowledgements

The editor and publishers wish to thank the following for permission to use copyright material:

David Aers, for 'Representations of Revolution: From *The French Revolution* to *The Four Zoas* in *Critical Paths: Blake and the Argument of Method*, ed. Dan Miller, Mark Bracher and Donald Ault (1987), by permission of Duke University Press; Gavin Edwards, for 'Repeating the Same Dull Round' from *Unnam'd Forms: Blake and Textuality*, ed. Nelson Hilton and Thomas Vogler (1986). Copyright © 1986 The Regents of the University of California, by permission of the University of California Press; Jean H. Hagstrum, for 'Babylon Revisited, or the Story of Luvah and Vala' from *Blake's Sublime Allegory: Essays on the Four Zoas, Milton, and Jerusalem*, ed. Stuart Curran and Joseph A. Wittreich, Jr (1973). Copyright © 1973 by the University of Wisconsin Press, by permission of the University of Wisconsin Press; Laura Ellen Haigwood, for 'Blake's *Visions of the Daughters of Albion*: Revising an Interpretive Tradition', *San Jose Studies*, 11, 2 (1985). Copyright © 1985 San Jose State University Foundation, by permission of *San Jose Studies* and the author; Nelson Hilton, for 'Blake in the Chains of Being' from *The Literal Imagination: Blake's Vision of Words* (1983). Copyright © 1983 The Regents of the University of California, by permission of the University of California Press; David E. James, for 'Angels out of the Sun: Art, Religion and Politics in Blake's *America*', *Studies in Romanticism*, 18 (1979), by permission of *Studies in Romanticism*; W.J.T. Mitchell, for 'Visible Language: Blake's Wond'rous Art of Writing' from *Romanticism and Contemporary Criticism*, ed. Morris Eaves and Michael Fischer (1986). Copyright © 1986 by Cornell

University, by permission of Cornell University Press; George Quasha, for 'Orc as a Fiery Paradigm of Poetic Torsion' from *Blake's Visionary Forms Dramatic*, ed. David V. Erdman and John E. Grant (1970). Copyright © 1970 by Princeton University Press, by permission of Princeton University Press; David Simpson, for 'Reading Blake and Derrida: Our Caesars Neither Praised nor Buried' from *Unnam'd Forms: Blake and Textuality*, ed. Nelson Hilton and Thomas Vogler (1986). Copyright © 1986 The Regents of the University of California, by permission of the University of California Press; Brenda S. Webster, for 'Blake, Women and Sexuality' from *Critical Paths: Blake and the Argument of Method*, ed. Dan Miller, Mark Bracher and Donald Ault (1987), by permission of Duke University Press.

Every effort has been made to trace all the copyright holders but if any have been inadvertently overlooked the publishers will be pleased to make the necessary arrangement at the first opportunity.

General Editors' Preface

The purpose of this series of New Casebooks is to reveal some of the ways in which contemporary criticism has changed our understanding of commonly studied texts and writers and, indeed, of the nature of criticism itself. Central to the series is a concern with modern critical theory and its effect on current approaches to the study of literature. Each New Casebook editor has been asked to select a sequence of essays which will introduce the reader to the new critical approaches to the text or texts being discussed in the volume and also illuminate the rich interchange between critical theory and critical practice that characterises so much current writing about literature.

In this focus on modern critical thinking New Casebooks aim not only to inform but also to stimulate, with volumes seeking to reflect both the controversy and the excitement of current criticism. Because much of this criticism is difficult and often employs an unfamiliar critical language, editors have been asked to give the reader as much help as they feel is appropriate, but without simplifying the essays or the issues they raise. Again, editors have been asked to supply a list of further reading which will enable readers to follow up issues raised by the essays in the volume.

The project of New Casebooks, then, is to bring together in an illuminating way those critics who best illustrate the ways in which contemporary criticism has established new methods of analysing texts and who have reinvigorated the important debate about how we 'read' literature. The hope is, of course, that New Casebooks will not only open up this debate to a wider audience, but will also encourage students to extend their own ideas, and think afresh about their responses to the texts they are studying.

John Peck and Martin Coyle
University of Wales, Cardiff

Abbreviations

All references to Blake are to *The Complete Poetry and Prose of William Blake*, ed. David V. Erdman (Berkeley, CA; most recent edn 1982), abbreviated throughout as E. The volume follows the usual convention of giving both text and page references.

The following abbreviations are used for specific works of Blake:

A	*America, a Prophecy* (1793)
ARO	*All Religions are One* (*c.*1788)
BA	*The Book of Ahania* (1795)
BL	*The Book of Los* (1795)
BU	*The First Book of Urizen* (1794)
E	*Europe, a Prophecy* (1794)
EG	*The Everlasting Gospel* (*c.*1818)
FR	*The French Revolution* (1791)
FZ	*Vala, or, The Four Zoas* (1795–1804)
J	*Jerusalem* (1804–20)
M	*Milton, a Poem in 2 Books* (1804–8)
MHH	*The Marriage of Heaven and Hell* (*c.*1790–3)
NNR	*There is no Natural Religion* (*c.*1788)
PA	*Public Address* (*c.*1810)
SE	*Songs of Experience* (1789–94)
SI	*Songs of Innocence* (1789)
SL	*The Song of Los* (1795)
Thel	*The Book of Thel* (1789)
Tir	*Tiriel* (*c.*1789)
VDA	*Visions of the Daughters of Albion* (1793)

Introduction

DAVID PUNTER

This book contains ten essays written about Blake's poetry between 1970 and 1990. In this Introduction, I shall comment briefly on the essays and, more generally, on the nature and diversity of Blake criticism during those twenty years; but first it is necessary to set the scene, because criticism of Blake has a curious history. Much of it is by now well known. William Blake was largely unknown in his lifetime; very few of his poems were published, and most of the later work only saw the light of day, if at all, in enormously expensive limited editions, hand-produced by Blake himself. Towards the end of his life he was 'taken up' by a small group of younger men, including Edward Calvert and Samuel Palmer, but he was only really 'discovered' as a writer later in the nineteenth century.[1] A long critical essay by the poet Swinburne, and a substantial edition of his work by E.J. Ellis and W.B. Yeats, were turning-points in his reception,[2] and through the first half of the twentieth century his reputation steadily increased.

The Blake found by Ellis and Yeats was, of course, a very specific Blake, a Blake of Neoplatonic wisdom and arcane hermetic ideas. Many different Blakes have been discovered since then, perhaps most notably the prophet of liberation some of whose poems became hallmarks of the 1960s. Since then there has been a still increasing amount of critical activity; between 1974 and 1984 some 50 full-length monographs were published on Blake, together with a huge number of essays and articles, in English alone; this is to say nothing of criticism in other languages – there is, for instance, a thriving critical industry on Blake in Japanese, which is regrettably not represented in this collection.[3]

And the critics have had many difficulties to deal with. There is, for a start, the effect of the hand-produced nature of many of the texts, which means that no two copies of the major works are precisely the same. Even more importantly, there is the diversity of the Blake canon itself; the question, as we might put it, of what Blake's textuality is. For Blake was not only a poet: he was also a painter, in oils and watercolour; an illustrator of other writers' work; an engraver; he also wrote a few prose pieces and left behind him a number of annotations to key books of his age.

All of these activities were, for Blake, deeply and complexly interlocked; and therefore there is a preliminary danger in trying to separate the poetry out from the remainder of the 'text' which is Blake, this despite the fact that when his written work is put together, the whole output only comes to a few hundred pages, nothing that one could remotely compare with, for example, those giants of first-generation romanticism, Wordsworth or Coleridge. But then, was Blake a romantic? His writing evades literary categorisation. His openness to influences from the past was remarkable; but when it comes to his contemporaries, it has often been remarked that it is as though he worked in a bubble of his own devising, as uninterested in what was going on around him in literary circles as he was embroiled in the social and political life of his day.

In this collection, I have restricted myself to essays which deal with his poetry, although in at least one case the visual art is strongly alluded to and should ideally be seen as part of the same text as the verbal.[4] I have selected the essays according to three principles. First, they attend to a variety of poems, or more to the point, to a variety of Blake's modes of poetry, from the early songs to the later Prophetic Books. Clearly they cannot be comprehensive in this respect: but the student looking for a starting-point in, say, a Song of Experience or in the massive *Jerusalem* (1804–20) should be able to find something here which will open debate. And that has been my second principle of selection: each of these essays forms part of a larger debate within Blake studies. I have tried to choose the provocative rather than the bland, the questioning and the suggestive rather than the attempted final statement. And thirdly, and perhaps most important, I have chosen essays which reflect a diversity of modern approaches to criticism and to writing.[5]

Some of Blake's poems – 'London', for example, or *Visions of the Daughters of Albion* (1793), or *Jerusalem* – have been focal points for critical thinking about Blake during these twenty years. There are often good reasons for this: as we may glimpse when we come to discuss the essays themselves, the privileged poems are often ones which abut in significant ways onto contemporary concerns. Other areas of Blake's poetry – the Songs of Innocence, some of the books of the Infernal Bible, *Vala, or, The Four Zoas* (1795–1804) – have been less well attended to: this is sometimes because of historical factors, sometimes due to the sheer difficulty of the works themselves. For Blake is a difficult poet. There have been many ideas expressed about the nature and causes of this difficulty. More traditionally minded critics have talked about the extreme difficulty of pinning down Blake's intentions in his work. For reasons which we shall go into later, the search for authorial intention has been now all but abandoned by critics; we now hear more of the contradictory political pressures acting upon his writing, or about the psychological ambivalences which lie at the heart of his work, or about the involuted concern with textuality which always threatens to disrupt that work, to prevent it from achieving organic unity or a polished poetic surface.

But whatever the reasons, the difficulty remains; and alongside it an apparently endless fruitfulness. Perhaps indeed, as I have hinted above, we should abandon the task of trying to speak of 'Blake' and try instead to conceive of a multiplicity of 'Blakes', some of them already co-existing during his lifetime, during the span of his production, others being continually superimposed on the writing, rewritten and reread, as the poems themselves often were, before coming together into the apparently final form in which we now have them, the form in which they are set in the pages of the authoritative editions. For the student, I believe, this offers an unusual opportunity; Blake's work has so far managed, in a most remarkable way, to resist the process of 'becoming classic'. This is not to say that Blake has not been canonised; it would be a most unusual university or college course in literature which did not represent Blake's work. But there is, it is fair to say, still no settled unitary opinion about Blake, still no agreement as to quite *where* in the body of literature he belongs; and it is this sense of an open space in Blake which has made his work both peculiarly available, and simultaneously peculiarly resistant, to recent changes in critical awareness.

What there is, however, is a body of classic Blake criticism, which was already well in place by 1970, although this classic criticism pointed already in several different directions and reflected different concerns, different emphases, different readings. We can get our bearings, for example, by pointing to two of these classic works, Northrop Frye's *Fearful Symmetry: A Study of William Blake* (1947) and David V. Erdman's *Blake: Prophet Against Empire* (1954). Both of these books are brilliant; both represent years of engagement with Blake and research on his context and on his sources. Yet the Blakes which emerge from these two works seem almost wholly incompatible. Erdman's Blake is a man of his times, and a poet with a message to give to his times: a stubbornly engaged social thinker and responder, immersed in his daily environment as a London artisan at a time when the artisanate was unprecedentedly involved in thoughts of revolution.[6] Frye's Blake is an inheritor of great historic traditions: a myth-maker, deeply in touch with eternal sources of wisdom, engaged in his poetry in 'forging' – the metaphor is peculiarly Blake's – new ways of recounting old knowledge, asserting, whether consciously or not, his continuity with archetypal thought down the ages.

Perhaps I caricature two eminent books; but only slightly. What is clear is that the classic criticism of Blake left behind it certain questions unanswered. It left unanswered the question, as we have said, of Blake's intentions: what did he really mean by, on the one hand, professing violently strong beliefs while on the other clothing his expression of them in languages and forms too rebarbative to gain him any but the most minute of audiences? To put this in a slightly different form, it left unanswered the question of Blake's level of consciousness: to what extent did he know what he was doing, are the complexities of especially his later work the visible outcroppings of some deeply laid poetic and political scheme, or are we witnessing the products of a mind, if not deranged, then at least unaware in crucial ways of what it was up to? How could, we might say, a man with Blake's small education have known some of the things he seems to have known; or are we seeing coincidences, mirages, when we sense the correspondences between Blake's work and that of various groups of his forebears – literary, political, religious?

Thirdly, there were unanswered questions about the actual content of Blake's opinions, particularly in the fields of politics and sexuality. How, to put it crudely, can a radically advanced liberationist cohabit within the same psyche with a male chauvinistic despiser of strong femininity? Or, how can a poet with a message to give revise his work, again and again, in such ways as to make it more rather than less obscure to the very people to whom he professes to wish to speak? This could be put, fourthly, as a question about the 'forms' of Blake's texts: for opposite reasons, neither Erdman nor Frye approach textuality itself very closely, Erdman because he is primarily an interpreter, a critic who wants to know what things *mean*, Frye because he is primarily a systematiser, a critic who wants to know how things *fit*; but what this leaves open is the question of what Blake's texts actually *are*.

In speaking of literary critics before 1970, it can often be assumed that there was such a thing as 'traditional criticism'. This is, of course, a fallacy; and I hope that what I have already said is enough to show that it is a quite particular fallacy as far as Blake is concerned, for there was no one dominant view which prevailed. Blake the radical, Blake the revolutionary, Blake the mystagogue, Blake the satirist, Blake the madman, even Blake the failure, all of these Blakes were fully on view. Therefore the revolution in literary criticism which I am dating, for convenience, from 1970 came at Blake more obliquely than it struck the recognised classics, George Eliot, say, or Shakespeare, or even Wordsworth. Yet in or about 1970 there was, nonetheless, a revolution in literary criticism; and before proceeding with Blake we need to pay brief attention to what this revolution was.

Two images suggest themselves. The first has been coined by Catherine Belsey: it is of a 'Copernican revolution', whereby all the things which had been held to centre life and thought came to be seen as radically decentred.[7] Just as Copernicus infuriated his contemporaries by alleging that the earth goes round the sun rather than vice versa, so the various revolutions in thought from 1970 on confounded received views by insisting on a parallel process of decentring: decentring thought itself, decentring the conscious mind, decentring the male, and so on. The other image is of waves on a shore: this might initially sound too gentle for what actually happened during these decades, but perhaps we need to be reminded of the erosive power of waves, of the way in which even the most stalwart of rocks will succumb in the end to a succession of repeated shocks.

Where both images fail is in their attempt at symmetry or ready succession; for the critical revolution has not been like that. It has not been a matter of one change arriving, being absorbed, and then being neatly followed by another change. On the contrary, part of the problem of keeping one's feet over the last twenty years has been the vortex-like swirling, to use a Blakean image, of different and not always compatible ideas, almost always imported from apparently extra-literary disciplines – sociology, psychology, anthropology – which has provoked controversy, opened up opportunities, yet without providing a firm footing.

But if we cannot break this revolution into the neat symmetries of successive decentrings or successive erosions, we must nonetheless try to see what the key elements in it have been. My version of it has six; other versions will have a different number. These six, as I have said, cannot be chronologically precisely ordered, although I shall name them in the order in which I believe they affected criticism; and particularly, since this is our field, criticism of Blake. First, then, was Marxism. The crucial act performed by Marxism was the decentring of thought, which became a conditioned activity, within the more general realm of ideology and at the mercy of material life. For the Marxist, the crucial intellectual revolution involved the realisation of the non-primacy of the intellect itself, the acceptance that thought was conditioned by the economic process, that the products of thought could always be referred to the conditions of production of those thoughts, and ultimately to the class and economic nature of the society within which those thoughts were formed.

Second came the revolution effected by the absorption of psychoanalysis. Here the revolution was within the psyche itself: no longer could it be believed that the ego, the force within the psyche which sought intellectual control over the outer world, was primary or independent; there was something which lay at a deeper level of psyche and which interfered with all of the ego's projects, which was known only through dream, through parapraxis, and through the analytic process itself, and that something, variously known as the subconscious, the unconscious, the id, the 'That', was at the centre like a dark sun around which the pretensions of the ego revolved.

Compared with these two massive changes in thinking, the revolution of structuralism might seem tamer, more cerebral, but it was in fact not so: for the principal claim of structuralism was that below all the claims of independence of mind and individual power there lay a set of codes, embodied in myth but more importantly in language itself, which determined the limits on, the possibilities of, thought, speech and action. The roots of structuralism lay in anthropology and linguistics, in Lévi-Strauss and Saussure: its claim was to be able to find a super-system, a set of master-codes which would provide a solid ground for interpretation.

The fourth wave, sometimes called poststructuralism, but of which the most distinguished and present representative is the deconstruction fathered by Derrida, came at us from precisely the opposite direction. Where structuralism had threatened us with a master-narrative, with a story which would explain all other stories, with a narrative from which all other narratives must spring, deconstruction announced an end to all master-narrative. Its claim was for the importance of the marginal, the symptomatic, the misplaced and the displaced, the 'minute particular', in Blake's term, as against the sweep of pattern. Individual integrity, the notion of 'nature', the supremacy of political action, all disappeared in deconstruction into a maelstrom consisting of texts and the shattered shards of texts, words in endless play one against another, a dream or nightmare of textuality beside which all other human pretensions seemed bare and lame.

In turning now to feminism, the process of decentring is obvious: namely, the decentring of a patriarchal view, and of the practical and power-laden enforcement of that view, of history and of contemporary society and language. Feminism from the beginning undercut and continues to undercut the other revolutions, asserting that they are in the end partial, reflections of the masculine narcissism which has brought all systems – or even anti-systems – into being in the first place. At the same time, feminism has been strategically eclectic in its choice of insights and weapons, now turning to attend to the historical 'reality' of women's lives, now to versions of poststructuralism which would cast that very historical reality itself under radical doubt.

Finally, and despite other chronological vagaries certainly most recently, the new historicism comes as a further revolution which has already absorbed much of the territory claimed by its predecessors. In particular it comes as a materialism which is more enlightened, more flexible than its Marxist forebear, whose principal categories are not the crude ones of economics and class but the more general ones of power, regime, subjection; but at the same time it comes as an approach to textuality which claims to be more engaged than deconstruction, more alive to historical nuance, more alert to the mutual relations between text and context, more concerned with conceiving of the text as an active rather than a passive object in social and cultural history.

Turning back to the criticism of Blake, it has to be said that these revolutions often appear in Blake criticism in slightly muffled form. This is partly to do, as I have said above, with the already established multivocality and multipositionality of 'Blake'; but it has also something to do with what can be seen as a certain protective attitude which critics of Blake have towards their textual 'master', who is often also, as it turns out, their mentor as well. There have been two journals devoted entirely to the study of Blake, *Blake: An Illustrated Quarterly* and *Blake Studies;* both of them contain plenty of interesting material, and certainly neither has been immune to the successive critical shocks I have mentioned above, but to read them is nevertheless to discover that there is a great deal at stake in Blake criticism: it is tempting to say that the old nine-teenth-century sense of a *coterie* remains, infused and modified as it has become with theoretical advances.

Alongside these journals, however, there has to be set a further enormously significant element in Blake studies during the 1970s and 1980s, which was a number of important conferences which resulted in the publication of collections of essays (which are detailed in the Further Reading section[8]): here one can find genuine-ly new awarenesses pushing through, and it is in fact from these collections that many of the essays in the present volume are taken.

And we can, of course, find reflections, or perhaps better refrac-tions, of these theoretical advances in the essays I have reproduced. To begin with Marxism: this is the basic terrain of the essays by David E. James and David Aers (essays 3 and 9). James' piece, indeed, engages very explicitly with a Marxist argument. He is pri-marily concerned with the problem of historical reflection; with the question of what the relation might actually be between a poem and the context from which it emerges. He takes issue with those earlier critics, Erdman primary among them, who have implied that the relation is a simple one, that the interest of a piece of writing may be located in its relation to its own times, as though the media-tion, the essential mediation which makes a poem into a poem, is to be ignored or bypassed in the attempt to discover the historical truths which the poet embodies.

This is too simple for James, who, in a prolonged and detailed analysis of *America* (1793), continually draws our attention to the vital 'difference' of Blake's project, the way in which we can only apprehend the specificity of this project if we attend not only to history but also to form. We might say that such a model is, however, not too simple for Aers, whose essay is a full-throated appeal for us to take Blake's dealings with social revolution serious-ly. Where James argues for a relative autonomy of the realm of writing, Aers makes the contrary claim that since Blake dealt in the concepts of revolution it is open to us to judge his work accordingly, and to say that this or that poem does indeed advance a socially helpful or progressive argument, while this or that other one does not: his test case is *Vala, or, The Four Zoas*, on the site of which he enacts a set of discriminations about attitudes to society and change.

There is a larger argument behind this, which I hope will be obvious to the reader: to put it simply, it is an argument about whether writing can deal in revolution or only in 'revolution', change in the real or change in the imaginary. Clearly Blake's work can be seen as a crucial site for this argument, for to Blake, as we know, the imaginary was the real, or so he claimed in a series of formulations which have vexed us ever since.[9] What we have to deal with here is an extreme version of the imagination, the version which could drive Blake to castigate Wordsworth for being over-affected by 'natural objects' rather than by the 'visionary forms' which to Blake were more true avatars of the 'real' than the trivial evidences to be garnered in the course of everyday life.[10]

The psychoanalytic debate in this book goes on between Jean Hagstrum and Brenda Webster (essays 2 and 10). Hagstrum's piece is contentious, and he knows it. In the course of detailed discussion of *Jerusalem* and *Vala, or, The Four Zoas*, he advances a case for seeing Blake's view of the perversions of human sexuality against a Freudian background; but the centre of his reading lies in his implicit claim that Blake was essentially percipient about those perversions which he saw all round him. At root, Hagstrum believes, there is a sane and healthy Blake peering out at us from around the branches of the Tree of Mystery; there is a benevolent Blake who knows the deep ironies of his problems with the 'Female Will'; and beyond that there is a happy version of sexual love, marriage and family to be vindicated if we can only tell aright the 'Story of Luvah and Vala'.

Webster's perspective is altogether different. Blake, she would not be alone in saying, is embroiled in contradictions. He loves women; he hates and despises women. He scorns violence; but he admires that violence which is for a 'just cause', while reserving to himself what the justification of that 'just cause' might be. Certainly Blake has a 'psychology' in mind; but again there is a larger question here behind the argument, which can be put in two different ways. First, we might recast it in Marxist form: how can we possibly say that Blake knew more than his prevailing ideology could permit him to know? Second, we can put it in psychological form: to what extent is Blake able to get free from the psychic constraints of his own times, any more (we might now ask) than Freud was later able to free himself from the constraints of turn-of-the-century Vienna?

Whether a structuralist debate is here properly presented is rather harder to discern. I would point to two of the essays, although in both cases with degrees of hesitation. In the first place, George Quasha's essay (1) engages with a basically structuralist position, in so far as it takes on some of Frye's claims in the aptly titled *Fearful Symmetry*. Symmetry can be seen as the principle which underlies all structuralism, with its fixation on binary opposites; thus it also underlies Frye's mythic approach to Blake. Quasha's attempt is to set alongside this emphasis on symmetry an alternative, a concept of 'torsion', which he represents and justifies as a more modern way of thinking through crucial issues about identity and difference.

The argument of W.J.T. Mitchell's essay (7), I would say, also develops in part from structuralism; for Mitchell's concern, both here and elsewhere, is essentially with structure. But in this case it is curiously and significantly inflected; for the structure so beloved of the structuralists becomes radically problematised in Mitchell's work. For what, after all, is this 'structure' if not mere replication of the assumptively primal structure of language? Mitchell's radical interrogation of this assumption, carried out in the name of and on the textual body of Blake, consists in a reassertion of the rights of the image; firstly as a restatement of the importance of the visual arts, in Blake and elsewhere, but secondly and more importantly as a relativisation of the all-importance of verbal language, as a salutary reminder of the uncertainty which attends our efforts – although Mitchell does not say this – when we try to recast the dream, the unconscious, that which unsettles structure, in terms of language alone.

Deconstruction in this collection could be said to be the privileged mode of the essay by Nelson Hilton (essay 4); to be the site of argument in the essay by David Simpson (essay 8); and to be the contestant in the essay by Mitchell. To turn first to Hilton, what we find in this essay (as in much other work by Hilton and Thomas A. Vogler[11]) is an extraordinary in-depth attention to words. Although I believe that Hilton's essay is deconstructive, there are points where I am perilously inclined to call it instead 'ultra-etymological'; and I mean this as a compliment, because what is here evident is a remarkable grasp on the power of words: words as material objects, words as signifiers, words as living histories of their own times and of times before. If this is deconstruction, one is tempted to say, then its sense of history surpasses that of many historians.

Simpson, a very fine critic of the romantics, is perhaps unfairly represented by the rather short and occasional essay reproduced here; nevertheless, I believe that in the course of it he raises a number of crucial issues and, more importantly, draws together Blake, Rousseau and Derrida in one of those important but unexpected collocations which provide the spark of criticism. Neither Hilton's nor Simpson's essays are, we might say, 'pointed'; in other words, they do not seek to place Blake's texts at the service of a linear critical narrative, yet it is also true that they reveal that within those texts, especially according to Simpson's reading, whole acts of instituting are continually going on, and these acts of instituting are obviously of wider importance. I have mentioned Mitchell's essay above; suffice it to add that Derrida's complex and ambivalent logocentricity is here also attacked, and the peculiarities of Blake's artistic practices again prove an intriguing test case for contemporary theory.

The feminist argument in this collection is carried largely by Laura Haigwood and Brenda Webster (essays 5 and 10), although it has an Ur-text, which is the perceived celebration of married love in Blake by Hagstrum, to which Webster makes direct reference. Haigwood's piece seems to me of the first importance because it advances the case for a wider definition of 'feminine positions' than is customary in Blake criticism: particularly in the figure of Oothoon, Haigwood advances the case for seeing woman not as victim alone but also as wielder of power; in this respect it seems to me that she gets closer to the ambiguities and reticences of Blake's thought than many another.

Rather as in the relationship between James' and Aers' essays above, Webster is rather firmer about this, and inclined to reside less in ambivalence than in the available political value of the texts. The fact of the matter is, as Webster reminds us, that whatever Blake's professions – or perhaps more importantly the professions of various of his critics – there is a deep-lying problem in Blake, or perhaps a problem of deep 'lying' in another sense of that word: women are after all only 'emanations' in Blake; if they escape from that soft trap, from that golden cage, then they are evil, they are Rahab, they are the consummation of corruption, the source of infection and contamination. This is, of course, not directly to assign blame to Blake (although under the circumstances of [intermale?] mentorship alluded to above a discourse of blame is hard to avoid no matter what the theoretical underpinnings); but the texts tell their own story, and we must be prepared for it to be an unpalatable one.

Perhaps there is room for a further comment on Blake's texts and the issue of the relations between the sexes. It is, possibly, a very obvious one: but it is that there appears to be a disjunction in Blake between what we might think of as clearly sexual activity and the activity of the emotions, or even the passions. It seems to me that it would be difficult to deny that Blake is one of our most important poets of the passions; but when we see what passions are upper-most for him, then we inevitably enter into a world where gender difference is all-consuming, because primary among those passions are jealousy, envy and, as Blake himself said, hate, the passions of the infant. Although it is also true that Blake is a great poet of for-giveness, there can be no forgiveness unless there is something to forgive; and the inner worlds presented by Blake are rather full of things to forgive, of angers and inward violences; and in all of these inner-world scenarios, masculine/feminine patterning takes its part.

It is probably a little early to pin down the new historicism in the world of Blake criticism; but three of these essays clearly touch upon its main premises. James (essay 3) gives us the sense that power is not mediated through politics alone; he touches on the crucial role of religion in the power politics of Blake's books, and this is a salutary reminder of what we might be always tending to forget in a secular age as we watch religion and its attendant cer-tainties and problems sliding off against a historical backdrop. Hilton's essay (4) also necessarily touches on new historicist con-cerns, partly through the profound historical sense which informs it but also through the prevailing awareness of the ways in which texts are material objects that make an intervention in history as much as being at the mercy of it. In terms of this argument, the question of the extent to which Blake was read – or rather, not read – is obviously important, but it is not the end of the matter; some texts in history are like time-bombs, waiting to explode at a later date, and this does not necessarily defuse the historical anxiety from which they speak.

Finally, and I know that it might seem very contentious to take it under the heading of the new historicism, there is the essay by Gavin Edwards (6); the main underpinnings of this essay come from linguistic philosophy, and particularly from the speech-act theory of

J.L. Austin and others. Yet I think it can be argued that this does indeed fall within the broad remit of the new historicism; for Edwards' intention is to pursue Blake's linguistic usages into the crevices of their historical realisation, and indeed what could be more redolent of historic power than the perennial action of performatives, their jamming, their effectivity, their embeddedness? Edwards' chosen backdrop is an unusual one in the last twenty years, but it is one which undoubtedly fructifies a crucial area of Blake, as perhaps it does of all our lives, by daring to utter the name of that element within us which persists in the 'same dull round'.

If we are to take up in general the issue of contemporary criticism and its relation to Blake, then we are confronted with an intervening question, which is about the relation of these theoretically grounded approaches to poetry in particular. For poetry is the hardest nut to crack. This is so partly because many of the new theories rely crucially on a notion of narrative to underpin them; it is so also because the new theories are interested in disruptions, but of course disruptions are the very stuff of poetry from beginning to end. There is therefore a danger of a kind of mirror-imaging going on when we hold up Derrida to Blake, as Simpson so ably points out;[12] and there is also a danger that the categories in which theoretical models try to work might always be outflanked by the poets themselves.

If we are to ask the question of where purchase on Blake's texts might be found, then we are immediately and emblematically outflanked by the question which comes back from Blake, which is about the nature of 'purchase' in the first place: where might we buy wisdom, and how might we buy it for a song? Yet if we are to resist these metaphors of purchase, or indeed to resist, in the sense of deconstructing, all metaphorising, then we find ourselves in a terrain far from Blake. Perhaps this is one of the crucial questions that we need to address back to the critics: what is it to invest such effort into de- or reconstructing the works of a single 'author' (and, indeed, it is true that the criticism is dominated, as it is not in, for example, the case of Wordsworth, by single-author critics)? One of the questions not addressed in this volume is this: what does it mean to be a critic of Blake? Where is it that one situates oneself? And, perhaps most important of all, against what is it that one is situating oneself, in fantasy – for there are crucial questions of fantasy identification here which need more address.[13]

I shall conclude this Introduction with two practical points. The first is one which I have already broached above: which is to do with the 'illuminations'. Blake was, to reiterate, not a poet only: he was a maker who saw the verbal and visual arts as moving in close counterpoint – some would say in close harmony, but that would be to beg several questions. If asked about his occupation, Blake would have said that he was an engraver; an artisan who brought to a certain material point designs already executed by another. This obviously has strong resonances with the decentring projects of contemporary criticism: we have here a question about the voice and what speaks through the voice, and unlike his romantic contemporaries Blake had first-hand knowledge of what it is like not to be an *auteur*, to be rather one who executes that which has been pre-thought, pre-imagined. His flights of imagination might now seem to us extraordinary, but they were achieved against the most pragmatic of backgrounds.

The second point, which is even more practical, should constitute a note on Blake texts. There are two essential Blake texts. One is that edited by Geoffrey Keynes; the other is that of Erdman.[14] They differ in crucial ways. The Keynes text is accessible; the Erdman is much less so. This difference derives very largely, not from a difference about which of Blake's texts might be 'authentic', but rather from the fact that Blake did not use ordinary punctuation. A lot of the time he does not punctuate at all; sometimes he uses punctuation marks which are not known to modern punctuation and which are difficult to reproduce typographically.

Thus the two texts are different, but both are indispensable. Advice to the student is to use the Keynes text wherever possible and for ordinary work on Blake; although a great deal of the punctuation is supplied by Keynes himself, very few have queried his results: he had an editorial and bibliographical rapport with Blake which we would now find hard to challenge. But if you wish to go deeper into Blake, to see some of the problematic incoherences of his work at first hand, then you must look at the Erdman text, which is without punctuation, and which therefore suggests many more startling verbal and imagistic connections which the Keynes text would forbid.[15] In conclusion, it should also be added that if you need, and you should in the context of this volume, a version of Blake which includes a substantial amount of the visual material, then you need *The Illuminated Blake* (1974), also edited by Erdman.[16]

NOTES

1. Despite more recent attempts at a very difficult task, the most reliable and readable biography of Blake is probably still Mona Wilson, *The Life of William Blake* (London, 1927); see also Deborah Dorfman, *Blake in the Nineteenth Century* (New Haven, CT, 1969).

2. A.C. Swinburne, *William Blake: A Critical Essay* (London, 1868); *The Works of William Blake, Poetic, Symbolic, and Critical*, ed. E.J. Ellis and W.B. Yeats (3 vols, London, 1893).

3. See, on this as on many other matters, the continuing bibliographical work of Gerald E. Bentley, Jr, beginning from Bentley and Martin K. Nurmi, *A Blake Bibliography* (Minneapolis, 1964).

4. See W.J.T. Mitchell, 'Visible Language: Blake's Wond'rous Art of Writing' (pp. 123–48 below).

5. I should also say that to avoid duplication I have not reprinted any of the essays already available in the excellent *Essential Articles for the Study of William Blake 1970–1984*, ed. Nelson Hilton (Hamden, CT, 1986).

6. The most important background book here is E.P. Thompson, *The Making of the English Working Class* (London, 1963).

7. See Catherine Belsey, *Critical Practice* (London, 1980), pp. 130–46.

8. For example, *Blake in His Time*, ed. Robert N. Essick and Donald Pearce (Bloomington, IN, 1978); *Interpreting Blake*, ed. Michael Phillips (Cambridge, 1978); *Unnam'd Forms: Blake and Textuality*, ed. Hilton and Thomas A. Vogler (Berkeley, CA, 1986).

9. See, for example, Blake, 'There is No Natural Religion', Second Series (*c*.1788) (E 2–3) and 'All Religions are One' (*c*.1788) (E 3).

10. See Blake, Annotations to Wordsworth's *Poems* (1826) (E 665).

11. See Further Reading – for example, Hilton, *Literal Imagination: Blake's Vision of Words* (Berkeley, CA, 1983); Vogler, 'Intertextual Signifiers and the Blake of That Already', *Romanticism Past and Present*, 9 (1985), 1–33.

12. See pp. 160–1 below.

13. See David Punter, 'The Sign of Blake', *Criticism*, 26 (1985).

14. *Blake: Complete Writings, with Variant Readings*, ed. G. Keynes (London, 1966); *The Complete Poetry and Prose of William Blake*, ed. David V. Erdman (Berkeley, CA, 1982).

15. There are also, of course, some very useful selected texts; see, for example, *William Blake: Selected Poetry and Prose*, ed. Punter (London, 1988).

16. *The Illuminated Blake*, ed. Erdman (Garden City, NY, 1974).

1

Orc as a Fiery Paradigm of Poetic Torsion

GEORGE QUASHA

THEORY: A MYTH OF THE FUNCTIONING ARTIST

For the darkness of Asia was startled
At the thick-flaming, thought-creating fires of Orc.
(*SL* 6:6–7:E 67)

When I make sculpture all the speeds, projections, gyrations, light changes are involved in my vision, as such things I know in movement associate with all the possibilities possible in other relationships. Possibly steel is so beautiful because of all the movement associated with it, its strength and function. Yet it is also brutal, the rapist, the murderer, and death-dealing giants are also its offspring... . I have carved marble and wood but the major number of my works have been steel, which is my most fluent medium and which I control from start to completed work without interruption. There is gratification in being both conceiver and executor without intrusion.

(David Smith)[1]

The birth of rising of Orc, seen in archetypal perspective as the first phase of a cycle, has come to seem an inevitable component of Blake's meaning. Yet 'the Orc cycle' may be a more characteristic creation of Northrop Frye's cartography than of Blake's poetic system, which strove for escape from circular closure in space and time. A careful reading of *America*, either from a strictly historical perspective, as employed by David Erdman, or from the perspective established by intrinsic structural analysis, seriously raises the question of the relevance of any cyclic symmetry to the poem engraved in 1793.[2] Frye himself is careful to leave Orc in his first appearance some breathing space: '... Orc is the power of human desire to achieve a better world which produces revolution and foreshadows the apocalypse; the "Preludium" to *America* represents him as having arrived at puberty determined to set the world on fire as a promising youngster should do. To the reactionaries, of course, he is a demonic and hellish power, rising up to destroy everything that is sacred and worth conserving.'[3] Careful, further, to indicate the auspicious aspect of the cyclic view: '... Orc, then, is not only Blake's Prometheus but his Adonis, the dying and reviving god of his mythology. Orc represents the return of the dawn and the spring and all the human analogies of their return: the continuous arrival of new life, the renewed sexual and reproductive power which that brings, and the periodic overthrow of social tyranny.... Orc dies as the buried seed dies, and rises as it grows; winter nights become long and gloomy, but at the depth of winter the light slowly returns.'[4] The 'cyclic' inseparability of Orc and Urizen, however, records Blake's 'pessimism' about actual political revolutions, though opposing principles do maintain their separate identities and potentialities: 'If the dragon is itself old Orc, then surely is not Orc simply a dragon who has the power to shed his skin from time to time?'[5] Frye, finally, notes the probability that Blake came to emphasise Orc's identity with his opposite only *gradually*.

If we are to consider the full poetic implications of this evolution of the archetypal perspective, we must define not only Orc's function in the early prophecies but also the principle inherent in his particular action there. Clearly we must identify Orc with political revolution, mainly in its productive role, but to discover the principle involved we must explore its more complex psychological and aesthetic operations as well.

Blake's mode of visionary thought, as Frye demonstrates extensively, involves each poetic meaning in the furthest possible ranges of a dynamic metaphoric system. His mental habit of seeing every Particular as containing the cosmos – ontogeny recapitulating phylogeny – relates him to the earliest mythopoeic thinkers. Recognition of the creative act (*poiein*) as a metaphor for its own process – a Zagreus-Dionysus myth – is characteristic of the ancient oral-traditional prophetic poet, who sees his art – the very powers of tradition, order, truth, and vision – as a craft and as literal performance.[6] Art delights in art (to paraphrase Blake's 'Life delights in life') and is self-begetting. It is the duty and burden of such a poet to realise continually the human capacity for skilful self-renewal in the here and now, to *make* history. The future, as a perception within the generative poetic act, is continuous with past and present. So Blake resembled the primordial poets he honoured, while to an unexampled degree he converted phenomenological awareness into creative principle. Verbal invention came to imply perpetual revolution within the expanding vortex of human consciousness. And the violent birthlike experience of apocalypse he embodied in a language structure which from our vantage point resembles organic evolution: a cumulative, temporally linear, unpredictably irregular progression toward more complex forms.

Early in his work Blake embraced an affirmative principle of growth:

> ... the ratio of all we have already known is not the same that it shall be when we know more....
> The desire of Man being Infinite the possession is Infinite & himself Infinite....
> As the true method of knowledge is experiment the true faculty of knowing must be the faculty which experiences. This faculty I treat of.
>
> (E 2)

Over the years his description of Intellectual and Imaginative expansion varied, emphasising Poetic Genius and Prophetic Character and de-emphasising 'experiment', but the fundamental notion endured: that the prophetic poem is the vehicle of visionary travail, the Chariot of Genius. If art is the process of evolving spirit, the working artist is the agent of remodelled man, at his best conceiving or inventing unexampled forms, expanding the medium:

> I know my Execution is not like Any Body Else. I do not intend it should be so; none but Blockheads copy one another. My Conception & Invention are on all hands allowd to be Superior. My Execution will be found so too.
>
> (*PA*: E 571)

In no respect does Blake seem more contemporary than in this conception of man (metaphorically the working artist) as the willing inhabitant of a universe of open possibilities: 'Every thing possible to be believ'd is an image of Truth' (*MHH* 8:E 36). There is practically no end to parallels with Blake in our contemporary world of artists, and even the manner of expression of a sculptor like David Smith seems Blakean: 'Everything imagined is reality / The mind cannot conceive unreal things.'[7] In one stream of the 'modern' – the structurally 'open' and experimental – form does not obey paradigm but takes the particular impress of the creative act, which shapes 'barren' nature into human identity. 'Invention depends Altogether', insisted Blake, as do many artists and poets of our time, 'upon the Execution or Organisation; as that is right or wrong so is the Invention perfect or imperfect' (Annotations to Reynolds: E 626). And in this definition, perfection means accurate *function*, the flawless transmutation of medium into shape; it is 'relative' in Einstein's sense of particularity in a universe without geometric paradigm, but 'absolute' in the aesthetic sense of irreducible formal identity. For creative man, as for his analogue the body politic, erection of a standard of authority outside the imagination is an absurdity, an enslavement by perverse religion or commercialism, a failure to realise the potentials of indeterminate direction. Falsely closed form is a Narcissistic parody of creation.

Orc in *America*, I intend to argue, is a specific manifestation of a principle of renewal through 'thought-creating fires', the basis for enduring social and political revolution: primal (and primordial) Energy released as *formative power*, the creative force of the universe alembicated by human vision-in-action, metaphorically the generative action of a dying-reviving god. To be sure, Orc, the active creative principle, must ultimately be 'married' to the principle of poetic prophecy or message, its 'contrary' in a fallen, self-divided world. The early Los, as he emerges in *The Book of Urizen*, exemplifies the worst tendencies of passive intellect subserving misguided prophecy and false authority; having 'shrunk from his task' (5:1:E 76), he is trapped in Urizen's circle of dead forms until he finds courage to heat up his smithy with Energy's transforming fires. In this symbolic drama of the poet's struggle toward material message, the later 'Orc cycle' enacts a failure of generative power to unite with stable and relevant social vision. Culture gives way to inertia; evolutionary progression grinds to a halt from the pull of historical gravity.

A partial realisation of the Orc principle is Fuzon, an inferior poet, so to speak, who leaves Urizen's Egypt but lacks the genius to forge a new orb (in *The Book of Ahania*). He confuses or fuses mere novelty, and consolidates rather than transcends the Urizenic limits. His Robespierrean perversion of generative action to destructive ends[8] illustrates for Blake the tragic failure of imagination, on every level, to discover appropriately functional order. The result is empty rhetoric, Narcissistic self-deception ('I am God, said he, eldest of things!'); fire in tyrannical hands – Orc as pyromaniac – dramatises the reversibility of any principle in the absence of vision: Orc failing into cycle is the medium without the message.

Yet a message not continually rediscovered through an evolving medium is a still greater risk, and the Orc cycle is paralleled in Blake's cultural ecology in the failure of the main English poets, starting with Dryden, to carry on where Chaucer, Shakespeare, and Milton left off. Settled in a socially unrealistic and poetically limiting passivity, the Neoclassicists saw nothing new under the sun, and their technique knew, from Blake's point of view,

> Enough of Artifice but Nothing Of Art. Ideas cannot be Given but in their minutely Appropriate Words nor Can a Design be made without its minutely Appropriate Execution.... Unappropriate Execution is the Most nauseous of all affectation & foppery.
>
> (*PA*: E 565)

Johnson's disdain for the streaks of the tulip, the poetic unit of discrete evolution, meant settling for the tautology of mere literature, 'Pope's Metaphysical Jargon of Rhyming', abstraction rather than 'Knowledge ... by Perception at once' (E 565, 653). To the inertia of poetic closure Blake posed the prosodic counter-principle, symbolised by Orc, of forced progression through the fertile penetration of *any* closed system.

On the level of the medium itself, *poiein* is the Orc-Poet's breaking *into* the mind of the reader who 'sees all things thro' narrow chinks of his cavern': 'this I shall do, by printing in the infernal method, by corrosives, which in Hell are salutary and medicinal, melting apparent surfaces away, and displaying the infinite which was hid' (*MHH* 14:E 38–9). As by a Cubist painting, a Surrealist movie, or Brechtean-Artaudean theatre, the reader-viewer is not permitted to be a serene spectator of the cultural artifact; he must enter directly the infernal, transforming process which 'rouzes the faculties to act' by alienating him from the comforts of conventional literary form. As Orc shatters the stony law and scatters 'religion' to enable the inhabitants to rush together with renewed force, Blake would confuse the faculties – Rimbaud's 'dérèglement de tous les sens' – to enable the imagination, through a fortunate fall of the senses, to hatch from its shell of Innocence: once revived by its fiery entrance into perilous passage, the expanded inner eye gazes, from a perspective of the infinite, at the world outside the poem.

This translation of Zagreus-Adonis into aesthetic function metaphorically extends both the surface-piercing heat of the 'infernal method' and its equivalent in verbal action, which I suggest calling *poetic torsion*. Torque, a turning or twisting force, is what produces a rotary effect or torsion. Its prosodic and syntactic dynamics characterise the poetry of 'process', as distinguished by Frye from the poetry of 'artifact'.[9] If the latter is Aristotelian, aesthetic, and structurally conventional, the poetry of process is Longinian, psychological, and often unconventional or nonparadigmatic. Linguistically, the poem conceived as conventional artifact refines the model of 'intensive' syntax, in normalised grammar (rational or closed discourse); the poem conceived as psychological or visionary process develops out of the associational or 'extensive' syntax of the spoken language (expressive or open discourse).[10]

If we define poetic structure as the concrete embodiment of the principles which generate it, we can say that an ideal reader re-enacts those principles by following the temporal sequence of the text and of any variant accompaniment such as Blake's illuminations. Within their symbolic drama, the plots of Blake's narrative poems direct the reader-viewer along the curve of visionary experience, generally that of an opening circle or series of epicycles leading, ideally, to human action in the literal world. An expanding vortex of 'centrefleeing' force in the poem must be alembicated by a 'centreseeking' force in the reader's mind. In other terms, the movement from artistic fission – a splitting or rending action – to perceptual fusion or reconstitution repeats the process of human redemption, the movement from fall or self-division to reunion, wholeness, incarnation. Poetry saves man by energising the spiritual process that revives the bonds of communication, and Blake's Orclike attempt to arouse young men of the new age seems, from today's perspective, to herald the action-poetry of 'howl', the oral art-form of anticultural defiance, or the poem as rapist and death-dealing giant.

AN ALLEGORY: OPENING THE MIND

The plot or mythos of *Visions of the Daughters of Albion* essentially resembles that of *America* (Preludium and Prophecy) as an imitation of the action of universal propagation, human progression and, by implication, evolution. The general paradigm of penetration–fertilisation–birth specifically modulates in *America* to a pattern of sexual, political, and poetic redemption which may be followed on several dramatic levels: a potent young man rescues his mother from a cruel and illegitimate father (an 'Oedipus complex' myth); a national hero saves a fallen continent from a fierce dragon (an epic myth, comparable to *Beowulf* or the story of St George); youth defiantly steals the source of power from the aged (a Promethean myth); the Male Will to change triumphs over the Female Will to stasis (a yin-yang analogue of organic and poetic process). In bare outline the allegorical action is:

rape – forced break in a closed system; human touch; friction or the traction of contraries in contact;

outcry – human sound, initially lamentation; verbal 'seed' of fertile human identity in 'barren' natural ecology; torsion; a system of forces, released in waves;

prophetic form – the increment of formative power or the birth of new form itself; poetry; revolution; eventually, apocalypse.

It is my working hypothesis that Blake intends us to read the dramatic action of *Visions* as foreshadowing and, in a sense, producing that of *America*, and I see the Preludium, written after both poems, as a mythical regression to a time 'earlier' than either drama that structurally bridges the two.

In the narrative of *Visions*, Oothoon's apparently willing but precarious passage from Innocence toward Experience is redirected by Bromion's rape to produce her rapid and powerful self-actualisation, which supplies the controlling dynamics of the poem. Consider her new perception of the distortions of appearance: '... Theotormon is a sick mans dream / And Oothoon is the crafty slave of selfish holiness.... the youth shut up from / The lustful joy shall forget to generate & create an amorous image.... Are not these ... / The self enjoyings of self denial? ... Can that be Love, that drinks another as a sponge drinks water? ... Such is self-love that envies all!' (6–7:E 48–9). It is hardly accidental that brutal 'interference' has engendered this poetic expression of Blake's own revolutionary psychology, since the price of true vision in the fallen (modern) world is a harsh exaction. And by the redeeming logic of the fortunate fall, Oothoon by facing that rending with clarity and courage rises a step higher in the spiritual evolution of mankind.

The poetic rite of Oothoon's passage repeats the Orc paradigm:

rape – forced division of her virgin world ('in twain') despite her good intentions in leaving Leutha's vales;

outcry – her call, first, to Theotormon's eagles and, second, to Theotormon himself, lamenting his refusal to accept her;

prophetic form – her new identity and long final speech, symbolic of the birth of poetry, the language of Blake's own thought.

Dramatically, her function is that of revolutionary Orc and of the Prophetic Character generally, to voice a Declaration of Independence from the manacles of slave morality and church oppression and to state the grounds of positive morality, 'for every thing that lives is holy!' (her concluding words: 8:10; cf. A 8:13). Poetry here is the Adamic naming of newly perceived realities, deepening from psychological to political perspectives.

Structurally the allegory presents the seed of prophetic Orc, as fertilised in the body of America: 'the child / Of Bromion's rage, that Oothoon shall bring forth in nine moons time' (2:1–2) – implicitly the poetic body of *Visions*. The later poem will 'bear' the mature Orc visibly, struggling from the womb-earth in the second Preludium page, then liberated, in the upper left corner of the first Prophecy page – as if phallically entering the body of *America*. Oothoon's morning song celebrates this approaching realisation: 'Red as the rosy morning, lustful as the first born beam' (*VDA* 7:27:E 49).

In a modulating poetic sequence, Oothoon metaphorically becomes the shadowy daughter of Urthona ('American plains': A 2:10), much as Orc transfuses into Fuzon, or as visual figures metamorphose from plate to plate – e.g., the leaping female at the top right of the *America* title page transforming into a leaping male at the top left of *America* 3 (the *spirit* of Oothoon inhering in Orc?). And a still more important bridge between the poems establishes the dramatic necessity for a second rape of the American body, this time by her own child. In *Visions* Oothoon's psychological liberation is ultimately unsuccessful, never progressing beyond mere words, the same dull round of lamentation over and over ('every morning':8:11). And her role as Echo to a Narcissus-Theotormon, reaching us as the echoing voices of enslaved Daughters, is twice removed from effective prophecy. What is this feminine self-enclosure in complaint but a more insidious form of the self-enjoyings of self-denial? And how can this cry for 'little glancing wings' (of poetry?) do other than petrify, finally, into an 'iron tongue' (A 1:9)? Blake's meaning – like Ezra Pound's in his insistence on 'ideas into action' – is that a poetry which deplores the evils of a time, without offering a positive vision of action, is but a disguised version of the basic evil of intellectual passivity, a self-satisfied withdrawal to literary cloisters. True poetic lament, like Enion's (FZ II 35:E 318) which voices Blake's own anguish over art's failure to transmute evil, figures only as a moment within evolving prophecy, which transcends pathos.

If self-pitying Oothoon cannot bring 'Expansion to the eye of pity' (VDA 8:3), she does sing poetry's tortuous struggle to break the closed circuit of self. In its torque of genesis her language expresses the tragic joy of Orc, and of poetry that sometimes has to function within the isolated self as both male and female. Yet Blake's kind of poetry is not parthenogenic, any more than the upward curve of the Orclike twining in D'Arcy Thompson's description below is a pure phenomenon of willpower. Both vine and poem must climb through uncertain torsions, their traction resulting from actual confrontations of contraries. Unlike Wordsworth, Blake did not suffer a direction-reversing disillusionment over political revolution. Appalled by its failures, he re-enacted it himself, in mental rather than corporeal warfare. Orc may dwindle allegorically into cycle, but the Orc principle fires the smithy of the major prophecies.

VERBAL TORSION

In 'twining' plants, which constitute the greater number of 'climbers', the essential phenomenon is a tendency of the growing shoot to revolve around its vertical axis.... This tendency to revolution – circumvolution, as Darwin calls it, revolving nutation, as Sachs puts it – is very closely comparable to the process by which an antelope's horn (such as the koodoo's) acquires its spiral twist, and is due, in like manner, to inequalities in rate of growth of the growing stem: with this difference between the two, that in the antelope's horn the zone of active growth is confined to the base of the horn, while in the climbing stem the same phenomenon is at work throughout the whole length of the growing structure. The growth is in the main due to 'turgescence', that is to the extension, or elongation, of ready-formed cells through the imbibition of water; it is a phenomenon due to osmotic pressure.... The essential fact ... is that in twining plants we have a marked tendency to inequalities in longitudinal growth on different aspects of the stem.... There is very generally to be seen an actual *torsion* of the twining stem – a twist, that is to say, about its own axis.... When a stem twines around a smooth cylindrical stick the torsion does not take place, save 'only in that degree which follows as a mechanical necessity from the spiral winding': but ... stems which had climbed around a rough stick were all more or less, and generally much, twisted.... The mechanical explanation would appear to be very simple.... In the case of the roughened support, there is a temporary adhesion or 'clinging' between it and the growing stem which twines around it; and a system of forces is thus set up, producing a 'couple'.... The twist is the direct result of this couple, and it disappears when the support is so smooth that no such force comes to be exerted.... The effect of torsion will be to intensify any such peculiarities of sectional outline which [the twining stem] may possess, though not initiate [them] in any originally cylindrical structure....

(D'Arcy Wentworth Thompson)[11]

By no means an orderly Dantescan rising
but as the winds veer
    ... as the winds veer and the raft is driven
  and the voices ...
    as the winds veer in periplum ...
      (Ezra Pound, *Canto LXXIV*)

Vinelike torsion – pictured literally in the vine of *America 2* – is manifested in the dramatic structure by, for example, a persona's reaction to brutal waves of outside force, the 'interference' of selfhood by Experience. Oothoon, deflowered and newly pregnant, registers the penetration-action of Bromion ambivalently as both her suffering and her sexual excitation: 'But she can howl incessant writhing her soft snowy limbs' (2:12); 'can' implies the capacity she is discovering for both kinds of experience. Similarly in *America* a counterpoint of anguished writhings in response to antipathetic or antithetical forces produces the couple and twist Thompson describes. Fertile and

progressive engagement of contrary forces is seen as the involvement
of a dramatic character in definitive action brought about by a sort of
Darwinian 'resistance' – though the notion is opposed by Thompson's
specific morphology. In this sense prophecy becomes what Yeats,
thinking of poetic drama, called 'Character isolated by a deed'.

Structurally the couple is a temporal point in language, a node
of verbal energy which by its recurrence defines the poetic plot, an
irregular pattern of vectors in a self-fulfilling but inconclusive
poetic process.[12] In *Visions* and the Preludium of *America* the
recurrent couple is the action of rape which centres in image-
words of tearing and rending. Both Argument and Preludium initiate the pattern in an overturelike prefiguring which provides the
prophetic poem that follows with the ordering effect of strong
poetic closure, without resort to such conventional dramatic resolution as Fortinbras' ceremonial entrance or the terminal couplet
of a Shakespearean sonnet. Oothoon's initial monologue, spoken
from a point of vantage above or beyond her chained lament at
the end of the poem, provides a *generative* verbal order by establishing the plot of *rending*: 'But the terrible thunders tore / My
virgin mantle in twain.' This mythic overview of primordial rape,
recurring in the Preludium, gives an evolving poetic meaning both
to dramatic inconclusiveness (Oothoon's failure to actualise her
liberation) and to structural open-endedness (her endless daily
cycle of lamenting). The effect of the poem's thus seeming to spill
out of its aesthetic frame is to suggest opposing possibilities: unity
and unlimited gnomonic extension of a pattern. While the perverse body-and-mind-opening rape by Bromion results in aimless-
ly circular open-endedness, its repetition by Orc corrects and
redirects it toward the gate-opening of the affirmatively unresolved termination of *America*. (Compare the end of *Europe*: 'Till
morning ope'd the Eastern gate.')

The *rending* plot of these poems is borne along on a terminology
of torsion of which the Minute Particular or discrete terminological
unit is any dialectical verb (the 'action word' of grammar) such as
'rend'. Because of semantic ambiguity, such a verb generates both
extensions of itself and of its opposite, which in turn regenerate the
original word. The result is a 'logological' system, to use Kenneth
Burke's vocabulary, wherein each verbal operation stands for the
whole poetic machinery in which it functions.[13] A particle serves as
catalyst of a changing Gestalt, which in turn redefines the particle.
Thus the *term* (a torsion word) is the ontogenetic embryo of the

grammar (the 'logic' of torsion language) which is the phylogenetic pattern embodying its own operative principles. That pattern is the process symbolised by Orc.

Thus 'rend' generates, first, images of itself, analogues or synonyms ('tore my virgin mantle in twain') emblematic of the whole class of divisions of being (Fallen Man, separation of continents, split of mind and body, etc.), sexual and aural 'piercing', physical and verbal 'writhing' and 'wrenching', and so on. Second, it generates different levels of opposing principles or antonyms: reunion or reconstitution of the liberated body politic, sexual union of revived youth, 'rushing of th' inhabitants together', etc. Generation of contraries on a verbal level is tantamount to an 'identity of opposites' in poetic process based on metaphoric thought. From this perspective the Orc cycle is one extreme of poesis, modelled on the theological doctrine of circumincession, that each member of the Trinity inheres in the others – Orc and Urizen being reciprocal, because interdependent, human possibilities. In Blakean metaphoric process the Orc *cycle* is a failed marriage of contraries, a loss of identity due to a double misunderstanding of the creative process, the false assumptions being that marriage means a passive union of opposites rather than active engagement and that a dialectical system (of thought, language, life) seeks a binding synthesis. Properly it seeks a purer extension of its dynamics in newer and newer visionary orders; metaphor, like the Trinity, is the work of the creator, and all created things bear the essential stamp of his mind: the rending is the marriage and true marriage is perpetual visionary rending.

By 'expanding' the poetic dialogue of *Visions of the Daughters of Albion* into a full-scale prophetic opera in *America*, Blake demonstrates creative powers of Genius in the phono-aesthetic resources of language. The rape–outcry–prophecy paradigm develops as the course of evolving human communication, beginning with Orc's conversion of cosmic silence into primal verbal presence, in the shadowy daughter's newborn words, and continuing through Washington's courageous speech, Orc's Declaration of Independence, the verbal apocalypse of Plate 8, and the pure musicality of the rest of the poem. Aesthetically the highest stage of this evolution of communication is the poem itself, its verbal-visual-musical modality.

Structurally the Preludium appears to *produce* the Prophecy, the primal rape generating the antithetical torsion of mental warfare, the symbolic drama of apocalypse. As if to test the medium of poetry itself – its presumption, for example, that 'Mental things alone are real' – Blake presents an instance where mental struggle must turn into human action or lose a portion of the infinite. Orc, though chained, spiritually accumulates the revolutionary energy to save the continent: '... Rivets my tenfold chains while still on high my spirit soars' (A 1:12: see the illustration of *MHH* 4). And his suffering contains the plot of the paradigm he must later enact (emphasis added):

> ... & sometimes a whale I *lash*
> The raging fathomless *abyss*, anon a *serpent folding*
> *Around* the pillars of Urthona, and *round* thy dark limbs,
> On the Canadian wilds I *fold*, feeble my *spirit folds*.
> For chaind beneath I *rend* these *caverns*; when thou bringest food
> I *howl* my joy!

'Fold' is the dialectical verb here, which generates both the 'awful' circularity of the shadowy female and the vinelike torque of the serpent whose winding is indeterminate – and creative – and whose movement *around* pillars and limbs is also a movement *up*, eventually to 'burst the stony roof' (8:9) and pierce the 'Invulnerable tho' naked' womb. Similarly, elsewhere, 'infold' can suggest both Los's false creation – 'Human Illusion ... involvd' (*BL*, last line: E 94) – and his true creation, the 'infinite infolding' of *Jerusalem*. Positive rotary action opens into progression, by virtue of waves of centrifugal creative force:

> The hairy shoulders rend the links, free are the wrists of fire;
> Round the terrific loins he siez'd the panting struggling womb;

and of penetrative power: 'It joy'd'; and of reactive torque: 'then burst the virgin cry'.

SELF-INTERFERENCE AS SELF-GENERATION

> For nothing can be sole or whole
> That has not been rent.
>   (Yeats, *Crazy Jane Talks with the Bishop*)
>
> Poetry Fetter'd, Fetters the Human Race!
>   (*J* 3)

By using the Orc paradigm of opening a body (inward and then outward) as its mode of operation, prophetic poetry becomes a self-extending system with a built-in procreative mechanism, a verbal torque of self-interfering process. Thus in 'A Prophecy' soul-piercing 'sullen fires', reported in ear-rending sounds, produce Orc fires and revolutionary diction, and so on. Blake evidently was thinking of evolution on the level of organic morphology and embryology,[14] and his Orc initiates the chief cosmic event in biological terms: 'the Zenith grew' (4:4). The human organic system, no less than freed slaves (Pl. 6), breaks out of apparent limits, and the image of *bursting* stands for birth out of the womb of closed systems (2:2, 6; 6:5, 8:9, etc., leading to 15:19: 'The doors of marriage are open'). Spiritual evolution is phylogenic progression, the entropic cycle breaking into epicycle and moving on the track of actual time. Apocalyptic expansion of Man's body is 'human blood shooting its veins all round the orbed heaven' (4:5), a massive torsion that modulates into the open circuit of nerves and vines:

> They feel the nerves of youth renew, and desires of ancient times,
> Over their pale limbs as a vine when the tender grape appears
>
> (15:25–6)

This visionary rebirth foreshadows the drama in *Jerusalem* of Man's hatching the egg of his limited world: 'There is a Void, outside of Existence, which if enterd into / Englobes itself & becomes a Womb' (*J* 1:1–2:E 143).

Higher human form, a sort of Superman 'Wonder' (5:7), is engendered by the power of heat, which penetrates the body, as opposed to light, which reveals the play of appearances:

> Intense! naked! a Human fire fierce glowing, as the wedge
> Of iron heated in the furnace; his terrible limbs were fire ...
> ... heat but not light went thro' the murky atmosphere
>
> (*A* 4:8–11)

Orc as phallic wedge in the smithy of human re-creation links with Los as artist of 'infernal method'. At every stage of development from generative principle to prophetic principle, true creation is born of some sort of marriage of the two. Orc-Los, the poet-prophet, as a man-transmuting alchemist uses the traditional and clearly sexual Rod of Fire[15] to effect a transcendent form: man's 'feet become like brass, / His knees and thighs like silver, & his breast and head like gold' (8:16–17). The journey toward *Jerusalem*, locomoted by torsion, is a marriage of heaven and hell, a vinelike spiritual 'ascent', blossoming in sunlight, and a magical 'descent' through the condensed heat of smithy, body, and imagination.

The body-piercing and surface-rending heat, extending the metaphor of infernal *poiein*, suggests that Blake as primal poet sees his function as releasing the energies and 'desires of ancient times' pent up beneath closed surfaces. Closer to eighteenth-century pseudo-science than to the poetics of contemporaries who accepted the 'bondage' of a prosody of restraint, his Visionary Forms of tactile release suggest a hidden metaphor of ritual friction. For the pseudo-scientist (such as Blake's 'Inflammable Gass') 'Everything that rubs, that burns, or that electrifies is immediately considered capable of explaining the act of generation'.[16] A treatise by Charles Rabiqueau of 1753, *The Spectacle of Elementary Fire or A Course in Experimental Electricity*, for example, develops 'an electrical theory of the sexes' based on a theory of friction. Torque itself – of demonic winding serpent, coupling vine, or twisting fire – relates to the electrifying friction of contraries. Frazer cites friction-caused ritual fires, with sexual significance, and Bachelard[17] cites a fire ritual 'which unites the Sun festival and the harvest festival ... above all a celebration of the *seeding* of the fire. In order that it may have all its force, this seeding must be seized in its first intensity, when it comes fresh from the rubbing tool'. As ritual, the progression from Orc to Los moves from fire-seeding Minor Prophecies to harvesting Major Prophecies – as the wheat-yielding illumination of 'A Prophecy' visually suggests. In the terms I have been using, poetic self-interference is the ritual self-seeding and -firing which leads to the self-reaping of prophecy (message) and myth (structure).

The marriage of Orc and Los or process and message, dramatised in Plate 8 of *America*, justifies a poetry of 'terrific form' (7:7), analogue of 'fearful symmetry'. The dialogue of Orc and Albion's Angel, a traction of verbal contraries, intensifies the dialectics of *Visions of the Daughters of Albion* to apocalyptic breaking point. The progression is electrically generated from verbal pronouncement (Orc's speeches, *A* 6 and 8), to increasingly violent reactive verbal torsions (the Angel's augmenting hysteria in 7 and 9), then on to waves of expanding force (the Angel of Boston's 'rending off his robe', Pls 11 and 12, involuntarily seeding the flame that 'folded roaring fierce'), and finally beyond discourse to pure verbal action (flames magnetising citizens, etc., Pl. 14). Plate 6, Orc's Declaration, is the agent of primary force, but Plate 8 is the fertilised seed, the strongest node in a moving field of forces. The latter defines revolutionary identity: the *cognito* or self-naming ('I am Orc'), the serpentine torsion ('wreath'd round the accursed tree' – kernel of the 'wreaths' of renewal in 15:21), the fiery acceleration of history toward collapse into apocalypse ('The times are ended'), and, by implication, the rending of all temporal and mind-forged chains as rehearsed in the Preludium. In the spiritual birth process the open discourse of Orc contrasts symmetrically with the closed shriek of Albion's Angel, held within the envelope of musical refrains in Plate 9. The visibly stony womb of Plate 8 encloses Orc's apocalypse, with Urizen sitting over it like a hen on an egg, until two plates later it 'gives birth' to fiery Orc, as though verbal seeds had burst into visionary flames.

This link between Plates 8 and 10 suggests further that pregnant *America* contains the kernel of *Europe*. As the womb that 'Heaves in enormous circles' (9:10) crosses the Atlantic in widening force-waves, poetic systems interpose in a larger self-interfering system. *America* 10 may, as Erdman suggests, illustrate the concluding lines of *Europe*; or rather, the serpent-hair of Orc pictured in *America* 10 emerges verbally in *Europe* 15 as the 'snaky thunders' on the *reared* head of Los. And *America* climaxes in renewed vines and opened gates of perception that reopen into *Europe* as 'Five windows' lighting 'the cavern'd Man' (viz., the reader) and as 'the eternal vine' (*E* iii:1–2). *America* 8 is, I suggest, the main generative torque for both poems and the vector determining their open endings – structurally the ontogenesis of their phylogenesis.

The Minute Particular of this long-range linking is Orc's fertilising action within Plate 8. The stony law he stamps 'to dust' becomes ejaculated seed that 'scatter[s] religion abroad / To the four winds as a *torn book*' – the Holy Bible itself rent and impregnated within this Bible of Hell. Taking the Book into its smithy, *America* disseminates seeding sparks to 'make the desarts blossom' and reincarnate God in the living body of religion (Man as Jesus, Poet as Creator). Man returns to inner sources as the 'deeps shrink to their fountains', waking Albion to 'infinite infolding'. Again Orc-seeding leads us to Major Prophecy; the image of fires that 'inwrap [cf. Milton's 'instruct'] the earthly globe, but man is not consumed', will grow into the vision of Night IX of *The Four Zoas*:

How is it that we have walkd thro fires & yet are not consumd
How is it that all things are changd even as in ancient times ...
The Expanding Eyes of Man behold the depths of wondrous worlds
(138:39–40, 25:E 391)

Poetic alchemy reverses, as if by magnetic repolarisation, 'life by magic power condens'd; infernal forms art-bound' (*Ab*:14:E 57), and the poet becomes Prometheus unbound.

As an allegory of poetics, Orc embodies the principle of expansion by prosodic and structural unfettering, the opening inward by syntactic, rhythmic, and other formal means directly to energies of creative process. The self-interfering poem and book become a self-regulating economy, like the bird learning its limits by soaring on its own wings. 'Allegory' is a term hardly adequate to this perception. Herbert Weisinger argues in his essay on 'The Mythic Origins of the Creative Process' that the archetypal dying-reviving-god pattern of myth and ritual, viewed in the light of evidence from both literature and science, becomes 'the symbolic representation of the creative process, that is to say, the mind's figuring forth of itself ... the mode of operation of the mind ... as essentially dramatic and dialectical, of proceeding by what amounts to leaps, falls and higher leaps....'[18] Orc initiates a process which, in authentic prophecy, must determine poetic structure by enacting 'the primal law of the inner life of man' that

> ... *ontogeny recapitulates phylogeny*, ... as it would appear that that
> is the law of history and nature itself. As I try to visualise the move-
> ment of the mind during the creative process, I see an *unfolding from
> within, a reaching beyond, another unfolding*, and another stretch;
> an ever *shifting centre radiating out* to ever *widening circumferences,
> not circular, but irregular*, with deep bays of regression, flat beaches
> of futility, and sudden promontories of achievement. In any event, I
> do not see the movement as a circle, of a beginning returning in on
> itself, but rather an *uneven ascending spiral*. I suppose that from the
> point of view of God as he looks down on the process it is a circle (as
> I suppose it is too from the point of view of Satan as he looks up at
> it) but from the point of view of man standing midway and looking
> head-on, the circle is a spiral, and what hope he has comes from the
> difference in location and angle of vision.... The creative process is
> therefore by its nature profoundly *revolutionary*, a *built-in device
> which immediately upsets any state of equilibrium or stasis* it
> encounters. By its *interposition* it transforms rest into motion, alter-
> ing and recasting, until the *friction* of *resistance* and effort slows it
> down into form or formula, a new state of rest whose balance it
> again upsets, so that now each new mirror in the corridor reflects
> one subtly altered image after another....[19]

Together with the vine morphologue from Thompson, this account gives us a vocabulary for self-correcting verbal action and structure in Blake which lead us beyond the poem, where the poet would have us go, and then back into its evolving economy, equipped then with expanded critical tools. We may learn thereby the full meaning of the 'going forth & returning' of *Jerusalem 99*.

From *Blake's Visionary Forms Dramatic*, ed. David V. Erdman and John E. Grant (Princeton, NJ, 1970), pp. 263–84.

NOTES

[George Quasha's essay first appeared in the important collection of essays on Blake, *Blake's Visionary Forms Dramatic*. It takes as its starting-point a revision of the classic mythopoeic approach to Blake taken by Northrop Frye, principally in his *Fearful Symmetry: A Study of William Blake* (Princeton, NJ, 1947), from the standpoint of modern developments in thinking in both the arts and the sciences. It concentrates particularly on the role of Orc within Blake's texts, and pays particular attention to two of the early Prophetic Books, *Visions of the Daughters of Albion* and *America*. It is here reproduced in a slightly abbreviated form, omitting the 'Note on the Bard's rending of His Harp' with which the original essay concludes. Ed.]

1. 'Notes for David Smith Makes a Sculpture', *Art News* (Jan. 1969), 48.

2. See David V. Erdman, *Blake: Prophet Against Empire* (2nd edn, Princeton, NJ, 1969), esp. pp. 6–7 and 53–60.

3. Northrop Frye, *Fearful Symmetry: A Study of William Blake* (Princeton, NJ, 1947), p. 206.

4. Ibid., p. 208.

5. Ibid., p. 210.

6. See Albert B. Lord's study of oral-traditional poetry, *The Singer of Tales* (New York, 1965), from which my assumptions about tradition-al poetry derive.

7. *David Smith by David Smith*, ed. Cleve Gray (New York, 1968), p. 67; see also pp. 132–35. Celebration of the open artistic mind in an open universe of possibilities relates Blake's world to that of such con-temporary poets as Charles Olson and Robert Duncan and such a composer as John Cage – the latter notably in his application of *I Ching* chance and indeterminacy principles to musical procedures. Some 'new' directions in modern thought similarly are quite Blakean, often consciously so, as in Thomas J.J. Altizer's important application: *The New Apocalypse: The Radical Christian Vision of William Blake* (East Lansing, MI, 1967). Blake's faith in the formative power of

human identity has striking parallels in Lancelot Law Whyte's *Accent on Form: An Anticipation of the Science of Tomorrow* (London, 1955), and R. Buckminster Fuller's *No More Secondhand God and Other Writings* (Carbondale, IL, 1963).

8. See Erdman, *Blake: Prophet Against Empire*, pp. 289–90.

9. See Frye, 'Towards Defining an Age of Sensibility', in *Fables of Identity* (New York, 1963), pp. 130–7.

10. The perception that 'process' and 'organic' poetry are orally structured relates Blake and much modern poetry to ancient oral verse (see Lord, *Singer of Tales*). Blake's vision of future 'harmony' is an aural perception 'Within the unfathomd caverns of my ear' (*J* 3: E 144). Cf. Walter J. Ong's application of Auerbach's belief in a Hebraic-Christian 'wellspring of mankind's genuine historical awareness' – a heritage 'rooted in an oral-aural notion of knowledge, not in the more visual Hellenic …', a verbal world of 'ineluctable interiority, related to this irreducible and elusive and interior economy of the sound-world' ('A Dialectic of Aural and Objective Correlatives', *Essays in Criticism*, 8 [1958], 166–81). Cf. also Marshall McLuhan's *Verbi-Voco-Visual Explorations* (New York, 1967).

11. D'Arcy Wentworth Thompson, *On Growth and Form* (Cambridge, 1959), vol. II, pp. 887–92.

12. Recurrence appears to be the basic feature of poetic, as of musical, structure, and the high incidence of repeated key words and motifs in Blake ought to be definable in linguistic terms. Such 'nodes' may be related to the 'summative' words which linguists have found to be the centre of phonic patterns in certain sonnets and other short forms: see J. Lynch, 'The Tonality of Lyric Poetry: An Experiment in Method', *Word*, 9 (1963); Dell Hymes, 'Phonological Aspects of Style: Some English Sonnets', in *Style in Language* (Cambridge, MA, 1960), pp. 109–31. Claude Lévi-Strauss offers a broader definition of recurrence: 'La répétition a une fonction propre, qui est de rendre manifeste la structure du mythe' (*Anthropologie structurale* [Paris, 1958], p. 254).

13. My method here derives from Kenneth Burke's notions of poetry as 'symbolic action' and the 'dancing of an attitude' in *The Philosophy of Literary Form* (New York, 1957), and in *The Rhetoric of Religion: Studies in Logology* (Boston, 1961).

14. Carmen S. Kreiter, 'Evolution and William Blake', *Studies in Romanticism*, 4 (1965), 110–18, suggests that Blake had knowledge of early theories of evolution, embryology, and the biogenetic law; however, Kreiter's analysis does not go beyond linking the diction of *The Book of Urizen* to contemporary science, except to offer the curious argument that Orc represents a 'devolution' from the 'higher' state of innocence symbolised by the worm.

15. See Gaston Bachelard's *The Psychoanalysis of Fire* (Boston, 1964), a key (along with Bachelard's other works, mostly untranslated) to a phenomenological analysis of poetry – and apparently an important influence on the method of Northrop Frye (who supplies an Introduction). Bachelard discusses the sexual meanings of alchemy – the phallic Rod of Fire and the smithy which was often shaped as a sexual organ.

16. This and other relevant passages quoted by Bachelard, ibid., pp. 26ff.; cf. 'The equation of fire and life forms the basis of the system of Paracelsus ... [and] Boerhaave. It is the hidden fire that must be utilised for the curing of sickness and for procreation. Nicolas de Locques [1665] bases all the value he attributes to fire on its inwardness. Fire is "internal or external; the external fire is mechanical, corrupting and destroying, the internal is spermatic, generative, ripening"' (p. 73).

17. See Bachelard, *Psychoanalysis of Fire*, pp. 31–2.

18. Herbert Weisinger, *The Agony and the Triumph: Papers on the Use and Abuse of Myth* (East Lansing, MI, 1964), p. 250.

19. Ibid., pp. 252–3; my emphases.

2

Babylon Revisited, or the Story of Luvah and Vala

JEAN H. HAGSTRUM

The subtitle of this essay locates its temporal bounds: we are concerned with love and passion in the period of the great prophecies – *The Four Zoas, Milton*, and *Jerusalem*, when Satan has replaced Urizen as the archvillain and the anti-man, when Orc has been sexualised and the political serpent has become phallic, and when the forgiveness of sins has replaced revolutionary indignation as a redemptive value. It is the period when Ona, Lyca, Thel, Leutha, Oothoon live on in the mind of the artist as emanations he fights to preserve for all eternity – as spirits that can emerge from the presses of art to help constitute the Wine of the Ages. But our immediate concern is not with these lovely and now sometimes shadowy recollections of past Innocence and Experience but with the Zoa of passionate love, Luvah, and his consort, Vala, who dominate a social-political-psychological landscape that is less like Urizen's rocky, stony, cavernous lunar death and more like Milton's lake of fire, with agonising forms rising from its burning marl.

It would be hard to exaggerate the importance of the theme. Blake the older poet-prophet is more concerned than ever with those staminal virtues of humanity, the sexual appetites. He has shifted the emphasis from love as a singing joy in nature and from love as a force for revolutionary release to 'the torments of Love & Jealousy', a preoccupation so central he made that phrase the subtitle of *The Four Zoas*. Innocent sexuality produced some of Blake's loveliest pages of composite art, and revolutionary sexuality some of his most memorable. But for richness of meaning and breadth of implication, both in its positive and negative aspects, it would be difficult to match even in Blake the love story of his late prophetic pages. The first adjectives that come to mind to describe this achievement are 'powerful' and 'inescapable'. But 'delicate' will also have to be used, since Blake is concerned with emotions that are evanescent and changing as well as searing, with creatures as gorgeous as they are dangerous, whose shifting forms are – if we may listen to a voice uncongenial in this setting –

> Dipt in the richest tincture of the skies,
> Where light disports in ever-mingling dyes,
> While ev'ry beam new transient colours flings.[1]

Friendship is robust and can tolerate severe contentions. Love cannot – it flies into error, perversion, extremity, change.[2] Delicate in Innocence, it can become a glittering poison in Experience, tending toward death. And around the lovely, bestial, and protean forms of the late prophecies Blake weaves a complex network of meanings that coalesce, their main outlines, however, remaining firm and clear.

Our main concern is with fallen love, so vivid as picture, so salutary as prophecy, so close to our business and bosoms. It will help us see our fallen condition clearly if we begin with the ideal original and the ideal restored condition, though we intend no temporal sequence here, recognising that the ideal and the real are states to which the prophetic vision – or its lack – can consign us here and now, at any moment of insight – or error. Vala, to begin with the derivative or secondary female principle, was, first, a city, a temple, or a garden. She was also the bride of Albion, the Eternal Man, and was, at the time of her birth, 'the loveliest of the daughters of Eternity'. The superlative perhaps ought to be toned down, since it comes from the mouth of the fallen goddess herself as she recalls her past. And when the fallen demons pay her the tribute of once having been a 'fair crystal form divinely clear', we should of course pay them heed, remembering, however, that they are under the spell of the seductress. Luvah, from whom Vala emanated as from a primary and more basic force, was her father, her lover, or her husband – always some kind of consort.[3] He was given the title of 'prince of Love', a ruler over the east, the realm of the rising sun. But though he possesses a lofty title and a beautiful and extensive realm, his manner was more Christ-like than monarchical, for he was the 'gentlest mildest Zoa'.

And his activities were rather those of servant than ruler: a cupbearer to the gods, he poured wine of delight and love, his pure feet stepping on the steps divine; a charioteer, he drove the horses of light and warmth; a weaver, he assumed a kind of feminine role, weaving fibres and threads for others to use.[4]

Considered ideally, these two – the Zoa of love and his consort – possess attractiveness and grace. But there is clear indication that their position is not the highest, the myth placing them more often than not in positions of service. All this, of course, befits a faculty or an appetite that is a part not the whole, that is powerful but not supreme, and that is gracious only when it is subordinate. Luvah and Vala in great eternity are not mighty monarchs but gentle angels ranged in order serviceable.

It is important to stress the qualities of gentle subservience ministering to harmony and proportion in the ideal state, because in the fallen state these beings assume the opposite characteristics. They become raging tyrants – burning, destroying, dominating. What could have been the nature of the fall that toppled them from a modest but noble station to swirl in vortexes of uncontrolled energy? Like all myths, Blake's provides alternative versions, each of which contributes an insight or an emphasis to round out the whole. There are at least four related but differing accounts of how Luvah and Vala got to be what we know them to be in life.

1. Luvah intoxicated Urizen, the god of light, with stolen wine – stolen, apparently, because the legitimate portion was of insufficient quantity to accomplish Luvah's mischief, which recalls Phaeton's, for he seized Urizen's horses and drove the chariot of the day.

2. While Albion and Urizen slept, Luvah and Vala awakened and flew up from the heart, their proper place, into the brain.

3. Luvah now aggressively assumed Urizen's territories to the south, leaving the east a gaping void.

4. Luvah and Vala divided into separate forms. Luvah was sealed in a furnace, as Vala fed the flames.[5]

These several versions say that the fall resulted in displacement and separation. The separation of Luvah and Vala need not mean anything so outlandish as that we were once literally androgynous and that in falling we became men and women. It means, more simply and relevantly, that passion is separated from tenderness, desire from affection, a disaster not unlike the one Freud described in 'Degradation in Erotic Life'.[6] The effect of separation is to leave tenderness a victim and passion a raw aggressor, both in the female and the male. The displacement does not mean literally that climates have been disordered at certain points of the compass, but metaphorically that heat has replaced light, that some places have become void and that others howl in thunder and cyclone. That is, some people most of the time and other people some of the time lament in loneliness and frustration, empty and deserted; and still other people most of the time and some people part of the time burn and freeze in passion. Blake is psychologist first and cosmologist second; the doctrine that all things fall to the centre, leaving the east hollow, the south burning up in heat, and the west raging in storms is vastly more metaphorical than the modern tentative cosmology that disappearing stars have created black holes in the universe, small concentrations of matter of incredible density. As cosmology the modern formulation may turn out to be true. Blake's could not, though his psychology is valid. What Blake is saying in his four versions of the fall of Luvah is that within the human personality passion has supplanted reason, excess has supplanted control; the gentle passions have been replaced by violent ones, compassion by cruelty, love by prostitution.

All this is traditional enough, having been more or less present in human thought from the Book of Genesis to *Paradise Lost*; but Blake, radical humanist that he is, gives it a particular twist. The fall is a revolt not so much against God as against man. Luvah's ultimate blasphemy was that he murdered Albion, who is at once Blake himself, his culture, his nation, and, by extension, the eternal man in all of us. Luvah's own account reveals the full extent of his demonic and inhuman delusion, which was also close to Blake's own activities in the nineties. Both Blake and Luvah attack Urizen, Luvah believing that he would be able to blot out the human delusion of reason. Just how mistaken and impious he was, Luvah himself reveals when he says that he hoped 'to deliver all the sons of God / From bondage of the Human Form' (*FZ* II:311). A tragic flaw and a hideous blindness! For Christ is the Human Form Divine. The attack on Urizen had turned round and become an attack on Jesus, that is, on man himself. Luvah, in what at the end of the eighteenth century seemed to be a justified aggression against the rational faculty, succeeded only in crucifying Christ afresh. It is difficult not to believe that in the fallen Luvah's confession Blake is making his own.

The raging fiery furnace that Luvah and Vala have now placed in the world is the central heating and energy system of Babylon. For all its religious and political significance, Babylon is a highly sexual zone, more intensely sexual than the milder Beulah. Both places are created by Blake in response to the inescapable presence in man of sexual desire. Both are places of erotic blandishments, of the physical melting of the will. Both are places of veils, coverings, death, and ecstasy, and Luvah and Vala, the creators of Babylon, appear in Beulah. But for all their similarities Beulah and Babylon are, of course, distinctly separate regions. When Albion in Beulah faints on the bosom of Vala, this ecstasy causes a wall to be built by heaven around Beulah, which is endangered by an excess of its own qualities. Beulah is a place of 'soft Delight', of shadows, mirrors, delicate wings, crystal places, and 'mazes of delusive beauty'; of dreams 'in soft deluding slumber', a mild and pleasant refuge in 'soft slumberous repose' from the evils of Urizen-land. Essentially, it is a place of mercy created by the Lamb of God, who through it does what Los and Enitharmon as artists also do: here bodies are created for that 'insane, and most deformed' part of man that Blake calls spectral, bodies that can preserve the essential human being from eternal death, which is damnation.[7]

Babylon, on the other hand, drives inexorably on toward death or nonentity. It is a place, not where spectres are put in bodies or literary artistic forms, but where they remain pure spectres, unthwarted, preying on life. In Beulah the moon beams faintly; in Babylon, the sun – out of place, to be sure – is a fire that rages too close to the earth. Beulah preserves, Babylon consumes itself and others. Beulah is a place of soft coverings – of the womb, the vulva, the mother's arms enfolding the child. Babylon is a place where male and female energy bubbles and boils in vein and artery. Beulah is a place of sweet alluring dreams, Babylon of nightmares. In Beulah 'every female delights to give her maiden [that is, her maidenhead] to her husband'. But in Babylon, where all males become one male in a drastic sexual concentration, love is a 'ravening eating Cancer'. In Bunyan, Beulah is the last step on the way to heaven. In Blake, Beulah is the married state, the last station on the way to eternal bliss. But Babylon is prostitution, tottering on the edge of Blake's hell, Ulro. Beulah is Innocence, the place of Oothoon's palace, and of the grain of sand that Satan's watch fiends cannot find.[8]

And yet they do find it – in Lambeth. They call Beulah sin,[9] thus perverting it to Babylon. In the last analysis Beulah and Babylon, vastly different and yet mutually reminiscent, can best be thought of together: Babylon is a hideous perversion of Beulah. The coverings, counterpanes, sheets, and blankets of Beulah become Vala's veil in Babylon. The protection and tenderness of Beulah, with its 'dimm religious light',[10] become the mysterious and life-denying sexual religion of Babylon. The delicate sexual acts of Beulah, necessary for our salvation, are twisted into the Abomination of Desolation. Both places are profoundly autobiographical in ways we can only divine. Beulah was a distillation of the best moments of Blake's marriage with Catherine and his collaboration with that sweet and simple woman in creating the lovely forms – in word, line and colour – of *Innocence, Thel, Europe*, and *Albion*. In the hell of Babylon, Blake concentrated his worst moments with Catherine, his lusts, his own temptations, and the powerful conflicts that his creation of 'The Tyger', the early Orc, Bromion, Urizen, and Hell must have entailed upon his psyche.

There are two kinds of perversion, those that turn a pleasure from its normal course and those that drive it too far, past enjoyment to excess. We shall consider the second kind in discussing monomaniacal heterosexuality, perhaps the central characteristic of a Babylonian citizen. But there are also in Babylon the abnormal, deviant types of perversion, although these are rather hinted at than fully developed. Three such perversions can be distinguished: (1) the incestuous, (2) the narcissistic, and (3) the feminine-phallic.

1. Storge, *or love of parents for offspring.* The term *storge*, from the Greek στοργή, was known and used by Blake, his contemporaries, and his immediate predecessors, including Swedenborg, from whom the poet undoubtedly borrowed it.[11] The Swedish seer uses the term for a love that is physical and that is communicated by that same sense of touch that cements the physical bond between married people. But it is universal, providential, tender, peaceful, and innocent. In fact, it tends to recede as innocence itself does.[12] But the English seer, in the period of his major prophecies, sees *storge* as something other than beautiful and divine parental love. From 'all powerful parental affection' spring 'the silent broodings of deadly revenge', and Albion comes to loathe his sons in sexual jealousy as he sees them assimilate with Luvah and assume their man's estate. So Los, in an illustration to *The Book of Urizen*, looks with envious eyes on his son Orc. Blake has provided an unmistakable Oedipal triangle in visual form, as son and mother embrace while a bearded father (an unusual way to represent Los) looks on in deep love-jealousy as a red chain of envy binds his waist. In *The Four Zoas* the son provides ample reason for his father's jealousy,

for he has conceived an Oedipal love for his mother. The howling sexual serpentine Orc comes to love with a craving 'Storgous Appetite'. One would have to say that among the 'thrilling joys of sense', which the sexualised Orc enjoys in exploring the 'hidden things of Vala', is an abnormal affection for his mother.[13]

2. *Narcissus*. Before being incestuously enjoyed, Milton's Sin is narcissistically conceived, self-begotten from the head of her father Satan. Blake, too, conceives of sexual sin as narcissistic, a subcategory of that dreadful vice of Ulro, self-destroying self-love. That strange, perverted, grotesque beauty that Enion incestuously produced and that we have already commented on is also a 'self-enjoying wonder'. And one characteristic Albion acquires in his fallen state is a tendency to worship his own Shadow, which is only a 'watry vision of Man'. Paradoxically, this urge rises in him when he feels himself to be nothing. The pious man who sings in his chapel, 'Oh, to be nothing nothing, Only to lie at Thy feet', is perceived by Blake's penetrating eye (so like Swift's on the subject of dissenting hypocrisy) as self-idolatrous. Whomever Blake is thinking about – and it is undoubtedly more than pious Christians pretending to be nothing – the projection of self can absorb Albion entirely, a self-idolatry at which even Vala trembles and covers her face in shame; for of course it is a total negation of the heterosexual love by which this Venus subsists. It is a tempting vision, not to be taken lightly. Although 'watry', it is also a shadow of 'living gold, pure perfect, holy; in white linen pure'. However fair, it is no less evil. It springs from a 'wearied intellect' as an 'entrancing self-delusion'.[14]

3. *The phallic woman*. Freud believed that in the terrors of his uninstructed imagination a young boy might endow his mother with the male organ and masculinise the woman who sometimes threatens and punishes him as she denies him his wishes.[15] Blake too conceived of the phallic woman. In *America* (Plate 14) a submissive boy is being instructed by an early version of Rahab seated under a tree, her loins producing a phallic serpent whose forked tongue seems to spit menaces at the youth. The fully developed Babylon of the later prophecies includes a similarly perverse creation to express aggressive and unnatural female sexuality. In Luvah's own story of his past, he conceives of Vala's earliest condition in imagery that is phallic. He produces first an earthworm, who becomes a scaled serpent (hating him, incidentally); under his care she then becomes a winged dragon bright and poisonous – this phallic career preceding her birth as a weeping infant who grows up

to be a producing mother.[16] Vala has had, to say the least, a phallic origin that apparently remains with her, to keep her femininity aggressive and warlike. The mature Vala is even capable of the masculine act, for she at one point is conceived of as a 'Worm in Enitharmon's Womb / Laying her seeds upon the fibres' (*FZ* III:320).[17]

We must, of course, be careful not to insist always on literal sexual perversions when Blake, with his all-personifying faculty, is clothing other human monstrosities in vivid physical imagery. But Blake's personified figures, so unlike those of his eighteenth-century predecessors, are real and powerful in and of themselves; and there is no clear separation between tenor and vehicle as in allegory, which Blake loathed. Sexual perversion is a powerful metaphor in Blake for political and religious perversion because it is itself a real feature of Babylon. And the three irregularities we have noted – the storgous, the narcissistic, and the female phallic – are insistently present as realities. There may be others as well, and when Blake refers to 'detestable births', 'devilish arts abominable unlawful unutterable' (*FZ* VIII:364), he may refer to dark sexual perversions he does not choose to embody fully in his myth. Blake has a lot to say about Ulro. Of Alla, the errors of the heart, he has also much to say, even though he uses the term only twice.[18] This essay discusses the errors and perversions of Al-Ulro, the errors of the 'Loins & Seminal Vessels'. But of Or-Ulro, the errors of the 'Stomach & Intestines', Blake has virtually nothing to say – except that the imaginations that arise from these lower gates are not only 'wondrous' but also 'terrible, deadly, unutterable' (*M* 34:13, 15–18). Like Saint Augustine and Swift before him and like Yeats after him, Blake was conscious of the irony that man is born between the gate of seed and the gate of excrement. About this latter orifice Blake is reticent, but his own contemporary the Marquis de Sade and our own age of Freud can supply the details.

Relatively silent about the phallic woman, whose perversion is unnatural, Blake has much to say about the phallic predominance in heterosexual men, about the male who 'phallicises' all nature, including his own and his beloved's brain. This driving of a natural passion to absorbing excess is characteristic of the age of the phallic Orc, who has replaced the political revolutionary Orc.[19] (More precisely stated, the phallic-political Orc has replaced the political-phallic Orc; for neither manifestation is without the sexual and political combined.) When that frosty tyrant Urizen explores the world of the new Orc, he sees a world where his horses must feed in fiery mangers, where holy oil burns in fury within caverns and rocks, where the bulls of Luvah breathe fire, where lions howl in burning dens. It is a hell, a lake of fire consuming itself in the flames of Orc. In a brilliantly condensed description, it is called 'A Cavernd Universe of flaming fire'. One understands the sexual Babylon only if one realises that it is a place of both (1) raging fiery passion and (2) caverned restraint. Hence the individual sufferings and also the rages that tear nations and cultures apart. Los's mighty rivers must flow in 'tubelike forms' as they sink to the place of seed to be divided into testicles. Everywhere there is the pressure of passion on the veins and arteries of the body, and the moony escapes of Beulah are not adequate to provide relief.[20]

Love has become burningly sexual, as Luvah becomes Orc and as all nature becomes serpentine. Beauty becomes scarlet, separated from familial love; and lust rages in the heart that was once the seat of delicate sensibility and fine feeling. The 'new born king' does not rule in mercy mild but as the red Orc, 'the King of rage and death' (FZ V:333).

The paradox about love that we shall return to at the end emerges here. Blake allows Orc to enjoy his fires, at least to prefer them to the snowy death of Urizen. In fact, Orc's reading of the fall is very much like that of the earlier revolutionary Blake. Why does the phallic worm wrap the tree of life in the garden and lead Eve and mankind to destruction? Because he is 'A Worm compelld' – compelled by the restraints and deceits of Urizen. And now Orc 'organizes' a serpent body for all nature, becoming himself a 'dark devourer', precisely because rational and coldly moral limits have been put upon him.[21]

There is no evidence that Blake rejects Orc's analysis. But he does add a new dimension to it. The new Orc may be preferable to Urizen, but he is a tyrant nonetheless. He subjects Babylon to a new tyranny, that of obsessive phallic passion that burns alone, unattached to any love object, and that then stalks abroad seeking whom it may devour. Destructive, it is also nasty; and scaly monsters, bred in the swamps of Orc-country, vomit up creatures that 'annoy the nether parts of man'. It is the age of the phallic predominance. All who love, including the quondam King of Love himself, Luvah, are now 'reasoning from the loins in the unreal forms of Ulros night'.[22]

If men reason from the loins, they do so because of the dazzling beauty of the fallen Vala, because of the dominance of what Blake feared as an anti-human blasphemy, the dominance of the Female Will, made possible by sexual power. Vala is the *agent provocateur* of sex in the head.

Vala meets the old Orc in *America* as the nameless 'Shadowy daughter of Urthona'. She encounters the new Orc as a 'nameless shadowy Vortex', and the change in phrasing is eloquent. Vortex indeed! Swirling sexual energy meets the phallic Orc more than half way – in 'the Caverns of the Grave [a place of sexual commerce] & Places of human seed'. But, in actuality, she embraces his fire to dampen it. She apparently wants Orc to lose his rage and subside into meekness. Why does she stoop to the Urizenic tricks of beguiling humility? The reason is simple. She has become a tyrant, and like all tyrants she recognises the value of humility-inducing opiates. But the meekness is intended for her victim, for she herself is far from being lowly of heart. In Beulah, the creation of Los and Christ, the woman is a submissive receptacle, a handmaiden of her Lord. In Babylon she is an aggressive 'Sexual Machine', who, as we have seen, may be regarded as also a phallic mother, a glittering but threatening dragon-shape. She is a rival of the serpentine Orc himself. Small wonder he is jealous![23]

The aggressive Vala is a successful imperialist on a larger scale than we have hitherto seen. Conquering new territories, she takes on more than Orc, becoming even Los's harlot, poisoning and dominating the artistic imagination. She also becomes Urizen's harlot, adopting, as we have seen, his arts of 'Pity & Meek Affection', but extending these far beyond the task of subduing the serpentine fires of Orc. She penetrates Beulah with 'false / And generating Love'. She extends to all parts of the body, a 'hungry Stomach, & a devouring Tongue'. The fires of her loins invade cities, nations, families, languages. Man is reduced by her to a phallic worm and, paradoxically, an effeminate phallus at that, a breeder of seeds. Whoever he is – pope or poet, king or philosopher – he is 'Woman-born / And Woman-nourished & Woman-educated, & Woman-scorn'd!' The fallen Vala, or Rahab, conquers such a wide domain because through her daughter, the cruel Tirzah, she sexualises everything, creating breasts and testes ('tying the knots of milky seed into two lovely Heavens'), a brain heated white, and a 'red hot heart'. That is, in magnetising everything by sexuality, she can dominate it through physical attractiveness, thus perverting our staminal virtues.[24]

The effect of Vala's becoming both Orc-like and Urizenic needs to be examined further. Her all-naturalising power becomes responsible for two enormous perversions, sexualised religion and the sexualised state. These separate but related phenomena are the most prominent – and dreadful – features of Babylon. As the shadowy female, Vala has absorbed both the science and art of Urizen and the fiery aggressiveness of Orc. She is a double-threat tyrant, ice and fire at the same time, seductive and cruel. 'In the power of Orc', she insinuates herself into the state, altering the vortexes, changing the true centres of power, making both female attractiveness and female frigidity a motive power. As Urizen, she insinuates herself into religion; for she has, as we have seen, affected the arts of pity and humility. In different ways, then, venereal disease may be said to attack metaphorically the body politic and even the body of Christ. Christ's real body resisted 'the festering Venoms bright' that threatened it when he forgave the Magdalen and took on her sins to forgive them. But his false body, the established church, no longer had such immunity because it had forgotten the art of forgiving sin.[25]

Metaphors have a way of taking over in Blake, and the insistent use of sexual imagery for religion and religious imagery for sexuality (not unlike Donne, by the way) suggests an interpenetration of essences that can only mean that when one is corrupted the other is too. Woman-dominated man has created woman-dominated religious institutions – Hebrew, Christian, druidic, or natural. Puritanical religion enshrines female fears of sexuality and makes them holy – a perversion so gross that it causes the Eternals to laugh 'after their manner'. What provokes mirth in the heavens is a self-denying religious ethic by which a man 'dare hardly to embrace / His own wife, for the terrors of Chastity'. Hebraic religion, transmuted to Roman and Anglican Christian establishments, is also woman-dominated, but perhaps in another way. The magical ark of the Covenant and its equivalents in Christian altars, along with its attendant ceremonies and rites, is seen by Blake as analogous to secret, furtive, guilty sexuality. Freud noted that the holy and the forbidden are in many languages designated by the same word,[26] and in Blake sexual terror and sacrifice for sin are imagistically tied together. Both the sex act and the religious rite are done in secret, dark, covert places, incensed and perfumed; and the conjugal bed, with its hangings, counterpanes, and curtains, is like the altar, with its rich cloths, its protecting covers, and its vestmented priests. The tabernacle, the place of the sacred elements, is one of Blake's images for the enclosing of the male organ by the female. Both fallen sexuality and fallen religion hide the bread and wine from the light of common experience. Fallen religion can also be druidic, but that cruel religion is no less female-dominated than the puritanical and the Hebraic-Christian. Vala's daughters wield the stone knife of cruel sacrifice, becoming castrators and circumcisers, sacrificing innocent male lambs to their perverse delights.[27]

Such, then, is the 'Synagogue of Satan'. Such is Rahab, the 'False Feminine Counterpart Lovely of Delusive Beauty'. In the religio-sexual tabernacles of Babylon the true God, who is the true man, is buried.[28]

If sexualised religion is bad, the sexualised state is even worse. And in this aspect Luvah-Los may be worse than Vala-Urizen. Luvah tears forth from Albion's loins and flows in red blood all over Europe, and Blake intends us to understand that sexual energy has burst its dams and issued forth as aggressive warfare. 'The Beast & the Whore rule without control'.[29]

Let us consider the several stages that descend to this awful perversion of love into war, of Vala first into 'Mystery the Harlot' and then into 'Mystery the Virgin Harlot Mother of War, / Babylon the Great, the Abomination of Desolation!' The first stage, from Adam to Lamech, includes mighty hermaphrodites, menacingly narcissistic, full of evil promise. The second produces the 'Female-Males, / A Male within a Female hid as in an Ark & Curtains' – that is, the sexualised religion we have just considered. The final stage, to which Blake's age had arrived, is the 'Male-Females, the Dragon Forms / Religion hid in War'. This is the period when an inversion has taken place from the second stage: the male within a female has become 'A Female Hidden in a Male'.[30] We have already confronted one manifestation of this condition in discussing the aggressive phallic female who, assuming the role of a man, impregnates another female. We now confront the anomaly of the female-insinuated man. He is aroused by the female whose sexual attractiveness invades his whole being, dominating every nerve and limb; but he is without relief. The anomaly is that he has not only absorbed the female's seductive charms; he has also adopted the female ethic based on frigidity and, censoring himself, he becomes his own restrainer. He has been made effeminate, an old fear that Blake revives with new meanings. Man has, to use a Freudian term, 'internalised' the principle of feminine chastity and denial. The female in the male serves (1) to arouse and (2) to frustrate him. Unfulfilled love and unrealised desire produce one of the most prevalent discontents of civilisation. And man, drunk with his own swallowed passion, reels off to aggressive wars.

> I am drunk with unsatiated love
> I must rush again to War: for the Virgin has frownd & refusd
> Sometimes I curse & sometimes bless thy fascinating beauty.
> (J 68:62–4)

We have said that only Christ could rend the iron veil of Vala. Only Christ can overcome the devastations of the 'Female hid within a Male'.

> But Jesus breaking thro' the Central Zones of Death & Hell
> Opens Eternity in Time & Space; triumphant in Mercy.
> (J 75:21–2)

In studying Blake's concept of sexuality we confront a changing and paradoxical complex of attitudes that is a blend of personal joy and pain, prophetic rage and optimism, love of love and disgust with love.[31] That complex does, finally, organise itself into a pattern of Christian respect for the body that needs to be redeemed because it has been woefully perverted but that even in its fallen state, when sexual appetites are untrammelled and free, can provide an earnest of salvation.

So harrowing was fallen sexuality, but at the same time so full of delightful promise, that Blake always kept Babylon and Beulah in perilous balance. He could worry 'Lest the sexual Generation swallow up Regeneration' and declare 'Humanity knows not of Sex'; but he could also exclaim: 'O holy Generation [*Image*] of regeneration'.[32]

What is the place of the sexual body in Eden? Are there traces of the perilous balance even here? There seem to be; and these appear, if we try to follow Blake's hints about the hierarchical order of the four Zoas, as those eternal powers in man, none of which can be eliminated but all of which must submit to order, an order that may imply rank. Blake's ambivalent and changing responses to so powerful an instinct as the sexual seem to affect the position of Luvah. After the marvellous Titianesque bacchanal of the Last Vintage of the Nations, a purgative ritual act absolutely necessary to the restoration of the highly compromised human faculties, Luvah is spread by the sons of Tharmas and Urthona as dung on the ground. And in the majestic coda of Night IX ('The Sun has left his blackness & found a fresher morning'), there is a place for Tharmas and Urthona but none for Urizen and Luvah. The latter two had been active in harvesting the grain and in pressing the grapes; but the bread is made and the wine of the ages is refined by Urthona, assisted by Tharmas. It is as though the one-time tyrants of the mind and the passions must, in the restoration of order, return to their instrumental and subservient positions – reason below imagination, physical love below the sensibility of the heart. It may be possible to go beyond a subordination by pairs – Urizen and Luvah below Urthona and Tharmas – and say that Luvah stands below Urizen as undoubtedly Tharmas stands below Urthona, Blake reserving the highest role for the artistic and human imagination. Since *intellectual* war brings about the reign of sweet *science*, and since these are mental acts close to the imaginative, Luvah must take a place below Urizen. Albion turns Luvah and Vala over to Urizen with the command that as servants they are to 'obey and live', forgetting the wars of sexual violence and returning to peaceful love. They are remanded into their own place, 'the place of the seed not in the brain or heart'. In *The Four Zoas*, then, the ranking of these mighty faculties would appear to be: Urthona, Tharmas, Urizen, and Luvah.[33]

But that order hardly persists in Blake's other apocalyptic climaxes, and sexuality is given greater emphasis. The assimilation of the virgin Ololon into Milton is sexually conceived in a kind of climax that *The Book of Thel* lacked. The 'Clouds of Ololon' wrap around the Saviour's limbs as 'a Garment dipped in blood' – that is, as Luvah's garments, the garments of physical passion. And in the climax of *Jerusalem* the bow of salvation is masculine and feminine, the arrows are the arrows of love, and the chariot in which the new fourfold man rides is the 'Sexual Threefold'.[34] The East, the realm of Luvah, has its rivers of bliss, the 'Nerves of the Expansive Nostrils', nostrils perhaps being a polite substitute for enlarged sexual organs.[35]

Blake said of redeemed humanity that it 'is far above / Sexual organisation; & the Visions of the Night of Beulah.' In apocalyptic vision Beulah is transcended, and the sexual torments of the Luvah-Orc-Vala Babylon are burned away. Institutional marriage and the ritual giving in marriage do not exist in the fourfold Eden. But the body, threefold sexuality, clearly does. It is now on the periphery where it is prominent but not predominant; it is no longer at the centre where it does not belong. But the Zoas ride in their chariots, and Blake's final view is that the body must unashamedly be accepted and accorded its proper place in the intellectual and artistic life. 'Art & Science cannot exist but by Naked Beauty display'd.'

Sexuality remains and the body is redeemed, assuming an important though subordinate place.[36]

The final view, from the perspective of the imaginative eternity, upon the raging torments of love and jealousy is instructive. We have seen that one ordering places Luvah below Urizen in their eternal stations. But the positions are reversed in a retrospective glance on their fallen condition. For the production of pure mischief, essential and causative distress, the palm must go to the intellectual tyrant Urizen, whom Albion addresses as follows:

> My anger against thee is greater than against this Luvah
> For war is energy Enslavd but thy religion
> The first author of this war & the distracting of honest minds
> Into confused perturbation & strife & honour & pride
> Is a deceit so detestable that I will cast thee out
> If thou repentest not ...
>
> (FZ IX:375)

It is difficult not to believe that Blake shared Albion's view that it is better to burn sexually than to suffer, 'in misery supreme' and all alone, the deprivations of ungratified desire. If so, Blake's latest position reveals the essential integrity of his position on sexual love. The message of Lambeth had not been lost but modified to meet new individual and social conditions.

Philosophically, religiously, and artistically, the reason for Blake's preservation of the sexual body in Eden can be explained by the work of Los and Christ, who in the last analysis must sanction and support what is to be preserved. Los beats the 'terrific Passions & affections' into wedges and draws them into nerves. In the looms of Enitharmon the affections are endowed with 'the ovarium & the integument'. Both the man and the woman of art labour through adversity to create the sexual body with its 'milky fibres' of semen. Why? Not merely because generation is the image of regeneration, although it is that. More basically, because the sexual act and the sexual emotions belong to our essential humanity. Because art makes humanity its subject, the presses of Los could not make the wine of eternity without the grapes of Luvah. Art – and the salvation that it ministers to – depends as much on the presence as on the control and purification of the passions.[37]

Christ comes clothed in Luvah's red robes. In Great Eternity – when the faculties were in ordered stability – Luvah had been the most Christ-like of the Zoas, 'the gentlest mildest'. Even in his suf-

ferings on earth Luvah goes through a crucifixion, mocked as a king
of Canaan, wearing a crown of iron thorns. Christ assumed the
body of passion in the Incarnation, and when he forgave Mary he
also forgave that 'melancholy Magdalen', the fallen Vala. Blake's
belief seems to have been that Christ's nature was like ours even in
possessing the passions, that his manhood included the natures of
Luvah and Vala. When he put off his generated body (that is, the
body he acquired from his mother by natural, not supernatural,
generation) by dying on the cross, it was not to fly up to a shadow-
land of pure spirit but to reassume his position as fourfold man.
The Eternal Man, who is Christ, rides a sexual chariot and is
wrapped in a threefold sexual texture – the head, the heart, and the
reins; the forehead, the bosom, and the loins. In Babylon, as we
have seen, 'a pompous High Priest' enters religion and sex 'by a
Secret Place', and sexuality is confined to the genitalia as religion is
centred in the high altar. In eternity the genitalia remain and are
respected, but love is extended to the whole body: 'Embraces are
Cominglings: from the Head even to the Feet'.[38]

From *Blake's Sublime Allegory*, ed. Stuart Curran and Joseph A.
Wittreich (Maddison, WI, 1973), pp. 101–18.

NOTES

[Jean Hagstrum's essay is an attempt to trace a pattern of sexual and emotional relationships in Blake's texts, particularly in *Vala, or, The Four Zoas*
and *Jerusalem*, through a reading of the figures of Luvah and Vala. In the
course of his argument, Hagstrum draws on both mythic and psychoanalytic materials, thus pointing the way towards a debate on Freud and psychoanalysis which developed through the 1970s and 1980s, and engaging
also with a long-running controversy over Blake's sexual politics which
recurs in several later essays in this volume. The version given here is slightly abbreviated from the original. Ed.]

1. Pope, *Rape of the Lock*, II. 65–7.

2. 'Altho' our Human Power can sustain the severe contentions/Of
   Friendship, our Sexual cannot: but flies into the Ulro' (*M* 42:32–3).
   The statement just quoted is made by Ololon in despair, but it is a fair
   statement of Blake's own view in the years of tribulation.

3. See *J* 29:36–7, 40; *FZ* V:333; *J* 80:27; *FZ* V:337; *FZ* II:311.

4. See *FZ* I:302; *J* 24:52; *FZ* V:337; *Thel* 3:7–8; *J* 95:16. Milton O.
   Percival suggests that Luvah's role as weaver points to feminine

characteristics, since weaving in Blake is usually done by women. See *William Blake's Circle of Destiny* (New York, 1938), p. 29. The implication of the passage in *Thel* cited, where Luvah appears first, is that he was associated with Apollo, the god of light.

5. See *FZ* I:301; *FZ* V:337; *M* 19:17–24; *FZ* VIIA:351; *FZ* II:310.

6. Freud, like Blake, believed that ideally the two kinds of love are united. See the reprinting of his essay of 1912 in Sigmund Freud, *On Creativity and the Unconscious* (New York, 1958), p. 174.

7. *FZ* VIIA:351; *FZ* I:298–9; *FZ* III:320; *J* 37:21; *J* 33:4.

8. See *J* 69:15; *J* 69:2; *J* 35:1–2.

9. See *J* 37:19.

10. Milton, *Il Penseroso*, l. 160.

11. S. Foster Damon, *A Blake Dictionary: The Ideas and Symbols of William Blake* (Providence, RI, 1965), under 'Storge'. The *Oxford English Dictionary* lists uses of this term in 1637, 1764, 1809 and later.

12. Emanuel Swedenborg, *The Delights of Wisdom pertaining to Conjugial Love* (New York, 1949), sections 392–8.

13. See *J* 54:9–10; *BU* 21 (Trianon); *FZ* V:334.

14. The Blake references in this passage are as follows: *FZ* I:300; *FZ* III:320; *J* 43:35–43.

15. See Sigmund Freud, *New Introductory Lectures*, in *Standard Edition of the Complete Psychological Works of Sigmund Freud*, vol. XXII (London, 1933), pp. 24, 126, 130.

16. See *FZ* II:311.

17. John E. Grant has almost convinced me that the two figures on the huge lily (*J* 28) are Albion and Vala. But if, as I suggest, Vala in one aspect has a darkly masculine side, the illustration may indeed refer to Jerusalem and Vala assimilating. See Grant's 'Two Flowers in the Garden of Experience', in *William Blake: Essays for S. Foster Damon*, ed. Alvin H. Rosenfeld (Providence, RI, 1969), pp. 354–62. Grant, to whom I am indebted for several parallels, calls my attention to details of *J* 75, where the woman (perhaps Rahab) has genital scales and perhaps a penis.

18. See *M* 34:12, 14; and *J* 89:58.

19. Northrop Frye, who comments on the transformation of Orc, says that this erotic quality 'increases in proportion to the frequency with which Blake calls him Luvah' (*Fearful Symmetry: A Study of William Blake* [Princeton, NJ, 1947], p. 235).

20. See *FZ* VIIA:346; *FZ* VIIA:352.

21. See *FZ* VIIA:347; *FZ* VIIA:349.

22. See *FZ* VIII:369; *FZ* II:311.

23. See *A* I:1; *FZ* VIIB:395; *J* 39:25.

24. See *FZ* VIIB:395; *J* 17:25–6; *J* 64:8, 16–17; *M* 19:55–60.

25. See *FZ* VIII:361; *EG*, p. 514.

26. See 'The Uncanny' (1919), in which Freud discusses, among other words, the German word *heimlich*, which ranges in meaning from the familiar to the concealed, from the 'homey' to the holy; it finally becomes synonymous with its opposite *unheimlich* (Freud, *On Creativity and the Unconscious*, pp. 125–31).

27. The Blake references in this paragraph are as follows: *J* 32:43–7; *J* 44:11, 34–40; *J* 65:56–78. For a visual rendition of the castrators and circumcisers, see *J* 69.

28. See *FZ* VIII:363–4; *J* 30:25–35.

29. See *J* 47:4–5; Annotations to Watson, p. 601.

30. See *FZ* IX:375; *M* 22:48–9; *M* 37:35–43; *M* 40:20.

31. For a discussion of the persistence of Blake's preoccupation with sexual love and its shifting emphasis, see John Sutherland, 'Blake: A Crisis of Love and Jealousy', *PMLA*, 87 (1972), 424–31.

32. See *J* 44:33; *J* 90:37; *J* 7:65.

33. See *FZ* IX:390; *FZ* IX:391–2; *FZ* IX:380.

34. 'The chariot is actually the vehicular form of the driver himself, or his own body' (Frye, *Fearful Symmetry*, p. 273).

35. See *M* 42:11–12; *J* 97:9–12, 98:11, 16–17.

36. See *J* 79:73–4; *J* 32:49.

37. See *FZ* VIII:362; *J* 86:39. This last passage, Plate 86 of *Jerusalem*, establishes beyond doubt the sexual meanings of 'fibres'.

38. See *FZ* VIII:358; *J* 24:53; *J* 65:56–7, 66:23–6; *J* 65:38; *M* 4:4–5; 5:6–9; *J* 69:43–4.

3

Angels out of the Sun: Art, Religion and Politics in Blake's *America*

DAVID E. JAMES

> One madman printed his dreams, another his day-visions; one had seen an angel come out of the sun with a drawn sword in his hand, another had seen fiery dragons in the air.... The Lower classes ... began to believe that the Seven Seals were about to be opened.
>
> (Robert Southey)[1]

In the early 1790s, England seemed ripe for revolution. Economic disaster accompanied the war against France, and social unrest found a model for its aspirations in the events across the Channel. At that time Blake was an active member of various revolutionary intellectual circles, and he wrote two poems about the revolutions of his day. The first, *The French Revolution*, is relatively realistic, essentially accurate to historical events, and almost all its characters are historical individuals. The poem was to have been commercially published by Joseph Johnson, but only the first of an advertised seven books was set in type, and that was withdrawn before publication. Like *The French Revolution*, the second poem, *America*, is clearly sympathetic to the revolution it describes, and it looks forward to the renewal in England of the revolution in the colonies. Apparently encouraging the common people to rise and throw off the yoke of kings and bishops, it is Blake's most vehement political statement, and when it was made there seemed to be a real possibility of inciting the people to political action. But in *America*, Blake mixed historical characters with the 'giant forms' of his later symbolism, greatly distorted historical actuality, and produced a poem so difficult that, until the advent of modern scholarship, it remained as isolated as his later prophecies from all but a small group of initiated readers.

The issues involved in Blake's decision to abandon *The French Revolution*, as well as the style of that poem, become more pronounced when we recall that the formal innovations of *America* were concurrent with Blake's rejection of the advantages of easy reproduction afforded by the commercial printing press. Subsequently he hand-engraved and hand-coloured his work, juxtaposing the poetry with illustrations whose language is equally esoteric, and produced not an edition of a given poem but a small number of unique copies. Apart from miscellaneous catalogues and advertisements, *The French Revolution* was the last of Blake's works to be set in type and so the last which had even the potential for wide distribution. Blake's reversion to an artisanal, pre-capitalist mode of production, along with his elimination of the entrepreneur bookseller by selling his work from his own home, had important consequences. Most obviously, it affected the price; *The French Revolution* was advertised at two shillings, but Blake's 'Prospectus', *To the Public*, of October 1793 advertises *America* at ten shillings and sixpence,[2] thus limiting its readers not just to those fit to understand it, but to those fit to buy it. In fact he limited his audience to a small group of wealthy connoisseurs, specialists who have not left to posterity any indication of having more than the most limited comprehension of the poems, let alone any sympathy for revolutionary politics. In effect Blake revived for himself the system of patronage whose evils he so bitterly condemned, and by limiting his patrons to that class who had least to gain by a republican revolution he essentially ensured his own political ineffectiveness. By the style he developed, and by the means of production he adopted, Blake traded a popular audience for a hypothetical audience of initiates, and even that did not really materialise until a hundred years after he was dead. As a formally advanced work of art, *America* may seek to embody the paradoxes and contradictions of Modern Art in general, for the disparity between its difficult style and the reading abilities and interests of the general public raises issues which, while more than usually crucial in the case of a poem explicitly concerned with political events, have regularly recurred since the Industrial Revolution, and which polarise current critical theory.

Romanticism itself provides one approach to the problem, for the transformation of traditional spiritual beliefs into a religion of the imagination allowed non-didactic but formally sophisticated art to assume the morally renovative power previously ascribed to more orthodox religious observances. For the English tradition, the classic formulation of the belief in the moral, and hence social, function of advanced art is Shelley's, and in the *Defence*, as in *Prometheus Unbound*, Shelley described a model of the way in which art affects social behaviour that, with minor variations, became the great liberal defence of art. While Shelley allowed that 'religious and civil habits of action' as well as 'language, colour [and] form' were all 'the instruments of poetry', it was the works of the poet of verbal language that he finally found to be the more enduring. It was also to such a poet that he conceded the ultimate power over the moral nature of man: 'A man to be greatly good', runs the familiar passage, 'must imagine intensely and comprehensively; he must put himself in the place of another and of many others; the passion and the pleasures of his species must become his own. The great instrument of moral good is the imagination; and poetry administers to the effect by acting upon the cause.' And by acting upon the imagination, the cause of moral good, the poet becomes the prime mover in social melioration; he becomes the 'unacknowledged legislator'.

Versions of Shelley's argument have been used to explain the time-lag between artistic advances and their supposed social effects, and also to justify the disparity, at any given time, between avant-garde art (itself essentially a Romantic phenomenon) and popular consciousness. This latter disparity is now typically incorporated into our idea of the valuable in art, and modern art has become, almost by definition, inaccessible to the common person. Blake himself came to accept such a position. He admitted that he did not write for the common man ('You say that I want somebody to Elucidate my Ideas. But you ought to know that What is Grand is necessarily obscure to Weak men', letter to Trusler, 23 August 1799), and he realised that only in 'future generations' would he find his proper audience (letter to Butts, 6 July 1803). The apothegm, 'Empire follows Art & Not Vice Versa as Englishmen suppose' (Annotations to Reynolds) summarises a deep distrust of direct political activity that accompanied his evolution of an aesthetic idealism very much akin to Shelley's. As he laboured over the endless revisions to the manuscript of *The Four Zoas*, Blake realised that in Los, not Orc, lay the means to the redemption he sought and so he cleared the way for his analysis of Milton into two parts, the one Satanic in its political commitment, and the other divine in its commitment to art, to 'the Human Imagination / Which is the Divine Body of Jesus' M 3:3–4: E 96).[3] Blake's own commitment to the imagination alone is central to both the substance and the form of his late prophecies, which become then essentially auto-telic works, self-justifying by reference to the faith that the redeemed imagination must be the source of all positive change, personal and public.

The Shelleyan argument has not gone unchallenged, and the following extract from a preface by Sartre to a book on twentieth-century music raises the issue in a way that implies a quite different notion of the relationship between artistic and social developments.

> ... music has developed according to its dialectic, becoming an art which depends upon a complex technique. This is a regrettable fact, but *it is a fact*, nevertheless, that it demands a specialised public. To sum up, modern music requires an elite and the working masses require music ... the social revolution calls for a conservative aesthetic whereas the artistic revolution demands in spite of the artist himself, a social conservatism.[4]

It has not always been the case that the revolutionary in art has been in antipathy to social revolution – in the early years of the Russian revolution, for example, the two appeared to co-exist – but, typically, twentieth-century societies undergoing revolutionary social change have discovered Sartre's paradox to be true and, resolving it by sacrificing the artistic to the political revolution, have produced a spectrum of pragmatic theories, ranging from the rejection of formalism in the USSR after the mid 1920s to Mao's less extreme but equally pragmatic position described in the address to the Yenan Forum. Being subsequent to Marx's inversion of Hegel, these responses and others like them share a common rejection of Shelley's (and Blake's) basic premise. Following Marx in supposing that 'life is not determined by consciousness, but consciousness by life',[5] they reject the idealist postulate that radical social transformation can be produced by the visionary renovation of consciousness.

If we wish to approach Blake as a modern poet, possible responses to *America* will be polarised along these lines. If we adopt the idealist point of view, and accept the rejection of clear historical reference as inevitable in the creation of a great work of art, then we laud Blake as a spiritual mentor, allowing him such status not only because of the timeless content of his vision, but also because that vision is manifested in complex formal structures which themselves extend the reader's imagination. While such an attitude may be an appropriate way of approaching the late prophecies (though, since it derives its aesthetic from them, it can never be truly critical of them), to invoke such terms in approaching *America*, which seems to speak so directly to political activity, is perhaps more hazardous since it implicitly separates the poem from its specific historical reference and context. But the problem is even greater if we do not subscribe to the idealist principles of Romantic criticism and, prizing ready accessibility and fidelity to historical actuality, we regret the stylistic development *America* marks.

I do not wish to propose a Zhdanovist critique of *America*, but it is important to note that attitudes very close to the expectation that art should provide 'the truthful, historically concrete representation of reality in its revolutionary development ... linked with the task of ideological transformation and education of workers in the spirit of socialism'[6] have been implicit in the comments of those critics who, concerned to understand Blake in a social and historical context rather than a mystical or purely literary one, have found *America* problematical. David V. Erdman and Jacob Bronowski both perceive a disparity between the form of Blake's mature work and its social effectiveness, both regret the obscurity of Blake's style after *The French Revolution*, and both explain his retreat from realism as the result of his fear of prosecution.

Though Bronowski makes no comment on the form of *America* specifically, he does suggest that 'only after Napoleon betrayed the Revolution, sometime towards 1800, did [Blake] finally settle into that endless monologue of fantasy about a Biblical hereafter which we call his prophetic books'.[7] The style of the Prophecies (which, despite Bronowski's dating, is not significantly different from that of *America*) is elsewhere contrasted to the style of *The French Revolution*: '*The French Revolution* was given up between setting and printing, because what it said had grown to be disliked in that time; and it may have grown to be thought seditious. ... [It] was written to be read, and to be understood, by simple men'.[8] Erdman is more explicit and, while he gives full details of the climate of repression which was developing in the early 1790s, he thinks that

Blake was inclined to overestimate the consequences of publication. His remarks are very suggestive and, though lengthy, merit extended quotation.

> Failure to publish *The French Revolution* was a decisive failure for Blake. In this work, imaginatively high-flown as it is, he came closer than he ever would again to making his interpretation of history comprehensible to the English public of his own day. Withdrawal of this work was to mean Blake's withdrawal from any audience beyond a few uncritical or even uncomprehending friends, his withdrawal from the essential experience of communication, without which even the most richly significant and creative art cannot attain full stature and true proportions. Failure to communicate with the fraternity of citizens for whom and of whom he wrote encouraged Blake to pursue the involuted symbolism and obscure manner he had already made use of in *Tiriel* and *The Marriage*. (Yet today, as Blake's audience grows, we comprehend that the 'failure' was but for a season.)
>
> His isolation also gave free rein to his nervous fear of censorship, which was related to the political realities of his time only in an exaggerated form that interpreted the possibility of jail as a probability of hanging. ... Without the salutary corrective of public appearance in print, he assumed that his own republican thoughts would be considered deeply subversive and bring him to the scaffold. Yet in his bardic self he remained bold.[9]

Though Erdman does not pursue this line of thought in his later criticism,[10] here he implies that after *The French Revolution* Blake's poetry was not wholly successful, and also that the form of *America* can be explained as Blake's deliberate distortion of what he really wanted to say, the construction of a symbolism which concealed rather than revealed his true content. In light of Blake's subsequent evolution of a purely idealist aesthetic, Erdman's stress on his fear and especially on his isolation from the public implies an interpretation of Blake's whole career along the lines of Plekhanov's hypothesis about the relationship between style and social conditions, in which Blake's adoption of an 'attitude of art for art's sake' (rather than an attitude of 'art as a judgement on the phenomena of life' along with a concomitant 'readiness to participate in social struggles')[11] can already be seen as implicit in the form of *America*. Like the idealist approach, Erdman's argument, then, assumes that Blake saw history in the way that we do, and consequently, it presents Blake's choice between making art and writing history as an absolute one.

Contrary to both methods of interpreting Blake's stylistic innovations, I would like to argue that his view of history at this time was
quite different from ours, that the ontological dualism which for us
sunders reality into spirit and matter and so generates the two critical methods I have outlined, was not absolute for Blake, and that
the formal qualities of the poem, rather than manifesting a retreat
from history (caused either by fear or by the higher demands of art)
manifest a confrontation with history, the fulfilment of history as
Blake saw it. The form of the poem is the articulation of its specific
historical vision, a vision which is no longer current and of which
America was, perhaps, one of the last expressions. It was not until
after *America*, in fact not until Blake analysed Orc into Los and
Orc and rejected Orc, that for Blake the shape of consciousness
could be differentiated from the shape of history. At this moment
Blake became a 'Modern'. But at the time *America* was written,
Blake's conviction that the present moment was, in every sense,
'Eternal Death … the torment long foretold', where the poetic
genius was unified with practical action, produced a poem whose
formal qualities, while they invoke the problematics of modernism,
proceed from fundamentally different presuppositions.

A further remark by Erdman is illuminating. 'Both Paine and Blake,
living in a culture that still discussed politics in moralistic and Biblical
terms inherited from the English Civil War, viewed the American
Revolution as a sort of mass resurrection or secular apocalypse that
would overthrow poverty and cruelty and establish a new Eden.'[12]
Erdman is equivocal here, for, while he notes Blake's apocalyptic
expectations, the terms in which he elaborates them undercut them by
implying that Blake's discussion of politics in Biblical terminology was
merely metaphorical: Eden is defined as the absence of civil injustice
and the apocalypse is only a secular apocalypse. But the fact that we
no longer discuss politics in Biblical terms does not mean that Blake's
use of them was either metaphorical or a means of self-protection.
Living in a philosophic context that is essentially materialist, we can
tolerate such usage only by displacing it from reality, by distancing it
to some 'spiritual' realm of art or religion, categorically other than
historical actuality. We cannot take literally the suggestion that such
and such an event is a sign of the end of the world because we distinguish between spiritual (artistic) truth and events in political history,
and we know that among the latter the end of the world is not included. At this point in his career, such distinction was fallacious for
Blake, and his holistic vision of reality, which used to be interpreted as

evidence of his insanity, we now explain as metaphor. And by doing so, we essentially discount him. The cost of proving Blake sane is that we gloss as metaphoric (true only in the reflexive world of art) propositions which for him may well have been literally true.

America itself suggests that Blake's use of the terms of Biblical apocalypse was literal, for the revolution it anticipates is not another 'political' upheaval but the harbinger of the end of human time, and hence is apocalyptic precisely because it marks the coming together of temporal and spiritual history. The poem indicates Blake's expectation of the imminent consummation of 'the Jewish view of history', one which is 'linear, proceeding in a straight line from the six days of creation to the single Day of Judgement. During this progress from one end-point of history to the other, God manifests his purpose in and through everyday events, until at last all rivers of temporal history tumble into the vast ocean of eternity.'[13] *America* looks forward to such a confluence of the streams of human history, and consequently reveals political history as the outward sign of the impending Millennium. The revolution it expects is not a revolution in history in the usual sense of the word, but a revolution which would end history in the usual sense of the word; the conflict it describes is not one between rival political organisations, but rather a confrontation between God and the devil, between Christ and the Antichrist, whose successful resolution would end political organisations per se by containing the distinction between politics and religion in the revelation of a God who manifested himself equally in politics and religion and in fact in all areas of human experience.

As Erdman indicates, parallels to Blake's vision are not to be found in the rationalism of the justifications for the American and French revolutions, but rather in the expectations with which the English Revolution of the seventeenth century was approached. What Coleridge called 'that grand crisis of morals, religion and government'[14] engendered a whole spectrum of chiliastic creeds in the Puritan sects which brought an apocalyptic religious tradition into focus with the social changes attendant on the growth of modern capitalism. At that time, the reformation of morals, religion, and government were seen, not as separate issues, but as aspects of a single struggle to discover and put off the Antichrist in readiness for the end of the world.[15]

The continuity of the tradition of radical Puritan dissent through the eighteenth century has often been remarked upon, but its direct influence on Blake is hard to authenticate in detail outside the poetry, partially because of the paucity of biographical information and partially because the millenarian tradition was by that time largely an underground one. Nevertheless E.P. Thompson's assertion that 'the wilder sectaries of the English Revolution – Ranters and Fifth Monarchy Men – were never totally extinguished with their literal interpretations of the Book of Jerusalem descending from above' is, as he suggests, not without considerable importance for understanding Blake. Although, Thompson notes, the dissenting tradition as a whole split into those who pinned their hopes only on 'the kingdom within' and those who clung to the possibility of the restoration of 'the kingdom without', the latter group was revitalised by the political events of the end of the century: 'It was in the immediate aftermath of the French Revolution that the millenarian current, so long underground, burst into the open with unexpected force. ... Chiliasm touched Blake with its breath.'[16] Anticipating Thompson's point, A.L. Morton isolated four main groups of doctrine within the tradition that runs from the Ranters to Blake:[17] the belief that God had no existence apart from man; the belief that 'moral and ceremonial law is no longer binding on God's people ... and the orthodoxy which attempts to impose it is anti-Christian'; belief in the imminent revelation of the 'full truth of the Everlasting Gospel'; and 'the symbolism of the destruction of Babylon and the building of Jerusalem'.

These doctrines are clearly central in *The Marriage of Heaven and Hell*, and the introduction to that work invokes the French Revolution in eschatological terms: 'Now is the dominion of Edom & the return of Adam into Paradise' (Plate 3). The references to Isaiah XXXIV and XXXV direct the reader to an account of the 'day of the Lord's vengeance' (XXXIV.8) during which a peaceful return to Zion is accomplished after the destruction of the nations and the dissolution of the heavens. Thus, though the central substance of the *Marriage* is ahistorical and concerned with correcting the errors of traditional Christianity so as to create true insight within the individual consciousness, it frames its revision of Christianity with political references at the beginning and at the end ('The Song of Liberty'), which make its religious revolution at least synchronous if not synonymous with contemporary political events.

The particular terms by which the new heaven is a revival of 'the Eternal Hell' indicate another way in which the poem identifies the coming of the 'kingdom within' with that of the 'kingdom without'. As a critique of 'All Bibles or sacred codes' (including, especially, the idealist Swedenborg) the poem rejects the bifurcation of human experience into soul (good) and body (evil) upon which any distinction between spiritual and political revolution could be based. The very notion of a hereafter, or of a religion which allows mortification of the body as a means to spiritual redemption, is exposed as ideologically complicit in priestcraft's perpetuation of tyrannical social institutions. The inevitable implication of the poem's endorsement of bodily energy is revolution in the flesh as well as in the soul, and its ready acceptance of a Jesus militant leads easily into the recognition of contemporary revolutions as the war to end all wars. And so, in the 'Song of Liberty', after the 'new born terror' (a prototype of Orc) has routed 'the jealous king; his grey brow'd councellors, thunderous warriors' and the rest (Plate 25), 'Empire is no more', the very phrase that Orc uses in *America* to announce the inauguration of the new order.

Reading *America* as a religious poem, in which the political meaning of Orc is accepted as intrinsically artistic and spiritual, raises difficulties similar to those presented by the *Marriage*: it forces us to revise the limits of what is seen as specifically religious experience and also to reassess most of the values that we do think of within a religious frame of reference. Like the *Marriage*, *America* reveals orthodox pieties and institutionalised religion as party to tyranny of all kinds (Orc's speeches in Plates 6 and 8, for example, or Boston's Angel's speech in Plate 11), and in Orc values that we conventionally isolate into the separate realms of religion and politics are unified and identified. Similarly, accepting Orc as a religious force is initially difficult, and the violence of his energy has caused some commentators to feel that Blake was ambivalent about him,[18] especially since in *Europe*, printed only one year later, Blake had already begun to question the effectiveness of political revolution. The frequent references to both Jesus and Satan, when read undramatically, can cause added confusion. But, like the heroic principle of the *Marriage*, Orc includes the energy of both parties – the senses and the spirit – and the terms by which he is defined in the poem reveal political revolution as coincident with spiritual and aesthetic revolution.[19] Though his fires consume the five gates, we recall that the five senses are 'the chief inlets of Soul in this age' and that the body is 'a portion of the Soul discerned by the five Senses' (*MHH* 4). Nor should we forget that the devil who is Orc's prototype is Blake's first figuration of the Poetic Genius from which 'the body or outward form of Man' is derived (*All Religions are One*).

Like other radicals of his time, Blake interpreted the revolution in America as a conflict between the English rulers (and in fact the rulers of all the countries of Europe) and the people of England and America. The colonists' struggle was not an isolated or autonomous political event, but an ongoing one in which the revolutionary party had been victorious in the colonies, and, after a temporary setback in England, was soon to be victorious there also. This is important because it places the poem historically within the struggle it describes and so Plate 16 is not a coda to the main action, but rather the culmination of the main action, the point to which the whole poem looks. The poem's thematic structures are summarised there as Orc's fires consume 'the five gates of ... the law-built heaven' erected by the rulers of France, Spain, Italy, and Albion between 1776 and 1793. But replacing a war between nations by what is clearly an international class-struggle is the least significant of Blake's transformations of the orthodox view of history, for the specification of George as a tyrant over both England and the colonies is part of a more comprehensive definition of him as the Antichrist, tyrant over all God's people, and correspondingly the similarly comprehensive definition of Orc as the long-awaited redeemer.[20] Thus, while the values that are invoked in the definition of Orc and Albion's Angel include all areas of human experience, consistently these values are placed inside a controlling reference to the religious archetypes, God and Satan as they are redefined by Blake.

Of the main body of *America*, the Prophecy as distinct from the Preludium, only the last four plates are concerned with the military action of the war. Most of the poem is occupied by a debate, eventually involving the Americans as adjudicators, but primarily between Orc and Albion's Angel in which each party attempts to define himself as the true God and the other as the Antichrist. The method is dramatic and the entire section has a close structural and thematic reference to the *Marriage*, especially to the Memorable Fancy in which the Angel and the narrator each try to impose their 'phantasy' upon the other. Orc first appears over the Atlantic, 'a Human fire fierce glowing' and, like Milton's Satan, giving 'heat but not light'. Staining the temple with his blood and shaking it with his voice, he defines the moment of his coming as both that of the rising of Christ on the third day ('The grave is burst, the spices shed ...') and the Day of Judgement ('The bones of death, the cov'ring clay ... [awaken and] Spring like redeemed captives'). The metaphor's identification of political liberation in eschatological terms is extended to include further examples of liberation from tyranny: legal (the slave will be freed); personal (the 'inchained soul' will rise); and international ('Empire is no more'). Responding to this vision, Albion's Angel asks the so-far unnamed terror whether he is not in fact Orc, 'Blasphemous Demon, Antichrist, hater of Dignities; Lover of wild rebellion and transgressor of God's Law', his question affirming civil and religious transgressions as manifestations of a single source, parallel to and implicit in each other. Orc admits his identification with Satan ('I am Orc, wreath'd around the accursed tree') and as such proclaims his intention of restoring the 'fiery joy' that had been destroyed by the Urizenic Moses. His rejection of that 'stony law' is a rejection of false religions, preparatory for a renewal of the true hellish religion described in the *Marriage*. It naturally leads to a vision of man (derived from Daniel) walking through the fires of revolution which, as Bloom notes, presents 'Orc's man [as] one stage higher than Nebuchadnezzar's image'.[21]

Albion's Angel's reply to Orc's declaration of war identifies the American resistance as Satanic in similar terms. Looking across the Atlantic he sees the 'rebel form that rent the ancient / Heavens; Eternal Viper self-renew'd', and so he attempts to call his governors to arms. As they sit on the Atlantean hills, the governors thus find themselves in the position of having to choose between two figures each claiming to be the true God, each seeing the other as Satan. Speaking for the other twelve, Boston's Angel rejects Albion's Angel (as later the Americans 'reject' his plagues) and chooses Orc, basing his decision on the hypocrisy of Albion's Angel whom he sees as a false God, a restrainer of energies; under Albion's Angel, 'pity is become a trade, and generosity a science, / That men get rich by'. As in the *Songs* and the *Marriage*, orthodox Christian virtues are merely socially sanctioned forms of covert aggression; Albion's Angel is a God who 'writes laws of peace, & clothes him in a tempest'. Boston's Angel's decision marks the resolution of the debate and the acceptance by the Americans of Orc as the true God. The governors therefore throw down their 'golden sceptres' to join Washington and the active phase of the war begins.

While on the one hand the moment of history confronted by *America* is defined as a part of the conclusive battle between Christ and the Antichrist, it is also implicitly apocalyptic by virtue of the organisation of Orc and Albion's Angel into homogeneous 'sheaves' which allows the confrontation to take place. As in *Milton*, 'Separating What has been Mixed' (25:28) is the process which precipitates the consummation, and so the fact that, in the body of the poem, Orc is himself unified and then becomes unified with the American and the English people is itself a sign of his victory over the dualisms that the false God exploits in fallen time. Before the poem proper, Orc is divided. In the Preludium he is separated from nature, the 'shadowy daughter of Urthona', and he is himself split into a material and a spiritual form; Urthona rivets his tenfold chain to the rocks while his spirit soars on high. While Orc is in this condition, nature is moribund; the female is 'nameless' and her hostility and the armour she wears make her invulnerable. But after Orc liberates himself and copulates with her, she recognises as her lover not simply the Orc she had previously fed but also the forms in which his spirit appears; the 'serpent in Canada' courts her and 'a Whale in the South-sea' drinks her soul. By joining Orc, she becomes a nexus which unifies his disparate forms, and it is in this condition that Orc is revealed to her as 'the image of God', and his appearance as the sign of 'eternal death ... the torment long foretold'.

As an address to Orc's coming, *America* recapitulates its hero in that the dualisms which characterise fallen time are systematically replaced in the poem by a holistic vision in which political, social, and psychological events are all determined by a spiritual infrastructure. It is from this fact, from the elaboration of the defining qualities of Orc in the form of the poem, that its characteristic difficulties follow. Specifically, we may isolate three formal aspects which may be explained by reference to the combination in Orc of political and spiritual apocalypse: the nature of the symbolic figures themselves, the relation between the figures and their environment, and the relation between the events described in the poem and material history.

The debate between Orc and Albion's Angel is anomalous in that it presents as ontologically equal entities whose reference to material history are quite different. While Albion's Angel does invoke a specific historical figure, Orc himself lacks such a material reference. An allegorical reading can translate Albion's Angel as George, but an interpretation of Orc along the same lines confronts only another abstraction – revolutionary religious energy or something of that order. The conversation between an abstract symbol and a real person, which to us must appear as a paradox – the sign of a tension between history and art (or idea) – is possible in the poem because, since *America* is in a basic sense neither a fiction nor simply a history, it marks (to use Sidney's Aristotelian distinction) the coincidence of *kathekaston*, the particular, with *katholou*, the universal consideration. In the interpenetration of what we call art and history, of symbol and concrete reality, the metaphorical world is made real and the historical world is revealed as metaphorical. The historicising of mental, analytic forms like Orc is accompanied by a corresponding but inverse extension of figures like George into metaphysical agents. Consequently we find in the poem, not a rigid distinction between spiritual forms and historical figures, but rather a continuum of figures in whom the pressure of abstract, general significance is more or less intense. Between the extremes of abstraction and mere historical specificity represented by, say, Orc and Paine respectively, we find a range of figures whose significance is generalised to a greater or lesser degree; in order of decreasing abstraction a sample list would run something like: Orc, Albion's Angel, London's Spirit, the scribe of Pennsylvania, and Washington. In such a sequence, there is no point at which a precise line can be drawn to separate abstract analytic forms ('Gods') from humans, no line between *katholou* and *kathekaston*. Though our conception of history would suggest a more acute reference outside the poem for Washington than for Orc, within the dynamics of the poem, they co-exist as ontological equals. Though Boston's Angel (to take an intermediate case) is a human being in history (Samuel Adams, according to Erdman),[22] he is as unconstrained by time and space, by the materiality of his source, as Orc; he addresses Orc as an equal and is able to fly through the dark night (11:3). 'Unrealistic' acts like this, of which all characters are capable, are significant because they indicate the total absorption of material history into the spiritual perspective of the poem.

The lack of differentiation between characters and what we would expect to be symbols, analytic of character, is paralleled by a similar lack of differentiation between character and environment. All distinctions between spiritual values and materially descriptive qualities are condensed in a landscape that is itself simultaneously material and analytic. Statements like 'the Priests in rustling scales / Rush into reptile coverts, hiding from the fires of Orc' (15:19–20) or 'Sick'ning lay London's Guardian, and the ancient miter'd York / Their heads on snowy hills, their ensigns sick'ning in the sky' (15:9–10) include both figure and ground in an ontology that is, in our terms, purely metaphorical; the figures and the landscape are extensions, symbolic amplifications, of each other. Nature is itself symbolic; the symbolic becomes nature.

This identification of material and spiritual values in space, in geography, is paralleled by a similar identification in time of historical events themselves with their significance, for while the history that Blake presents is not a strictly 'factual' account, neither is it a poetic embellishment or distortion of the facts. Rather, it presents the interpenetration of material history with the meaning of history in such a way that specific events are seen to manifest the larger metaphysical happenings which control and produce them. Details from history are selected in so far as they illustrate the metaphysical conflict that is the poem's real subject. Consequently, in examining Blake's relation to his historical sources, what is most important is not the extent to which he conceals historical fact, but the extent to which he includes it.

From *Studies in Romanticism*, 18 (1979), 235–52.

NOTES

[David E. James' essay takes as its starting-point the major historical and political readings of Blake, David V. Erdman's *Blake: Prophet Against Empire* (revised edn, Garden City, NY, 1969) and Jacob Bronowski, *William Blake and the Age of Revolution* (London, 1972). Through a detailed analysis of *The French Revolution* and more particularly *America*, James seeks both to draw out the hidden assumptions of these critics and also to mount an argument about 'realism' and prophecy with a view to establishing the particularity of Blake's views of the events of his time and his unique approach to the textual representation of these events. It is here reproduced in abbreviated form. Ed.]

1. Robert Southey, *Letters from England* (2nd edn, London, 1808), vol. III, p. 238. Quoted in Jim Borck, 'William Blake: A Prophetic Tradition' (dissertation, University of California at Riverside, 1969), p. 52.

2. By 1827 it cost six guineas. See Blake's letter to Cumberland, 12 April 1827.

3. This development is most clearly described by Morton Paley in *Energy and the Imagination: A Study of the Development of Blake's Thought* (Oxford, 1970). See David E. James, *Written Within and Without: A Study of Blake's 'Milton'* (Bern, 1977) for Blake's revision of his earlier political position.

4. Sartre, 'The Artist and his Conscience', in *Marxism and Art*, ed. Berel Lang and Forrest Williams (New York, 1972), p. 218.

5. Karl Marx and Friedrich Engels, *The German Ideology*, in *Marx and Engels: Basic Writings on Politics and Philosophy* (Garden City, NY, 1959), p. 247.

6. I quote from the First All-Union Congress of Soviet Writers, in Abram Tertz, *On Socialist Realism*, trans. George Dennis (New York, 1965), p. 148.

7. Jacob Bronowski, *William Blake and the Age of Revolution* (New York, 1965), p. 10.

8. Ibid., p. 77.

9. David V. Erdman, *William Blake: Prophet Against Empire* (2nd edn, Garden City, NY, 1969), p. 153.

10. By the time of his '*America*: New Expanses', in *Blake's Visionary Forms Dramatic*, ed. David V. Erdman and John E. Grant (Princeton, NJ, 1970), pp. 92–114, Erdman had adopted the idealist position: the text and the pictures 'both lead us ... from perception to Intellectual Vision, a last judgment in which fools perish' (p. 93).

11. George V. Plekhanov, 'Art and Society', in *Art and Society and Other Papers in Historical Materialism* (New York, 1974), p. 20.

12. Erdman, *Prophet Against Empire*, p. 50. Erdman's symbolist approach recurs in 'New Expanses', where he speaks of Blake's '*symbolic* fusion of military and political and psychic history, *heightened by apocalyptic imagery*' (p. 95, my emphasis). In what remains otherwise one of the most precise summaries of *America*, S. Foster Damon offered a dualistic reading similar to Erdman's approach: 'In *The French Revolution*, Blake endeavoured to describe history as seen by the visionary; in *America* he tried to describe eternity as it is symbolised by history' (*William Blake: His Philosophy and Symbols* [1924; reprinted New York, 1947], p. 109). My argument is that in this poem eternity is not 'symbolised' by history, but manifest in history.

13. C.A. Patrides, *The Grand Design of God: The Literary Form of the Christian View of History* (London, 1972), p. 6.

14. Coleridge, *Table Talk*, 9 November 1833.

15. For seventeenth-century apocalyptic thought I have found the following most useful: Norman Cohn, *The Pursuit of the Millennium* (London, 1957); Michael Fixler, *Milton and the Kingdom of God* (Evanston, IL, 1957); and Christopher Hill, *Antichrist in Seventeenth-Century England* (London, 1971).

16. E.P. Thompson, *The Making of the English Working Class* (New York, 1964), pp. 48 and 50 respectively. See also Erdman, *Prophet*

Against Empire, p. 50, and Bronowski, p. 12. Borck's 'William Blake: A Prophetic Tradition' is an exhaustive account of contemporary prophetic writing and Blake's relation to it.

17. A.L. Morton, *The Everlasting Gospel: A Study in the Sources of William Blake* (1958; reprinted New York, 1966), pp. 36–7. A collection of Ranter literature is conveniently reprinted in Cohn.

18. For example Paley: 'In *America* (1793) a double perspective is maintained, suggesting the ambiguity of Orc by his two forms: human and serpent' (p. 61). In 'A Note on the "Orc Cycle"' appended to 'New Expanses', Erdman correctly takes issue with Frye's notion of an 'Orc Cycle' which would implicitly invalidate any Orc-inspired revolution. Erdman is entirely right in affirming 'The cycle of history prophetically examined in *America* and *Europe* is not that of rebellion–vengeance–tyranny; it is of enslavement–liberation–re-enslavement, the prophet's concern being how to escape the re-enslavement' (p. 112), but it is important to notice that *America* itself contains no indication of cyclicism within Orc. As George Quasha remarks, 'A careful reading of *America* ... seriously raises the question of the relevance of any cyclic symmetry to the poem engraved in 1793.' [See p. 17 above. Ed.]

19. Cf. Erdman: 'in *America* Orc himself fulfils all the functions of Los and the latter is not mentioned' (*Prophet Against Empire*, p. 255).

20. Erdman's argument that Blake adopted the symbolic forms through fear of reprisal runs into some difficulty here. Though it is true that 'the final text of *America*, for example, eliminates all direct naming of George III and his Parliament' (*Prophet Against Empire*, p. 153), it hardly seems likely that 'The King of England' is less dangerous a locution than 'George III'.

21. Harold Bloom, *Blake's Apocalypse: A Study in Poetic Argument* (Garden City, NY, 1963), p. 131.

22. Erdman, *Prophet Against Empire*, p. 26.

4

Blake in the Chains of Being

NELSON HILTON

For the poet who hears 'mind-forg'd manacles' and who describes our planet Earth pleading for someone to break her heavy chain, such devices assume more than material reference; they present themselves as key links in the linear, univocal speech and lockstep thought process that Blake strives to replace by the four folds of his vision. A 'chain' is not simply a chain, but also an instance of what it refers to and (as a word) itself participates in: an image of order variously epitomised as the 'great chain of being' and its double the 'chain of discourse', with its verbal 'links'. These formulations and assertions of the intelligibility of world and communication are bound together through the sign of the chain; this sign Blake seizes on in order to explore its nature and unlock the reader from its implications.

The background of 'the Great Chain of Being' needs little comment after A.O. Lovejoy's seminal study of what he saw as 'the sacred phrase of the eighteenth century'.[1] The chain originates in the *Iliad* (8.19), is adapted and expanded by Macrobius and others, approved by Bacon, and memorialised in Milton's picture of our pendant world, 'hanging in a golden Chain'.[2] A passage from Pope sets the tone for the century's sense of the image:

> Vast chain of being! which from God began
> Natures aethereal, human, angel, man,
> *Beast, bird, fish*, insect, what no eye can see
> ....

> From Nature's chain whatever link you strike,
> Tenth, or ten thousandth, breaks the chain alike.[3]

Samuel Johnson, by contrast, was not at all comfortable with the 'presumptuous' notion or doctrine of the 'chain of nature'. He saw in it 'infinite vacuities', each of which gave room for the 'infinite exertion of infinite power': 'no system can be more hypothetical than this, and perhaps no hypothesis more absurd'.[4] Blake would perhaps have agreed; Northrop Frye finds, for example, that 'there is no "chain of being" in Blake and no trace of any of the creatures invented by those who believed in a chain of being'.[5] But, though there is certainly no positively valued chain, one can, remembering the lines from Pope, still see its presence in Blake: the icon cannot be broken without having been recognised. In *The Book of Urizen* it begins not 'from God' but as 'the linked infernal chain' (10:35) given Urizen for a backbone after he disintegrates in

> unseen conflictions with shapes
> Bred from his forsaken wilderness,
> Of *beast, bird, fish,* serpent & element
> Combustion, blast, vapour and cloud.
>   (3:14–17)

Blake transposes 'Beast, bird, fish', from Pope's series of nine links but completes Urizen's 'ninefold darkness / Unseen' (3:9) by breaking down Pope's 'Natures aethereal' into the infinite vacuities of 'combustion, blast, vapour and cloud'. Urizen is in the state – or rather, is the state – where Nature's chain is being (mentally) created: in 'an unform'd / Dark vacuity: here Urizen lay' (*BL* 5:49–50).

The Chain of Being is only the most memorable instance of Being in chains: 'Our thoughts are link'd by many a hidden chain', wrote Samuel Rogers,[6] while for Burke, 'There is a chain in all our sensations.' The French jurist J.M. Servan gave the power of association even more dramatic expression in 1767:

> When you have ... formed the chain of ideas in the heads of your citizens, you may then boast of leading them and being their masters. A stupid tyrant can restrain slaves with chains of iron, but a real politician fastens them much more strongly by the chain of their own ideas; it is to the firm ground of reason that he attaches the first end, a link all the stronger because we ignore its composition, and because we consider it our own work: despair and time corrode links of iron

and steel, but they can do nothing against the habitual association of ideas, except to strengthen it further, and on the soft fibres of the brain is founded the inalterable base of the firmest empires.

Hume wrote of 'that chain of causes and effects which constitute our self or person'; Berkeley drew on the Greek word for chain (*seira*) in the title of his *Siris: A Chain of Philosophical Reflexions*; and Alexander Campbell's discussion of Newton was presented as a *Chain of Philosophical Reasoning*. Young wrote of '*Reason's* Golden Chain', and, according to Erasmus Darwin, 'Love and Sympathy ... bind Society in golden chains', while 'thoughts to thoughts are link'd with viewless chains'. Hannah More felt in 1782 that the essence of sensibility still eluded 'the chains / Of Definition', and Boswell, saying that Johnson's understanding was cramped by 'his supposed orthodoxy', wrote, 'He was confined by a chain which early imagination and long habit made him think massy and strong.' Hobbes spoke of 'the chayn of a mans Discourse', which was for Albrecht von Haller an intrinsic aspect of human communication: *Natura in reticulum sua genera connexit, non in catenam: homines non possunt nisi catenam sequi, cum non plura simul sermone exponere* [*sic*]. Little wonder that Rousseau's famous words found such resonance; as Blake would have read in the 1791 translation of *The Social Contract*, 'Man is born free, and yet we see him everywhere in chains: and those who believe themselves the masters of others, cease not to be even greater slaves than the people they govern. How this happens I am ignorant.' William Godwin's answer, two years later, was that 'the chains fall off of themselves when the magic of opinion is dissolved'.

Bacon, seen as having liberated science from the tyranny of scholastic rhetoric by realising 'the false appearances that are imposed upon us by words', is praised by James Thomson as the one who

> Led forth the true philosophy ... long
> Held in the magic chain of words and forms
> And definitions void ...
> ....
> Investigating sure the chain of things.[7]

The intense concern for making words adequate to things is mirrored in an ongoing discussion of the 'bondage of Riming', which included both cognates, rhyme, and rhythm. Rhyme is in one sense the highest expression of its proverbial complement, reason (precisely *because* it offers 'a kind of fixative counterpattern of alogical implication'),[8] so that criticism of rhyme unavoidably involves a conception of reason and its link to words, and the relation of words to things. The discussions of rhyme are particularly interesting since, with the growing power of the doctrine of 'association', rhyme was, as it were, an assertion of the operation of *verbal* association opposed to connections 'really' in the world. Criticism of rhyme is then part and parcel of the attack on the pun, the concern over 'the abuse of words', and is expressed even by Pope:

> We ply the Memory, we load the brain,
> Bind rebel wit, and double chain on chain
> Confine the thought, to exercise the breath;
> And keep them in the pale of Words till death.
> Whate'er the talents, or howe'er design'd,
> We hang one jingling padlock on the mind[9]

Mark Akenside's Shakespeare justifies his 'hardy style' and locates its possibility in politics: 'I saw this England break the shameful bands / Forg'd for the souls of men by sacred hands'; England has spurned 'her Gothic chain' and so, turning again to style, should cease to regard as a model the French language 'which fetters eloquence'.[10]

Both the chain of association (via the physiological psychology of David Hartley) and its analogue, the chain of discourse or language (implicit in the concern with versification), lead back to book 3 of Locke's *Essay Concerning Human Understanding*, 'Of Words'. Here the first link of these chains is discovered to be '*a perfect arbitrary imposition*' in which 'such a word is made arbitrarily the mark of such an idea'.[11] This arbitrariness, however, far from being weak or random, is supported by a great and continuing power: 'But so far as Words are of Use and Signification, so far is there a constant connexion between the Sound and the *Idea* ... without which ... they are nothing but so much insignificant noise'.[12] The 'sound annexed' to a collection of ideas must serve 'as the sign of that precise determined Collection, and no other. This is very necessary'.[13] The relation between word and referent is arbitrary but 'very necessary', reflecting an enforced 'constant connexion'. The resulting links in the chains of association and language are thus the instruments of an arbitrary, dictatorial power that in its political form was 'an eighteenth-century obsession'[14] but that in its invisible semiotic (the word proposed by Locke[15]) or psycholinguistic expression passed with less regard.

Reporting that he read Locke 'when Very Young', Blake declares that 'Lockes Opinions of Words & their Fallaciousness are Artful Opinions & Fallacious also' (E 659). Blake's rape of Locke begins with *An Island in the Moon*; there Scopprell takes up a book and reads the following passage to his friend Obtuse Angle: 'An Easy of <Huming> Understanding by John Lookye Gent John Locke said Obtuse Angle. O ay Lock said Scopprel' (E 456). Hence Urizen, who perhaps makes a cryptic appearance in the exclamation 'Your reason Your reason ... I'll give you an example for your reason' (E 450), ends 'In chains of the mind locked up' (*BU* 10:25, et al.); so also the speaker of 'The Crystal Cabinet' is seized by the Maiden, put 'into her Cabinet' – like Locke's 'empty cabinet'[16] – and 'Lockd' (significantly capitalised) up to consider *reflections* that are moonlight. Locke's 'nominal essence' is, for Blake, no different than his 'real essence',[17] and so it stands as the terminal element of the infernal trinity 'Bacon & Newton & Locke' pointed to throughout *Jerusalem*.

'King Edward the Third', in *Poetical Sketches*, opens with the king commending 'Liberty, the charter'd right of Englishmen'. He exhorts the troops before Cressy, telling them that 'The enemy fight in chains, invisible chains, but heavy: / Their minds are fetter'd' (E 424). After listening to Blake's eponymous character, 'William, Dagworth's Man', identify the king's expedition as sinful ambition (scene 4) and Dagworth in turn label the field of battle as 'this prison house' (scene 5), we arrive at the obvious question: how do the king's auditors know that they, too, are not invisibly bound? And what is the nature of such unseen but heavy chains that fasten in the mind?

In 'London' we experience these questions for ourselves. Here chartered rights have produced 'charter'd streets' and a 'charter'd Thames', and are revealed through 'marks of weakness, marks of woe', marks that testify to an 'arbitrary imposition' based on some mysterious charter or 'any writing bestowing privileges or rights'. To gloss this definition, Johnson's *Dictionary* cites Sir John Denham: 'Here was that *charter* seal'd, wherein the crown / All marks of arbitrary power lays down';[18] but 'London' sees that power taken up again, as the chains binding the earlier 'enemy' are spoken by fellow-travellers who have also lost the ability to hear themselves:

> In every cry of every Man
> In every Infants cry of fear,
> In every voice: in every ban,
> The mind-forg'd manacles I hear
> (5–8)

The closing line of the stanza first read, 'The german forged links I hear' (E 796), referring more to the national ties of the Hanoverian king than the strength of German iron. The final version, a uniquely Blakean line, moves beyond the hint of simple political oppression to question the structure of our experience and our response to it. 'I hear', implicitly asks, 'do you hear?' 'He that hath ears to hear, let him hear', is the repeated refrain of Jesus, Blake's 'Divine Vision'. What do we hear? 'Forg'd' or 'fraudulent'? Mine or mind? Man in manacles? Whatever it is, it is everywhere mined and forged in the hearth of what is heard and seen. In this dungeon of London, Blake's strategy for unlocking the reader is the multiplication of significance, breaking the vocal chain at its weakest link, the univocal sign.[19] This deconstruction involves reorienting logic according to synaesthetic relations of eye and ear. Thus we are urged to hear here ('hear' is everywhere in this poem) the soldier's sigh running in blood, while the chimney-s/weeper's cry casts a pall over St Paul's:

> How the Chimney-sweepers cry
> Every blackning Church appalls,
> And the hapless Soldiers sigh
> Runs in blood down Palace walls
> (9–12, emphasis added)

Thus the opening line of the final stanza again emphasises 'I hear':

> But most thro' midnight streets I hear
> How the youthful Harlots curse
> Blasts the new-born Infants tear
> And blights with plagues the Marriage hearse

What is heard is not the 'curse' ending the second line, but how it blasts the 'tear' ending the third line and rhyming back to 'hear'. These words, hear–curse–tear, bring to bear the contradictions of sight and sound as we hear/see them coalesce in the final word, 'hearse'. The oxymoronic image of the 'marriage hearse' points to the impossibility of imagining that sight and sound, signified and signifier can be eternally 'linkd in a marriage chain' (FZ 58:13:

E 339), wedlocked. Gavin Edwards points to this impossibility in connection with stanza 3, seeing that the lines 'themselves join sound and sight, voice and matter, but in such a way as to suggest their radical *dis*junction'. Edwards also notes the 'very complex relations between reading, and hearing, and seeing' in the poem, and continues his discussion of the third stanza in terms particularly appropriate for our purpose: 'Blake links "sigh" and "blood" as immediately and magically correlative in a way that suggests the active exclusion of chains of cause and effect that might *really* link them.' What *really* links is, of course, the question. We do indeed 'converge on the final word [of the poem] like a Greek tragedy on its recognition-scene', not simply to encounter 'hearse' for an expected 'bed', but rather to experience 'literally' what Edwards himself senses, 'a liberating movement from off-stage, as a work of scription and vocalisation, an inscription of written characters.'[20] The univocal signifier, whether Lockean precision, instinctual cry, or unquestioned daily hearsay, is the cure of imagination, its hearse 'vehicle'; this poem literally marks and mars our single-visioned dreams of 'spousall verse' celebrating the mind fitted to the external world.

For Harold Bloom, '"London" centres itself upon an opposition between *voice* and *writing* ... [and] offers us a terrifying nostalgia for a lost prophetic *voice*, the voice of Ezekiel and religious logocentrism, which has been replaced by a demonic *visible trace*, by a mark.'[21] But Blake, who took more care than most poets with the 'visible traces' of his writing, hardly offers a compelling example of nostalgia for voice. As the example of 'hearse' illustrates, the 'Spirit of Prophecy', which is 'the Poetic Genius' (*ARO*), particularly manifests itself in language by using the additional freedom found at the intersection of voice and writing. The achievement of this transcendence of either category makes it impossible to consider 'London' an 'altogether negative and self-destructive ... text'. We might rather conclude that 'London' offers an affirming and self-deconstructing text, one that implicitly urges the reader to allow his or her eye to wander through its chartered lines, marking its marks, and hearing its 'every voice'. These invitations are conveyed through the contradictions in logic mentioned above and by dint of repetition: we simply cannot encounter 'charter'd ... charter'd', 'mark ... Marks ... marks', and 'every' six times in five lines without being driven to wonder what the words mean and *how* they mean. Our delight as these questions, and then their several 'answers', come to light at once proves and loosens 'the mind-forg'd manacles'. The poem's self-unchaining does not, of course, usher the delighting reader into any realm of absolute free-play, that 'allegorical abode where existence hath never come' (*E* 6.7). One could characterise the 'liberated' version of 'London' as merely proliferated chains of association, but such prolific 'chains' are no longer limiting, enslaving, 'devouring'; they become 'fibres ... a living Chain' (*FZ* 63:3; E 342).

In addition to expressing her desire for morning, 'EARTH'S Answer' asks for someone to

> Break this heavy chain,
> That does freeze my bones around
> Selfish! Vain,
> Eternal bane!
> That free love with bondage bound.
>   (21–5)

Her chain appears to be the creation of a Zeus-like 'Starry Jealousy ... Cold and hoar', who keeps her 'prison'd on watry shore'. The coldness of her keeper and the freezing power of the chain invoke the common poetic conception of winter locking everything in ice, and remembering the first lines, 'Earth raisd up her head', we are led to believe that the rest of her body is restrained by chains of 'the darkness dread & drear'. Similarly the children of Tiriel are 'chaind in thick darkness' and Ahania, like Earth, asks 'how can delight, / Renew in these chains of darkness' (*BA* 5:42–3). So the last line in the first stanza, 'And her locks cover'd with grey despair', involves more than the image of 'grey hairs' on Earth's head. Despair, in the *Visions*, is 'cold', while 'grey' associates 'hoary' (4:2, 7:19) and 'the grey hoar frost' (*FZ* 138:9: E 406). Her 'locks', then, also form part of the cold, frost-covered chain; her hair represents her 'mind-locks' (cf. E 10:29). This identity of Earth, linked to the Homeric and Miltonic golden chain, and the englobed, enchained mind – like Prometheus ('Forethought') in the original 'adamantine chains' – is also evident in Samuel Rogers's *Ode to Superstition* (1786): 'Thy chain of adamant can bind / That little world, the human mind' (1:1). The serpent pictured at the bottom of 'EARTH'S Answer' shows another chain. It is the bound form of free love: 'men bound beneath the heavens in a reptile form', 'Like a serpent! like an iron chain' (*Tir* 8:10, *BL* 5:16). Earth is held by chains, which jealously attempt to limit her to monogamous meaning and prohibit the free intercourse of signification. But it seems to be the nature of Earth and language not to endure restraint; her very locks transform themselves. The language of the third stanza manifests the earth's potential liberation from univocal syntax and meaning, as the various constructions in themselves contest the heavy chain:

> Selfish father of men
> Cruel jealous selfish fear
> Can delight
> Chain'd in night
> The virgins of youth and morning bear.
> ('EARTH'S Answer', 11–15)

The Marriage of Heaven and Hell goes into the nature of the chains in greater detail.

> The Giants who formed this world into its sensual existence and now seem to live in it in chains, are in truth. the causes of its life & the sources of all activity, but the chains are, the cunning of weak and tame minds. which have power to resist energy, according to the proverb, the weak in courage is strong in cunning.
>
> Thus one portion of being, is the Prolific. the other, the Devouring: to the devourer it seems as if the producer was in his chains, but it is not so, he only takes portions of existence and fancies that the whole.
> (Pl. 16)

This recapitulates Plate 11, which tells how 'the ancient Poets animated all sensible objects with Gods or Geniuses, calling them by the names'. However, 'a system was formed, which some took advantage of, & enslav'd the vulgar by attempting to realise or abstract the mental deities from their objects.' Hazard Adams has pointed out that the activity of 'the ancient poets' was 'the creation of language', but that 'the poetic verbal universe that holds subject, deities, and object together is destroyed by a competing idea of language that claims for itself only the power to point outward toward *things*'.[22] This is the language-chain, which limits us to 'portions of existence'; the chains in which the Giants 'seem' to live are, similarly, only our devouring perception. This relation between language, perception, and the giant man enchained underlies Blake's exclamation at the beginning of *Jerusalem* that 'Poetry Fetter'd, Fetters the Human Race!' (*J* 3). Such fetters, the chains of uninspired language and quotidian association, 'the soft fetters of easy imitation',[23] are like those binding the inhabitants of the cave in Plato's *Republic*. As presented by Blake's acquaintance Thomas Taylor,

'Suppose them to have been in this cave from their childhood, with chains both on their legs and neck, so as to remain there, and only able to look before them, but by the chain incapable to turn their heads around'.[24] So, in *Europe*,

> With bands of iron round their necks fasten'd into the walls
> The citizens: in leaden gyves the inhabitants of suburbs
> Walk heavy ...
>
> (12:29–31)

while *The Book of Los* shows 'the Eternal Prophet bound in a chain / Compell'd to watch Urizens shadow' (3:31–2).

The ground of perception, like language, generally goes unperceived, and this ignorance is an intrinsic attribute of chains, an aspect of the invisibility of the determining dimension of language that Ferdinand de Saussure called *langue*. Thus Milton 'wrote in fetters when he wrote of Angels & God' because 'he was a true Poet and of the Devils Party without knowing it' (*MHH* 5). Religion with its laws and mysteries is an instrument restraining awareness; its popular etymology, 'to bind back' (*re-ligiare*), testified to its enchaining function.[25] *America* sees 'the female spirits of the dead pining in bonds of religion; / Run from their fetters reddening' (15:23–4). The liberating message of Jesus was hampered by his disciples' fantasies of 'chains of darkness' and 'everlasting chains' to bind fallen souls until Judgment; but true language and true perception are of the Devil's Party, itself ultimately Jesus', because they reject writing in fetters and urge instead, as the 'Proverbs of Hell' witness, the free flow of significance. Both the concept of 'energy' in Blake's early poetry and that of 'imagination', which dominates the longer poems, are expressions of the desire to soar above a common bound, to copulate as freely as possible. The transition between these two terms marks Blake's realisation that such polymorphous, polysemous desire is to be acted and answered in unrestrained language: 'If in the morning sun I find it: there my eyes are fix'd / In happy copulation' (*VDA* 6:23–7:1).

The Book of Urizen tells the story of the binding of its subject like this:

> Forgetfulness, dumbness, necessity!
> In chains of the mind locked up,
> Like fetters of ice shrinking together
> Disorganiz'd, rent from Eternity,

Los beat on his fetters of iron
  (10:24–8; cf. *FZ* 54:4–5: E 336)

Urizen's chains are made by Los, 'the eternal Prophet'. Urizen
having separated from Eternity through his mournful discovery of
self-love, Los must for the time being bind him back by whatever
means possible – any Urizen being better than none. Los must bind
himself to Urizen, and it is precisely this act of sacrifice that holds
the key to their mutual resurrection. So, as things get worse before
they get better, 'the terrible race of Los & Enitharmon gave / Laws
& Religion to the sons of Har binding them more / And more to
Earth' (*SL* 4:13–15).[26] As part of his (Los/Urizen's) binding, Urizen
is given a body consisting of the chained changing world. The pun
is evidently intended since:

> [Los] watch'd in shuddring fear
> The dark changes & bound every change
> With rivets of iron & brass;
>
> And these were the changes of Urizen.
>   (*BU* 8:9–12)

Later Los sees Urizen, 'in his chains bound'. Perhaps the most
intriguing and spectacular aspect of this bound creation is the first
'change', Urizen's backbone:

> Like the linked infernal chain;
> A vast Spine writh'd in torment
> Upon the winds;
>   (*BU* 10:36–8)

or, as *The Book of Los* sees it, 'Like a serpent! like an iron chain /
Whirling about in the Deep.' These connections disclose the underlying identification that:

[Urizen's] *spine* = *serpent* [worm] = *chain* [gravity].

Links here are the idea that the spinal marrow of a dead man turns
into a snake,[27] the classical and Norse conception of the serpent
wound around the earth (Blake labels his title-page illustration to
Gray's *The Descent of Odin*, 'The Serpent who Girds the Earth'),
and the Homeric and Miltonic golden chain of being that binds the
earth. After Newton the image of gravity as a chain became
common; so James Thomson apostrophises the Sun in *Summer*:

> 'Tis by thy secret, strong, attractive force,
> As with a chain indissoluble bound,
> Thy system rolls entire.[28]

In a footnote on the 'golden everlasting Chain' of Jove in book 8 of the *Iliad*, the original source for chain-of-being imagery, Pope suggested that 'the *Aegyptians* understood the true System of the World', so that 'it will be no strained Interpretation to say, that by the Inability of the Gods to pull *Jupiter* out of his Place with this *Catena*, may be understood the superior attractive Force of the Sun, whereby he continues unmoved, and draws all the rest of the Planets toward him'.[29] This is the 'Back bone of Urizen', which appears in 'the dark void' as an iron chain 'whirling about in the Deep'. 'Chain'd to one centre whirl'd the kindred spheres,/ And mark'd with lunar cycles solar years', wrote Erasmus Darwin of the earth and its newly created moon.[30]

Los makes the Sun 'the chaind Orb' (*BL* 5:40) and casts it 'down into the Deeps'. Then

> He the vast Spine of Urizen siez'd
> And bound down to the glowing illusion
>   (*BL* 5:46–7)[31]

Urizen's sevenfold 'chainges' produce the biological body (*BU* 10:36–13:19), which we may describe today as bound in links of stimulus-response, tethered to the history of its evolving mutations. This is one aspect of the body 'obscuring the immense Orb of fire' as it encases Energy and Imagination in material forms – including language – necessary to prevent Urizen from disintegrating into the void he created. So the other spiritual suns ('sons of Eternity', *BU* 5:34) were changed to material stars:

> Thus were the stars of heaven created like a golden chain
> To bind the Body of Man to heaven from falling into the Abyss
>   (*FZ* 33:16–17: E 322)

At the same time, the perceptual 'Abyss' and the Body of Man are maintained in their present state by the chain; it is, after all, the mind of man that 'created' the images of the golden and other chains. They came into being with the cosmic fall from 'Unity' into the present ontological realities, or chains, of gravity, time, the nervous system, and language; and, having securely instituted these basic parameters, they cannot of themselves unlock their prisoners.

Like the image of the golden chain, these seemingly steadfast realities must also be understood in terms of their having been created and imposed, if not by an evil or naïve fabler then by some earlier and different form of consciousness. The further back we trace a chain (to the imposition of gravity, say), the more free of it we become. In the end, or beginning, our chains will be seen as vestigial appendages helping 'two Eternities meet together' (*M* 13:11).

On one level, for example, the existence of the astronomical orbs 'creates' time (e.g., moon: month); but for Blake, their existence is a function of our perception: *we* established them as markers of time:

> The Eternal Prophet heavd the dark bellows,
> And turn'd restless the tongs; and the hammer
> Incessant beat; forging chains new & new
> Numb'ring with links. hours, days & years
>
> The eternal mind bounded began to roll
>   (*BU* 10:15–19; cf. *FZ* 52: 29 ff.: E 335)[32]

Here again the (eternal) mind has forged its manacles, now as bonds of linked time. Eternity is no longer (the) present; all that remains for most is the unquestioning acceptance offered by one of Blake's contemporaries in 1790: 'The change of seasons, and the golden chain / That links the year, and leads the ages on / And joins them to eternity.'[33] The 'golden chain' points to the creation of time; one part of that chain began when the stars and planets became primary objects of speculation (hence 'the stars of Urizen', E 14:33; FZ 93:26: E 365), leading to the development of abstract reasoning ('*Reason's* golden chain', as Young wrote). Reasoning in turn created the clock and chain of linear, sequential time (tame time as opposed to Los's 'messenger to Eden', the deliciously synchronic, synaesthetic, polysemous 'Wild Thyme').[34] This process produced Stonehenge, already hypothesised by the mid eighteenth century as an instrument based on, and intended for, the measurement of time.[35] Blake erred with his contemporaries in attributing Stonehenge to the Druids, but was correct in identifying it as a temple to time and astronomical reasoning built by Newton's forebears:

> They build a stupendous Building on the Plain of Salisbury; with chains
> Of rocks round London Stone: of Reasonings: of unhewn Demonstrations
> In labyrinthine arches. (Mighty Urizen the Architect.) thro which

The Heavens might revolve & Eternity be bound in their chain.

(*J* 66:2–5)

So, in *The Four Zoas,* Urizen tries to make 'another world better suited to obey', where he would be king and 'all futurity be bound in his vast chain' (73.20: E 350).

The Book of Urizen also tells for the first time the story of the chaining of Orc. After Orc's birth, Los's jealousy appears as a girdle tightening around his own bosom. For a while his sobbings nightly break the girdle:

> The girdle was form'd by day;
> By night was burst in twain.
>
> These falling down on the rock
> Into an iron Chain
> In each other link by link lock'd
>
> They took Orc to the top of a mountain.
> O how Enitharmon wept!
> They chain'd his young limbs to the rock
> With the Chain of Jealousy
> Beneath Urizens deathful shadow
> (20: 16–25)

Plate 21 shows the chain of jealousy emerging from Los's chest, dropping past his loins to assimilate his erect penis as one of its rigid links, and disappearing into the ground at the base of an improvised anvil. The chain of jealousy mirrors the chain of generations (as the pictured chain mirrors the relation of Orc to Enitharmon), and again we witness the forging of a primal link, the enslavement of the child (and ensuing generations) to the psychosexual conflict his existence occasions.[36] This struggle, like that for the realisation of language, may be seen as a contest over 'perfect arbitrary imposition': a struggle, that is, for the unequivocal, unilateral possession (enchainment) of the signifier. 'The chains are, the cunning of weak and tame minds, which have power to resist energy' (*MHH,* above). The father's resentment of filial desire or energy comes to be internalised by the son, who so perpetuates 'the Links of fate link after link an endless chain of sorrows' (*FZ* 53:28: E 336). The oedipal chain doubles the body's biological one, and sexuality, cut off from its polymorphous, polysemous free expression, becomes another form of enslavement; Albion sees 'his Sons assimilate with Luvah, bound in the bonds / Of spiritual Hate, from which springs Sexual Love as iron chains' (*J* 54:11–12). The story of the chaining of Orc is retold and continued in 'Night the Fifth' of *The Four Zoas*. There 'Los & Enitharmon / Felt all the sorrow Parents feel', and return to release their son only to find that 'fibres had from the Chain of Jealousy inwove themselves / In a swift vegetation' (62:23–4: E 342) around Orc and the rock. Their attempt is in vain, since they cannot

> ... uproot the infernal chain. for it had taken root
> Into the iron rock & grew a chain beneath the Earth
> Even to the Center wrapping round the Center & the limbs
> Of Orc entering with the fibres. became one with him a living Chain
> Sustained by the Demons life
>
> (62:32–63:4: E 342)

Darwin's *Zoonomia* also suggests that the body's living fibres and nerves can themselves be seen as chains: 'This perpetual chain of causes and effects, whose first link is rivetted to the throne of GOD, divides itself into innumberable diverging branches ... like the nerves arising from the brain'.[37]

The fiery form of Orc merges into the energy of nature; the life-force repressed and used by the reasoning mind itself represses and uses the reasoning mind. The Earth has become a 'chained Orb' – Orc-sustained – like 'the terrible Sun clos'd in an orb' (FR 211). As Los offers an anagram of 'sol', so fiery red Orc may be his orb, his terrible son. In 'Night the Sixth' of *The Four Zoas*, Orc is explicitly represented as a sun, the focus of the comets' 'excentric paths' (75:28 ff.: E 345), further developing his role with *revolution* and its portents. The chain of jealousy becomes a feature of Blake's cosmography; *Milton* emphasises twice the old prophecy that its protagonist will 'ascend forward from Felpham's Vale & break the Chain / Of Jealousy from all its roots' (23:37–8; cf. 20:59–61). This same section of *Milton* tells of 'the fires of youth / Bound with the Chain of Jealousy by Los & Enitharmon', a formulation resonating with their having given 'Laws & Religion' to bind the sons of Har 'to Earth'. The chain of jealousy is more than Los's fear of loss of love. Though the chain belongs to Los, it exists *sub specie* Urizen, first appearing 'beneath Urizens deathful shadow'. Orc, in fact, confronts Urizen as 'the cold attractive power that holds me in this chain', so identifying him as gravity in the standard metaphor and also as the cold or gelid chain of 'Starry Jealousy'. The Sun, then, is jealous of its planets as Los is jealous of his fiery son. 'Ocalythron binds the Sun into a Jealous Globe' (*M* 10:19), that is, one imposing a gravitational chain; and 'EARTH'S Answer' from her chained condition has already been presented.

The astronomical bodies in their chains are an expression of the enslavement of Orcean energy. A mundane analogue for Blake was the slave trade, rooted in white ethnocentric claims for profit. Radical humanitarian though he was, we ought to recognise that for Blake, as in the following passage, the slave trade showed only another aspect of the universe in chains: 'And slaves in myriads in ship loads burden the hoarse sounding deep / Rattling with clanking chains the Universal Empire groans' (*FZ* 95:29–30: E 361). Here, for example, the deep becomes 'the Deep' of Urizen in the following line, the abyss in which is hung the Sun. 'Universal Empire' reflects back eleven lines to the 'Universal Ornament ... the ends of heaven' and still further to the one other instance of the imperial root in the poem, 'a bright Universe Empery' (3:10: E 301). The 'slaves in myriads' are another vision of Urizen's Sons or suns, 'his myriads' of two lines following. In this passage, the slave trade figures largely as yet another rattle of the 'clanking chains' from which the whole creation groans to be delivered (cf. *J* 16:26); such expanding cross-reference mocks the chains of criticism.

Orc contained his chains from the beginning. He cannot consume all since the structure that allowed his conception – language and imagination – cannot be burned away. His serpent form in *America* is but a step toward the 'living chain' of jealousy sustained by his life; similarly his binding, beginning with *The Book of Urizen*, must be seen as the complement to Urizen's. The only other instance of 'the infernal chain' rooting Orc to the Earth is 'the linked infernal chain; / A vast Spine' made for Urizen. To say that Orc is Urizen's spine or that Urizen is Orc's chain is to suggest the reciprocity (like the id and the superego, signifier and signified) that is both the backbone and chain of human experience. Confronting Urizen, Orc realises, 'now when *I* rage my fetters bind me more', yet at the same time he accuses Urizen: '*Thou* dost restrain my fury. ... *Thou* wilt not cease from rage' (*FZ* 80:36: E 356). Frye hints at the common chain when he observes that as early as *The Book of Ahania* (itself dated a year after *The Book of Urizen*), 'Blake is becoming increasingly aware that by "Orc" he means something inseparably attached to Urizen'.[38]

Jealousy is like a chain in that it will not release its object, its 'signified'. While Orc flames and Urizen freezes through *America* (1793), with the first appearance of Los in 1794 (*The Book of*

Urizen) both are enchained; Orc is tied down with the chain of jealousy under the auspices of the already chain-linked Urizen. Los
seems as jealous for himself as the newborn infant or ego; he chains
Urizen to give him form and restrains Orc to give *him* form. Rather
than a figure of prolific inspiration, Los looks very much like one of
the 'devourers' described in *The Marriage*; he is, in effect, the
source of the 'chains' circumscribing his experience, Urizen and
orbed Orc. As Being, Los – the self-realisation of being lost – must
first institute the chains of being to halt the fall into disunity, for
'Truth has bounds. Error none' (*BL* 4:30). But then the poet must
grasp these chains as openly and clearly as possible. For while
'Deceit', especially self-deceit, 'forges fetters for the mind', 'Love ...
breaks all chains from every mind' (E 472). Accepting the burden of
incarnation/incarceration[39] is the first step toward freedom:

> So Orc became
> As Los a father to his brethren & he joyd in the dark lake
> Tho bound with chains of Jealousy
> (*FZ* 90:47–9: E 371)

The ultimate of love is forgivingness, which also embraces our own
being linked to a situation (language, world, body) not knowingly
self-created, though in good measure we are created by it. To
forgive, for Blake, is the way to understand.

In 'Night the Ninth Being the Last Judgment', the shackles fall
from Urizen as he realises that the binding power of his chains was
a function of his having failed to see them. The image offers a
cracking mirror in which the reader may catch a glimpse of his or
her individual, chained experience:

> Urizen said. I have Erred & my Error remains with me
> What Chain encompasses in what Lock is the river of light confind
> That issues forth in the morning by measure & the evening by
>   carefulness
> Where shall we take our stand to view the infinite & unbounded
> Or where are human feet for Lo our eyes are in the heavens
>
> He ceasd for rivn link from link the bursting Universe explodes
> (122:21–6: E 391–2)

Urizen has taken that step so evidently feared by Edmund Waller,
where, 'one link dissolved, the whole creation ends'.[40] Precisely
this image of a chain that guards and overvalues its every link

must be broken; chains, connections of some sort there will undoubtedly be, but provision must be made for those 'links', like the incarnate word, that 'pass the limits of possibility, as it appears / To individual perception' (*J* 62:19–20). Blake would call Urizen's self-recognition a beginning of true creation, destroying the separate and separating links of the chain of being, the isolated moments of the seriatim progression of time, and the attractive, compelling power of gravity and reason. The chain's logic of restraint is finally located and manifested in the prison of prosaic language continuously forged by reason and memory (Samuel Rogers, praising *The Pleasures of Memory* in 1792, writes, 'Hail, MEMORY, hail! thy universal reign / Guards the least link of Being's glorious chain'.[41]) But this chain is always ready to be snapped by the divine or polysemous character of poetic, prophetic language. Urizen's confession explodes, as if deliberately, one of the most pertinent examples Samuel Johnson offers for 'chain': 'A line of links with which land is measured. A surveyor may as soon, with his chain, measure out infinite space, as a philosopher, by the quickest flight of mind, reach it, or, by thinking, comprehend it. Locke.'[42] In 'The Last Judgment', 'our eyes are in' Urizen; 'our' becomes 'are', and being 'Lo' we are nonetheless 'in the heavens', as our feet are no longer human but poetic. Locke's 'candle of understanding' – the regular canals[43] and channels of knowledge – has become a 'river of light', which in full flood rives the torch links and chain links of the Uni-verse.

Blake's treatment of chains directs itself toward an apocalyptic uncovering of language, an unchaining of thought and association: phonetic, semantic, and historical associations are stressed past their breaking points (the unchaining text bursts its semes). From being what we beheld – a link in the chain of being or discourse – we must become what we now behold: polysemous consciousness (fourfold perhaps) creating and created in, going forth and returning to language.

Such a consciousness will be still chained; but, using one chain to contest and transform another, it will find the validation of freedom, presence, and imagination in the moment of transition from one to another across the chain-strung void. Unchaining, like disenchantment, is finally relative; as 'it is impossible to think without images of somewhat on earth' (E 600), so there are links that cannot be broken while we are as we are. Blake offers instead an experience of 'words of Eternity', a language not of puns mocking or amusing, but one where plural meanings, image of the infinite, are equally present in finite words. Such proliferation of meaning points toward a state where the chains begin to dissolve and melt together, where, rather than a universe interlinked and netted with univocal lines of discourse, each in its very existence bespeaking absence or loss, we participate in the plenum of being-presence, 'the Universal Brotherhood of Eden'. By his chains, Blake gives us to understand that man serves as his own jailer, imprisoned by his vocabulary, culture, and perception; that the inexorability of a 'chain of events' derives from our labelling it so, the logic in a 'chain of reasoning' from our being bound to its premise. Neither reason nor understanding can wholly lift us from the realm of human bondage. Yet, though we ourselves are the chain of jealousy and the mind-forg'd manacles, already inscribed (as some might say) in the chains of signification, it is in an imaginative vision of the nature of those chains and fetters, the nature of present perception and its transmission, that we find the key to our release: a release when we shall again 'be changed, In a moment, in the twinkling of an eye' (1 Cor. 15:51–2).

From *The Eighteenth Century*, 21 (1980), 212–35.

NOTES

[Nelson Hilton's essay first appeared in the journal *The Eighteenth Century*; the text reproduced here is taken from the version which subsequently appeared as Chapter 4 of his *The Literal Imagination: Blake's Vision of Words* (Berkeley, CA, 1983). Hilton's analysis centres on a detailed reading of the trope of 'chains' across a wide range of Blake's work, in the course of which cultural and etymological histories are employed to deconstruct this key motif in Blake while situating it against a rich background of eighteenth-century textual practice. As in several of the later essays, verbal and visual texts are treated together, and the reader is referred to crucial pictorial material at appropriate points. Ed.]

1. Arthur O. Lovejoy, *The Great Chain of Being: A Study in the History of an Idea* (New York, 1960), p. 183. Donald Greene argues, however, that Lovejoy's emphasis on the 'great chain' is misleading: 'on the whole, the century was certainly not under its spell' (*The Age of Exuberance: Backgrounds to Eighteenth-Century English Literature* [New York, 1970], p. 126).

2. Milton, *Paradise Lost*, II. 1051.

3. Pope, *Essay on Man*, I. 237–9, 245–6 (my emphasis).

4. Johnson, 'Review of A Free Enquiry into the Nature and Origin of Evil', in *Johnson: Prose and Poetry*, ed. Mona Wilson (Cambridge, MA, 1950), pp. 361, 355, 356, 372.

5. Northrop Frye, *Fearful Symmetry: A Study of William Blake* (Princeton, NJ, 1969), p. 38.

6. Samuel Rogers, *The Pleasures of Memory*, in *The Pleasures of Memory, with Other Poems* (London, 1799), I. 170; the quotations following in the paragraph are from: Edmund Burke, *A Philosophical Enquiry into the Origin of Our Ideas of the Sublime and Beautiful*, ed. J.T. Boulton (Notre Dame, IN, 1968), p. 120; J.M. Servan, *Discours sur l'administration de la justice criminelle* (Geneva, 1767), p. 35 (my translation); David Hume, *A Treatise of Human Nature*, ed. L.A. Selby-Bigge (Oxford, 1978), I. 4. 6; Edward Young, *The Complaint; or Night Thoughts* (New York, 1853), 8. 1062; Erasmus Darwin, *The Temple of Nature* (London, 1803), I. 8; Dewhurst Bilsborrow, 'To Erasmus Darwin', in Darwin, *Zoonomia; or the Laws of Organic Life* (New York, 1796), I. 43; Hannah More, 'Sensibility: A Poetical Epistle', in *Sacred Dramas* (6th edn, London, 1789), p. 282; James Boswell, *Life of Johnson*, ed. R.W. Chapman (London, 1953), p. 425; Thomas Hobbes, *Leviathan*, ed. C.B. Macpherson (Harmondsworth, 1968), I. 7; Albrecht von Haller, *Historia stirpium indigenarum Helvetiae* (1768), quoted in Norwood Russell Hanson, *Patterns of Discovery: An Inquiry into the Conceptual Foundations of Science* (Cambridge, 1958), p. 69; Jean Jacques Rousseau, *An Inquiry into the Nature of the Social Contract* (London, 1791), p. 3; William Godwin, *Enquiry Concerning Political Justice* (London, 1973), p. 149.

7. Francis Bacon, *The Advancement of Learning*, ed. Arthur Johnson (Oxford, 1974), 2. 14. 11; James Thomson, *Summer*, 1545–47, 1549, in *Poetical Works*, ed. J. Logie Robertson (London, 1908).

8. W.K. Wimsatt, 'One Relation of Rhyme to Reason', in *The Verbal Icon* (Lexington, 1954), p. 153.

9. Pope, *The Dunciad*, IV. 157–62.

10. Mark Akenside, *The Remonstrance of Shakespeare* (1749), 11. 23–4, 47, 63, in *The Poems of Mark Akenside, M.D.* (London, 1772). In the prologue to *The Mysterious Mother*, first publicly printed in 1781, Horace Walpole also criticises the 'French model', asking, 'Can crimes be punish'd by a bard enchain'd?'

11. John Locke, *Essay Concerning Human Understanding*, ed. Peter H. Nidditch (Oxford, 1975), 3. 2. 8, 3. 2. 1.

12. Ibid., 3. 2. 7.

13. Ibid., 3. 9. 9.

14. See James T. Boulton, 'An Eighteenth-Century Obsession', *Studies in Burke and His Time*, 9 (1968), 905–26.

15. Locke, *Essay*, 4. 21. 4.

16. Ibid., 1. 1. 15; cf. Wordsworth, *The Prelude* (1805), 2. 228.

17. Cf. Locke, *Essay*, 3. 14. 2.

18. Johnson, *Dictionary* (6th edn, London, 1785), s.v. 'charter'. E.P. Thompson's astute essay, 'London', offers an illuminating and detailed commentary on the social context and implications of 'charter'd' (in *Interpreting Blake*, ed. Michael Phillips [Cambridge, 1978], pp. 5–31).

19. Stanley Gardner also argued that the '"mind-forged [sic] manacles" are the dominant sequences of word, thought and reaction. ... Blake began by breaking the shackles of language' (*Blake* [New York, 1969], p. 41).

20. Gavin Edwards, 'Mind-Forg'd Manacles: A Contribution to the Discussion of Blake's "London"', *Literature and History*, 5 (1979), 88, 87, 96, 102.

21. Harold Bloom, *Poetry and Repression: Revisionism from Blake to Stevens* (New Haven, CT, 1976), p. 40; the next quotation is from p. 44.

22. Hazard Adams, 'Blake and the Philosophy of Literary Symbolism', *New Literary History*, 5 (1973), 137, 138.

23. Young, 'Conjectures on Original Composition', in *The Works of Dr Edward Young* (5 vols, London, 1783), 4. 85.

24. *The Works of Plato*, trans. Thomas Taylor and Floyer Sydenham (4 vols, London, 1804), I. 357 [*Republic* 514a].

25. So Ambrosio, in Matthew Lewis's *The Monk* (1796), curses 'the weight of Religion's chains' (ed. Howard Anderson [London, 1973], p. 269).

26. Cf. Hobbes: 'they made Artificiall Chains, called *Civill Lawes*' (*Leviathan*, 2. 21).

27. See Richard Broxton Onians, *The Origins of European Thought* (Cambridge, 1988), p. 206; George Sandys discusses the idea in a note to Book 15 of his translation of Ovid's *Metamorphoses*, ed. Karl K. Hulley and Stanley T. Vandersall (Lincoln, NE, 1970), p. 706; see also Thomas Browne, *Hydriotaphia; or, Urne Buriall*, 3. 41, in *The Prose of Sir Thomas Browne*, ed. Norman Endicott (New York, 1967), p. 270.

28. Thomson, *Summer*, 11. 97–9.

29. Pope, *Homer's Iliad, Books I–IX*, ed. Maynard Mack et al. (London, 1967), pp. 396–7.

30. Darwin, *The Botanic Garden*, part 1, *The Economy of Vegetation* (London, 1791), 2. 91–2. Robert E. Simmons proposes that 'the rending of Urizen from Los's side suggests ... a geophysical theory of the origin of the earth as a chunk of matter thrown off by the sun, just as Enitharmon, the moon, is born ... after "Los's bosom earthquak'd with sighs"' ('*Urizen*: The Symmetry of Fear', in *Blake's Visionary Forms Dramatic*, ed. David V. Erdman and John E. Grant [Princeton, NJ, 1970], p. 153). This geophysical theory, right down to the 'earth-quakes', can be amply illustrated with quotations from Darwin and adds a new twist: not only Urizen's rending, but also his chaining are – on one of many levels – the story of our Earth's relation to Sol (see David Worrall, 'William Blake and Erasmus Darwin's *Botanic Garden*', *Bulletin of the New York Public Library*, 78 [1975], 407–13).

31. *FZ*, 96.9 ff.: E 361, offers a somewhat different version; there Urizen takes 'the Sun reddning like a fierce lion *in his chains*' and hangs it in his 'temple ... to give light to the Abyss'.

32. Knowing these stellar chains to be freezing cold and bound into the same dull round, one can see in 'numb'ring' a minute instance of Blake multiplying the content of a word to carry his vision. Peggy Meyer Sherry, 'The "Predicament" of the Autograph: "William Blake"' (*Glyph*, 4 [1978], 141) remarks of this passage: 'That these chains refer not just to the linear measurement of post-lapsarian time but also to the order of language and the structure of the body is the kind of trope we would expect.'

33. Francis Webb, *Poems*, quoted in William Powell Jones, *The Rhetoric of Science: A Study of Scientific Ideas and Imagery in Eighteenth-Century English Poetry* (Berkeley and Los Angeles, 1966), p. 225.

34. The pun is noted by Kathleen Raine in *Blake and Tradition* (2 vols, Princeton, NJ, 1968), vol. 2, p. 161.

35. See John Toland, *A Critical History of the Celtic Religion and Learning* (London, [1740]), pp. 122–3.

36. *The Gentleman's Magazine* (August 1790), p. 680 [for 684] notes 'those delicate links and chains that unite mankind together in the various relations of husband and wife, of parent and child, of brother and sister'. The Contents page of Darwin's *Temple of Nature*, canto 2, discusses 'Storge goddess of Parental Love; First chain of Society', and 'sexual love ... Second chain of Society'.

37. Darwin, *Zoonomia*, p. 393.

38. Frye, *Fearful Symmetry*, p. 214.

39. *Soma / sema*; Blake could have encountered this venerable formula-tion of an old debate in Thomas Taylor's 1793 translation of the *Cratylus*; there Socrates argues that 'according to some, [the body,

'soma'] is the *sepulchre* of the soul, which they consider as buried at present; and because whatever the soul signifies, it signifies by the body; so that on this account it is properly called σῆμα, a sepulchre [sema]' (*The Cratylus, Phaedo, Parmenides and Timaeus of Plato*, trans. Taylor [London, 1793], p. 37).

40. Edmund Waller, *Of the Danger His Majesty (Being Prince) Escaped in the Road at St Andero*, 11. 168–70: 'The Chain that's fixed to the throne of Jove, / On which the fabric of our world depends, / One link dissolved, the whole creation ends' (in *The Poetical Works of Edmund Waller and Sir John Denham* [Edinburgh, 1857], p. 6). Urizen's opening declaration resonates with Cowper's description of 'the pride of letter'd ignorance, that binds / In chains of errour our accomplish'd minds' (*Hope*, 11. 483–4).

41. Rogers, *Pleasures of Memory*, 1. 358–9.

42. The other definitions are '1. A series of links fastened one within another; 2. A bond; a manacles; a fetter; something with which prisoners are bound'; and '4. A series linked together, as of causes or thoughts; a succession; a subordination'. Significantly, in the preface to the *Dictionary*, Johnson writes that 'to enchain syllables and to lash the wind are equally the undertakings of pride, unwilling to measure its desires by its strength'.

43. William Duff, *An Essay of Original Genius* (London, 1767), writes of 'the various ideas conveyed to the understanding by the canal of sensation' (p. 7).

5

Blake's *Visions of the Daughters of Albion*: Revising an Interpretive Tradition

LAURA HAIGWOOD

Oothoon, the central character of William Blake's *Visions of the Daughters of Albion*, is often viewed as a victim of the more powerful men around her. In this essay I would like to challenge this view on two points: its accuracy vis-à-vis the text itself and its underlying assumptions. I will give particular attention to the readings of Harold Bloom, David V. Erdman and Alicia Ostriker because they are especially representative of trends in the interpretation of *Visions*. I will then offer a different view of Oothoon, supported by a discussion of some important details of the plot and of Oothoon's own rhetoric. My interpretation is informed by feminist theory and criticism, but this essay also offers a critique of the tendency in feminism to – at times – over-emphasise the victimisation of women and neglect their power. In my interpretation of *Visions*, I will argue that guilt is inextricably linked to power and that Oothoon has more of both than other critics have remarked.

Visions is concerned with both the sexual theme of *Thel* and the political theme of *America*. And, as Nelson Hilton's work suggests, it is possible, and even probable, that Blake's contemporary observations of the relationship between the feminist author Mary Wollstonecraft and the misogynist artist Henry Fuseli rendered his understanding of the connection of sexual oppression to other forms of political injustice more acute.[1] Certainly, the book may be read as a political or spiritual allegory as well, although neither allegory necessarily excludes the feminist interpretation I will offer here.

Although it is difficult to argue that *Visions* is a feminist poem, it is an important text for feminist criticism to engage because it is a good place to confront the implicitly sexist biases of certain ways of reading. Specifically, I contend that the interpretations offered by David Erdman and Harold Bloom may be inaccurate and that their inaccuracies may arise from unexamined assumptions about gender. Because Bloom's commentary, in particular, has become part of the standard scholarly edition of Blake's complete works, it seems especially important to articulate a dissenting interpretation in order both to facilitate a clearer understanding of this particular text and to deconstruct the sexist biases themselves.

I would like to start by re-examining some widely held assumptions about *Visions*, particularly those concerning Oothoon's rhetoric of free love (and the precise relationship of Blake's text to that rhetoric) and those concerning the nature of the sexual encounter between Bromion and Oothoon. These two rather different areas of assumption are crucially related in terms of where and how they locate and distribute power, and whom they recognise as 'powerful' – specifically, how much power they acknowledge in Oothoon. First, I challenge the assumption that Oothoon speaks 'for' Blake as a direct spokesperson for his personal views on free love and sexuality; on the contrary, I think the text presents her speeches with considerable dramatic irony. Second, I interpret Oothoon's sexual encounter with Bromion neither as an instance of free love in action nor as a rape, but rather as an act expressive of her already fallen consciousness – a re-enactment of her sexual oppression, with which she is complicit.

The first of the assumptions I wish to contest, that Oothoon speaks 'for' Blake, is most clearly articulated by Harold Bloom, whose general description of *Visions* is 'this hymn to free love' (E 900). But later in his commentary Bloom refers to Enitharmon's song in *The Four Zoas* as a 'hymn of triumphant female will', despite the fact that it contains very significant echoes of Oothoon's speeches.[2] Both the song of Enitharmon and those portions of *Visions* which most suggest a hymn to free love convey a celebration of nature and sexuality which is indeed more like a hymn of the female will triumphant than an unambiguously liberatory invitation to sexual experience. By giving them essentially the same language, Blake's oeuvre associates them in ways which an interpretation of either character must take into account.

For a feminist reading, in particular, it is important to bear in mind that sexual liberation, in itself, is not invariably liberating to women, either psychologically or socially. On the contrary, to liberate women sexually without liberating them politically and economically as well is at best insufficient and at worst, as feminists from the Owenites to Shulamith Firestone have observed, to deepen their oppression.[3]

With this in mind, let us continue our analysis of Bloom's interpretation by focusing on his understanding of the central conflict of *Visions*:

> [Bromion's] sadistic pride in the rape is tempered both by a bad conscience, and by a revulsion from the sexual awakening he has brought about in his victim. Theotormon's simpler conflict is between the torments of jealousy and continued love. ... Oothoon's reaction is the most subtle and complex of the three. ... Oothoon *begins* by seeming to accept the morality of her ravisher and her lover, but the acceptance is belied by the psychic actuality of her reaction to her new state. She cannot weep because she is not moved to do so, though she attempts to simulate despair. But the writhing of her limbs indicates instead that her sexual desire has been aroused, and that it only remains for Theotormon truly to fulfil her. His failure prompts the substitute gratification (for both of them) of her masochistic and momentary submission to a Promethean punishment. ... From that nadir on, Oothoon moves forward into the full rhetorical power of her new freedom.
>
> (E 901)

Bloom purports to be recording what the text shows. But what he most accurately records here is the assumption that rape facilitates 'sexual awakening' in its 'victims'. It is now common knowledge that rape and other forms of sexual abuse generally have exactly the opposite effect, and it is regrettable that this particular version of one of the most notoriously oppressive and consistently discredited myths about female sexuality should have been retained in the 'newly revised edition' of the commentary to Blake's works. But more to the point is the question of the usefulness and accuracy of Bloom's remarks as an interpretation of the text: How does the poem bear out, or fail to bear out, Bloom's hypothesis? Is the purely sexual resolution he proposes here – that 'it only remains for

Theotormon truly to fulfil her' – really appropriate to the conflicts revealed in the speeches of the three main characters?

I disagree with Bloom that the encounter between Bromion and Oothoon is a rape, for reasons I will give below, although I do agree that Theotormon has power. But the nature of that power, in my view, is much more political and psychological than sexual. In other words, it may be that Theotormon 'fails' to give Oothoon sex, but Oothoon does not ask for sex. Rather, she asks for recognition: she asks him to look at her. Moreover, the sexual offer she does make to Theotormon is not the gift of her own sexual favours but those of other women, and her over-riding motive seems to be to engage his eye. Though significantly different in some respects, David Erdman's view of Oothoon shares certain assumptions with Bloom's. On the title page of *Visions*, Plate ii, we see a fleeing female figure running across the waves, looking back over her shoulder. Erdman interprets this figure as Oothoon and suggests that here the text invites us 'to help her maintain the faith whereby she still walks on the waves, despite the menaces of Bromion and Theotormon under the aegis of the selfish father-god Urizen'.[4] Like Bloom's suggestion that Oothoon's problem is sexual frustration and that if Theotormon were to satisfy her the poem's central conflict would be happily resolved, Erdman's vision of Oothoon as a damsel in distress is disarmingly chivalrous but also, I would suggest, slightly condescending, bearing with it the implication that women intrinsically require champions, and inevitably suggesting that they are weaker, in mind and spirit and not merely in body, than men.

But even feminist critics can, I think, unintentionally disempower Oothoon in their efforts to rescue her from male readers' misperceptions. In response to Northrop Frye's courtly and trivialising characterisation of the sexual encounter between Oothoon and Bromion as an 'extra-marital amour', Alicia Ostriker concurs emphatically with Bloom in calling it a 'rape'. One of the things I most appreciate about Ostriker's reading of *Visions*, particularly in her essay 'Desire Gratified and Ungratified: William Blake and Sexuality', is her sensitivity to the moral seriousness of the encounter.[5] But to call it 'rape' is, I think, inaccurate, again implying that Oothoon has no real will of her own toward it. As I intend to show, Oothoon is not a rape victim but an active and aggressive participant in her experience.

The interpretations I have referred to vary in significant ways: Bloom sees Oothoon as sexually frustrated, the victim of

Theotormon's fallen consciousness and resultant prudery or impotence; Erdman sees her as a tragically ignored emblem of the spiritually (and politically) good, desirable and liberatory, victimised by the political fear and apathy of the man she loves; Ostriker sees her primarily as a rape victim, the object of male violence toward women. But what these very different interpretations have in common is their emphasis on Oothoon's victimisation, her relative helplessness. In all three readings, the men around her are assumed to have all the guilt – and power.

I think it would be worthwhile to digress here briefly in order to explore the implications of this pervasive view of women as victims, particularly for feminist criticism and the theory that underlies it. While it is important to acknowledge, analyse and deconstruct the undeniable social and political victimisation of women, it seems equally important to acknowledge, *where appropriate*, their guilt, wilful complicity and responsibility. No one doubts the essential innocence of an unambiguous victim, but total innocence implies total powerlessness; ironically, and perhaps paradoxically, guilt is power. Most important, guilt implies the power to do otherwise, which in turn suggests the hope of eventually exercising that power to make a positive difference, both for oneself and for others. Though a blow to the ego ideal – or the projected ego ideal, perhaps, in the case of literary interpretation – occasional emphasis on women's guilt and their power to comply in turn tends to highlight their power, and their responsibility, *not* to comply. And the recognition and acceptance of such a power offers its own, invaluable, liberatory *gestalt*.

So let us now examine the development of plot and character in *Visions* starting from the assumption that Oothoon may be, to some degree, guilty. Is there adequate evidence to support such a view? I believe there is. At the very beginning of the poem, Oothoon plucks the flower, saying 'I pluck thee from thy bed/ Sweet flower and put thee here to glow between my breasts / And thus I turn my face to where my whole soul seeks' (1:11–13). But when she goes to where her whole soul seeks, she ends up on Bromion's bed which, as it turns out, is not a very soulful place. Bloom's interpretation tends to sever her act from its consequences: 'To hide in Leutha's vale is to evade sexual reality, and to pluck Leutha's flower and rise up from her vale is to attempt to give oneself to that reality. The "terrible thunders" of the roaring Bromion intervene, *to ruin the voluntary aspect of that attempt*'

(E 901, emphasis added). Again, while I agree with Bloom about the nature of Leutha's vale, clearing Oothoon from blame also means robbing Oothoon of power. It seems to me more plausible to interpret Bromion's 'terrible thunders' as an unforeseen consequence of Oothoon's choice, but one for which she is nonetheless responsible. We know that she is 'the soft soul of America' (1:3) but, significantly and characteristically, Bromion describes her and addresses her in purely physical terms: 'Thy soft American plains are mine and Mine thy north and south' (1:3). He breaks her into parts, none of which suggests or contains her soul. The landscape or body is what he stamps, presumably because it is all he sees. As her subsequent speeches indicate, she seems to learn from him how to see herself or – more precisely – finds in his stamping a further confirmation of her earliest instruction.

As she confides in her brief autobiography, she has been told certain things about herself, adding up to the message that she is merely a biological and sensual creature:

> They told me that the night & day were all that I could see;
> They told me that I had five senses to inclose me up.
> And they inclos'd my infinite brain into a narrow circle,
> And sunk my heart into the Abyss, a red round globe hot burning
> Till all from life I was obliterated and erased.
>
> (2:30–4)

Oothoon attempts to resist but ultimately complies with this vision of herself, as I hope to show in an analysis of some of her later speeches. She does not escape from the materialist perspective (emblematised by Bromion) which has 'stampt' and shaped her; even her rhetoric of opposition is at times grounded in the same point of view, and shares some of the same oppressive assumptions – most significantly, the assumption that woman exists to serve and reflect man, specifically at the sexual level.

Early in the poem, Bromion describes slavery in the following terms: 'They are obedient, they resist not, they obey the scourge:/ Their daughters worship terrors and obey the violent' (1:22–3). Considered in his character as a slavemaster, Bromion may be assumed to have strong ideological reasons for reporting the attitudes and behaviour of slaves in this way, accurately or not. However, as it happens, this does accurately describe Oothoon's attitude and behaviour through the rest of the poem. That is, she does say that she wants to 'reflect' or worship the tormented and

tormenting character she refers to as 'my Theotormon', who flour-
ishes his scourge at her in Plate 6. And the significance of worship
and obedience is that they *can* be withheld. In his commentary to
the Trianon Press facsimile, Geoffrey Keynes interprets this illumination as Theotormon flagellating himself; however, I think it
looks much more as if his scourge is recoiling from or about to hit
Oothoon, who is shrinking and weeping as if in anticipation or
response.[6]

What ensues from Oothoon's plucking of the flower, then, is the
drama of woman's sexuality in a fallen context, in which desire,
complicity and victimisation are intricately and problematically
related. The argument (Plate iii) is Oothoon's version of what happened to her ('I loved Theotormon ...'). The narrative voice fills in
some significant details. Oothoon is discovered in Leutha's vale,
wandering in 'woe', seeking flowers to comfort her, and we are
forced to recall that 'woe' is Milton's characterisation of postlapsar-
ian human life in the opening lines of *Paradise Lost*.[7] Further, as
Bloom notes and as S. Foster Damon has also suggested,[8] plucking
Leutha's flower may be emblematic of a sexual act. From the beginning, then, perhaps Oothoon errs in seeking sexual comforts for
spiritual ills. And the ineffectiveness of her argument with
Theotormon may arise from the same cause: she tries to offer him
sexual solace for his spiritual torments.

Now, by placing such emphasis on the failure of sexual satisfaction alone to provide spiritual fulfilment, am I suggesting a dualism
between spirituality and sexuality? I would not say that Blake posits
a duality between the sexual and the spiritual, but neither does he
posit them as identical and interchangeable. Sex may be a metaphor
for spiritual union, without being the same thing as spiritual union,
and this is the crux of my argument about Oothoon. Both the irony
of her own speeches and their ironic conjunction with the illustrations tend to emphasise that body and soul, though equally valuable
and mutually necessary, are not conflatable.

Thus, the back-to-back bondage of Bromion and Oothoon (Plate
i) may be a parody of sexual intercourse from a materialist perspective: a joining of bodies but not of eyes, visions, spirits. This picture
does not portray a punishment for sex, itself. Rather, it is
specifically named the fate of an 'adulterate pair' (2:5). And this
term is provided by the narrator, not a character, a fact which tends
to suggest special authority, at least within the fiction of the narrative itself. In other words, if Oothoon and the other speakers seem

at times conspicuously unreliable as narrators, perhaps we may read the authorial voice as indeed slightly more authoritative, offering clues to a basic plot against which we may compare the versions of the characters in order to discover their distinctive perspectives and limitations.

In the light of this authorial characterisation of Oothoon and Bromion as 'adulterate', it is useful to remember that 'adultery' is not merely a synonym for 'sex'. Rather, it is a term for sex in a particular context – sex between people who presumably have other sexual commitments of exclusivity and trust that are implicitly or explicitly violated by the 'adulterous' relationship. Such a context inevitably suggests, at least, duplicity and 'division'. Thus it is clear (or, if it is not immediately clear to our own experience and observation, Plate i certainly makes it clear) that the self-dividing torments of adultery may differ from the joys of genuinely free love. Thus, what we see here are both – and simultaneously – the spiritual consequences of sex in a fallen context and a tragic sexual transgression offered as a metaphor for spiritual confusion and lapse. Of course, Oothoon's lapse or error also fulfils the potential of experience (refused by Thel) to test and to temper one's vision. It is a 'fall' which prepares the reader (and, presumably, prepared the author) for the prophetic visions of *America*. But it is not – and this is my central disagreement with Erdman and Bloom – a privileged state in itself.

In discussing sexual transgression in *Visions*, I particularly want to emphasise how active Oothoon is. The sexual aggressiveness implied by her act is what makes it difficult for me to concur with Bloom and Ostriker that what occurs between Oothoon and Bromion is a rape. It becomes a kind of 'rape', perhaps, after the fact, when he interprets it rapefully and she does not effectively protest. (By 'interpreting it rapefully', I mean when he assumes possession, assumes that sexual possession implies total possession.) But the events of the poem originate in Oothoon's own plucking of the flower and subsequent 'impetuous' flight.

The sexually wilful aspects of Oothoon are further emphasised by textual and visual allusions to Leutha in *Visions*, particularly the rainbow of the title page which, though often interpreted as an unambiguous symbol of hope and other good things, may also be, as Aaron Fogel notes, 'an ironic allusion both to Noah's rainbow [a veil over wrath] and to Newton's prisms', evoking and emphasising the limitations of single or material vision, or the veil of the 'Delusive Goddess, Nature'.[9] It certainly suggests, at least, that the 'fallen, fallen light' of experience and the limited material vision of Newton may be assumed to have an important presence in the poem.

Having shown that Oothoon's associations with 'female will' and lust, as well as desire, are established early in the text and render her more complex and ambiguous, less pure, Promethean and positive than other readers have considered her to be, I would like to turn now to an analysis of some aspects of her speeches. To borrow Lois Chaber's keen observations on Moll Flanders, I would like to suggest that Oothoon's rhetorical aggression becomes at once a justified defiance of the unjust system of sexual discourse and intercourse in which she embarks upon her experience and an embodiment, verging on parody, of the most alienating features of that system – specifically, prostitution (or white slavery) and the objectification of women.[10]

One significant feature of Oothoon's rhetoric is her particular way of asking questions, frequently based on an either / or construction: 'Is it this or this?' rather than 'what is it?' Because they are questions, they seem like authentic gestures toward dialogue: structurally, a question would seem to 'want' a response. But the either / or construction slams shut the door of dialogue at the same time that it seems to open it: that is, the possible responses are limited in such a way that if the answer doesn't fit the asker's pre-inscribed categories, the person addressed can only be mute. Certainly this muteness is the traditional relationship of women to the discourse of patriarchal culture, which excludes much of their experience – most notably, their erotic (as opposed to merely reproductive) and intellectual or spiritual experience, the aspects of her own experience which Oothoon seems most anxious to articulate and vindicate. But her vindication is finally undercut by the fact that she has adopted the same aggressive, totalising style of language she has heard from Bromion. She doesn't really ask Theotormon what he think and feels; she tells him, 'enslaving' his experience to her own 'system'. This can be seen particularly clearly in another pseudo-question based on a does / then construction:

> And does my Theotormon seek this hypocrite modesty!
> This knowing, artful, secret, fearful, cautious, trembling hypocrite.
> Then is Oothoon a whore indeed! and all the virgin joys
> Of life are harlots: and Theotormon is a sick mans dream
> And Oothoon is the crafty slave of selfish holiness.

> (6:16–19)

I don't think that the text necessarily invites the reader to share Oothoon's point of view at this point, nor to assume that everything she says or speculates about Theotormon is true. When Bromion says to her, as quoted above, 'Thy soft American plains are mine', etc. his total appropriation of the other is not unlike Oothoon's appropriation here of Theotormon's imagination and desires. In this respect, perhaps Oothoon inflicts something of the same verbal rape on Theotormon that Bromion has inflicted upon her. In other words, I think that the voice Blake gives to Oothoon in certain passages, such as this one, is far from liberating.

In Plate iv of the Trianon Press facsimile, Plate 4, the shape that appears to envelop Oothoon is painted the same green as the surrounding ocean, suggesting a wave rebounding from the rock whose rigid contours are echoed in Theotormon's posture. This illumination is the visual analogue of her rhetoric, a sort of chained flying, circular and repetitive, the oral and aural equivalent of 'the same dull round'.

Just as Oothoon's rhetoric has, at times, an undeniably oppressive and aggressive quality, her 'free love' seems to me to be less free in itself and less potentially liberating , for herself and for her beloved, than it has seemed to other readers. She offers to bind her desires to Theotormon's, implicitly demanding that he bind his desires to her. Of course, she is not asking that he catch boys for her as she offers to catch girls for him, but she does ask that he accept her gifts and her worshipful 'reflection', subtly insisting that he continue in the role of a tormenting god who can only be invoked by lamentation and placated by female sacrifices.

Alicia Ostriker and David Aers[11] have pointed out that Oothoon's language contains and perpetrates many patriarchal assumptions and sexist fantasies. And they tend to agree that these assumptions and fantasies come directly and uncritically from Blake himself. Without giving Blake credit for an unduly high feminist consciousness, I nonetheless interpret Oothoon's speeches somewhat differently, as instances of dramatic irony, the portrayal of a consciousness insufficiently distanced from the oppressive system it is ostensibly criticising. And, again, I am strongly persuaded by Nelson Hilton's work that Blake was familiar enough with both contemporary feminist theory and the personal life of one of its major proponents, Mary Wollstonecraft, to conceive and execute a subtle critique of feminism's internal contradictions and inconsistencies.

The most obvious and poignant inconsistency of Oothoon's rhetoric is that rather than freeing herself effectively from Bromion's domination, she continues asking for more domination from Theotormon; instead of rising toward the freedom which she professes to desire, she descends further into 'reflection'. By offering to procure girls for Theotormon, Oothoon protests against her slavery in terms which ultimately intensify it, protesting her enslavement to the sensual, physical and biological by asking for more freedom to be sensual, physical and biological, and to extend the slavery imposed by that limited view of woman to other women. The passage in which Oothoon articulates her sexual offer to Theotormon significantly echoes the passage where she talks about her own ready and undiscriminating responsiveness to beauty:

> Open to joy and to delight where ever beauty appears
> If in the morning sun I find it: There my eyes are fix'd
> In happy copulation; if in the evening mild, wearied with work;
> Sit on a bank and draw the pleasures of this free born joy.
>
> (6:22–3; 7:1–2)

This is a charming passage, suggesting a naïve or innocent conflation of the spiritual with the sensual. However, I see a sudden ironic debasement of the sexual metaphor in her second use of 'copulation':

> But silken nets and traps of adamant will Oothoon spread,
> And catch for thee girls of mild silver, or of furious gold;
> I'll lie beside thee on a bank & view their wanton play
> In lovely copulation bliss on bliss with Theotormon:
>
> (7:23–6)

Even more revealing of the psychology of women under male domination, the difference between these two passages seems to suggest that she is willing to give up her own capacity for happy spiritual 'copulation' with Beauty – that is, her capacity for autonomous, unmediated spiritual and intellectual pleasure – to become the voyeur of Theotormon's carnal 'bliss', 'obliterating' and 'erasing' herself from 'life' in unselfconscious compliance with her early indoctrination.

My intention here has been to show how Oothoon sets the action of the poem in motion and uses what power she has to criticise but also to maintain an oppressive political and spiritual order. In addition, as I suggested in my remarks about the shared assumptions which underlie Bloom's, Frye's and Ostriker's very different read-ings of *Visions*, I have wanted to show how a feminist criticism which reads feminine characters primarily as victims may uninten-tionally echo and reinforce assumptions which support the very oppression it opposes. My more general political motive for making such a point is to find new ways of empowering women readers by contributing to the refinement and clarification of our 'visions' of ourselves and of the internal and external sources of oppression.

In order to make my point briefly I have neglected the more posi-tive aspects of Oothoon. It is clear, I think, that Oothoon has a 'vision' which in many ways transcends her sense experience. But I have been concerned here with how effectively and consistently she is able to articulate, maintain and persuade others to share that vision. The image of Oothoon chained within the wave of her own rhetoric is indeed complemented by images of her in flight and walking on the water, openly defying the laws of a 'Nature' that has frequently been invoked to justify political and economic injustices toward women. Oothoon's *double* vision, emphasised rather pointedly by the two pairs of eyes in her name, is a fundamental theme of the poem. *Visions* does not invite the reader simply to decide whether Oothoon is 'good' or 'bad', 'right' or 'wrong'; rather, it offers an opportunity for analysis of the very complicated ways in which she may be right but perhaps in the wrong way, seeing both with and through the eye or, to re-phrase this idea in terms of the poem's motto, speaking alternately and inconsistently from the perspective of the eye and the apprehension of the heart. Relinquishing the long-cherished image of Oothoon as pure, innocent victim in favour of a more complex, well-intentioned but perhaps profoundly erring Oothoon will, I think, enable readers of Blake to achieve a more accurate and inclusive interpretation of *Visions of the Daughters of Albion* as well as a clearer understanding of the oppressive system of discourse and inter-course that enslaves all three of the poem's voices.

From *San Jose Studies*, 11 (1985), 77–94.

NOTES

[Laura Haigwood's essay is a detailed reading of the sexual politics of *Visions of the Daughters of Albion*, concentrating especially on the role of Oothoon and engaging with previous readings by Harold Bloom, David V. Erdman and Alicia Ostriker. 'Although it is difficult to argue', Haigwood writes, 'that *Visions* is a feminist poem, it is an important text for feminist criticism to engage because it is a good place to confront the implicitly sexist biases of certain ways of reading'; in the service of this confrontation she seeks to query Oothoon's presumed role as victim and to relate the thinking behind this interpretation to wider feminist issues. As with the Hilton essay above, visual texts by Blake are alluded to in support of the overall argument. Ed.]

1. See Nelson Hilton, 'Blake Sees More Than We Know: the *Visions of the Daughters of Albion*' (unpublished essay, April 1982). As Hilton's fascinating and provocative essay is still unpublished, it may not be widely known. In the manuscript I have read he offers detailed research into the relationship between Blake and Wollstonecraft and a new interpretation of *Visions*, both of which have greatly influenced my reading of the poem.

2. The 'female will' is an important element in Blake's symbolic system. In brief and general terms, it is both the will of the female to entrap the male in emotional and sexual bonds (usually depicted as narrow and limiting, and in conflict with a broader and more heroic destiny) and the will or desire of the male himself toward the female which makes him susceptible to her. These are the lines from Enitharmon's song in *The Four Zoas* which echo Oothoon's:

> Arise you little glancing wings & sing your infant joy
> Arise & drink your bliss
>
> For every thing that lives is holy ...
>
> (E 317)

It is beyond the scope of this essay to pursue the parallels between Oothoon and Enitharmon in detail, although to do so would be both interesting and fruitful. And, of course, 'For everything that lives is holy' is also the concluding line of *The Marriage of Heaven and Hell* (E 45). Now, it is true that just as the same gesture, or the same form (see W.J.T. Mitchell, *Blake's Composite Art: A Study of the Illuminated Poetry* [Princeton, NJ, 1978] and Janet Warner, 'Blake's Use of Gesture', in *Blake's Visionary Forms Dramatic*, ed. David V. Erdman and John E. Grant [Princeton, NJ, 1970], pp. 174–95) need not mean exactly the same thing in every context, neither should we assume that the same words mean precisely the same thing in the mouths of different speakers. Yet we must, I think, consider the other occasions on which Blake gives the same lines to another speaker as part of the larger context in which a given speech is uttered. If we do, we may perhaps see in Blake's oeuvre an evolution of certain words and phrases, a gradual debasement of the phrase 'everything that lives is holy', mimicking the process by which metaphors die, or by which words of originally liberatory 'power' and resonance are seized upon by self-serving demagogues. If so, then we must recognise that Oothoon's speech in *Visions* comes between *MHH* and *FZ* and may represent a stage in that debasement.

3. See Barbara Taylor, *Eve and the New Jerusalem: Socialism and Feminism in the Nineteenth Century* (New York, 1983), and Shulamith Firestone, *The Dialectic of Sex: The Case for Feminist Revolution* (New York, 1972).

4. *The Illuminated Blake*, annotated by David Erdman (Garden City, NY, 1974), p. 127. See also Erdman, *Blake: Prophet Against Empire* (Princeton, NJ, 1977), and 'Blake's Vision of Slavery', *The Journal of the Warburg and Courtauld Institutes*, 15 (1952), 242–52.

5. Alicia Ostriker, 'Desire Gratified and Ungratified: William Blake and Sexuality', *Blake: An Illustrated Quarterly*, 16 (Winter 1982–3), 156–65; see also Ostriker, 'Androgynous Concept? Misogynist Metaphor?', in *Blake and Criticism* (Santa Cruz, 1982), pp. 180–92.

6. Geoffrey Keynes, Commentary to the Trianon Press Facsimile of *Visions of the Daughters of Albion* (Paris, 1959).

7. 'Of Man's First Disobedience, and the Fruit / Of that Forbidden Tree, whose mortal taste / Brought Death into the World, and all our woe ...' (*Paradise Lost*, I. 1–3).

8. See S. Foster Damon, *A Blake Dictionary: The Ideas and Symbols of William Blake* (Boulder, CO, 1979).

9. Aaron Fogel, 'Pictures of Speech: On Blake's Poetic', *Studies in Romanticism*, 21 (Summer 1982), 217–43.

10. Lois Chaber, 'Matriarchal Mirror: Women and Capital in *Moll Flanders*', *PMLA*, 97 (March 1982), 212–26.

11. See David Aers, 'Blake: Sex, Society and Ideology', in Aers, Jonathan Cook and David Punter, *Romanticism and Ideology: Studies in English Writing 1765–1830* (London, 1981), and 'William Blake and the Dialectics of Sex', *ELH*, 44 (1977), 500–14.

6

Repeating the Same Dull Round

GAVIN EDWARDS

One of the aphorisms in *There is No Natural Religion* says:

> The bounded is loathed by its possessor. The same dull round even of
> a univer[s]e would soon become a mill with complicated wheels.
>
> (E 2)

This metaphorical sense of 'round' as routine was already commonplace, already routine, in Blake's time. Blake revives the metaphor
and the link between various senses of 'round' by applying the
phrase to those turning worlds and mills that divine and human
creators conceive (think up, give birth to). One implication may be
that the process whereby metaphors lose their life through repetition is a part of the process whereby life becomes 'everyday' life. To
remind us that they are metaphors, acts of imagination, is then an
integral part of revealing and contesting the alienated life that the
aphorism describes. At the same time that he brings the metaphor
to life Blake is revealing that metaphors that are not brought to life
take on a deadly life of their own: there is a sense in which the dead
metaphor of the dull round comes fearsomely to life as a real mill
with complicated wheels.

The aphorism on the 'Conclusion' plate of *There is No Natural
Religion* says:

> If it were not for the Poetic or Prophetic character, the Philosophic
> & Experimental would soon be at the ratio of all things & stand

still, unable to do other than repeat the same dull round over again.[1]

(E 3)

Is Blake aware that he has repeated 'the same dull round' over again? This is a question I am bound to ask but to which I can give no definite answer. Perhaps Blake's work is implicated in the deadening routine it castigates. On the other hand he may be rousing my faculties to act and to supply the missing quotation marks around 'the same dull round'.[2] One consequence of this uncertainty is that a problematic relationship is set up between saying something again (repeating) and doing something again (repeating).

Blake was certainly interested in repeated utterances, notably in two kinds of utterance that actively participate in the construction of everyday life by virtue of their repetitious, ritualised character. The first part of my argument will be about Blake's interest in what we now call 'performative' utterances, including those performatives that play a central role in the ritual practices of the Law and the Church.[3] The second part will be about proverbs, Blake's interest in proverbs, and his own aphoristic, proverb-like writing.[4]

PERFORMATIVES

'London' (and I am taking the word as the title of the poem beneath it rather than the caption of the picture above it) obviously involves a sequence of voices heard in the street, over and over again. But its interest is wider than that; it includes a whole range of acts of vocalisation and scription: sighs and charters and marks as well as curses and bans. Four of Blake's words are particularly interesting in the present context: 'charter'd', 'ban', 'curse', and 'mark'. They are all words that, in other grammatical forms, can act as performatives. Briefly, performative utterances are utterances that themselves perform the actions to which they refer. Thus:

> Lawyers when talking about legal instruments will distinguish the preamble, which recites the circumstances in which a transaction is effected, and on the other hand the operative part – the part of it which actually performs the legal act which it is the purpose of the instrument to perform. ... 'I give and bequeath my watch to my brother' would be an operative clause and is a performative utterance.[5]

This example is pertinent for a number of reasons. First, it demonstrates that written discourse (a charter, for instance) can involve performative utterances. Second, 'I give and bequeath *x* to *y*' is clearly a formula, a repeated phrase, and it needs to be if the instrument is to be legally binding. Furthermore such ritual performatives are clearly always of particular significance where conventional relationships are being established in a conventional context – such as the fixing of rights of property and inheritance (charters for the incorporation of companies or towns), social contracts between rulers and ruled (Magna Carta), articles of apprenticeship (such as those signed by James Blake and James Basire), marriage ceremonies (the 'I do' of William Blake and Catherine Boucher, the 'I declare you man and wife' of the parson), and baptisms ('I name this child ...'). Such situations provide most of J.L. Austin's examples, and Blake's poem is overwhelmingly concerned with the overlapping areas of Church, Law, property, generational inheritance, and marriage.

As for the words themselves, 'I curse' would be a performative, as would 'I ban', and the poem also alludes to the banns of marriage, which gives us the parson's 'I publish the banns of marriage between... .' Charters are legal instruments that have to involve performative utterances, though I have not come across a charter in which the word itself is used performatively (as in 'I/We charter'). Finally, 'mark' is a special case to which I shall return.

Evidently these words in Blake's poem ('charter'd', 'ban', and 'curse') are not themselves performative. But as nouns or participial adjectives, they are what Barbara Johnson has called 'deactivated performatives'.[6] And the particular force that seems to animate them in the poem derives, I believe, from their direct reference to situations in which those same words help to constitute performative utterances. Austin points out that in performative words there is an '*asymmetry* of a systematic kind [with respect to] other persons and tenses of the *very same word*'.[7] For instance, 'I curse you' is a performative utterance, whereas 'he curses you', like 'I hear you', is not since it refers to an event independent of the referring utterance. The words in the poem – 'charter'd', 'ban', and 'curse' – derive at least some of their force from how they embody this asymmetry. They refer to conditions in the world outside the poem, but how they so refer is determined by the fact that, as deactivated performatives, they are also existentially linked to actual performative utterances. The poem's words actually do bear the operative power of performative utterance within themselves, in a congealed form. Consequently the social conditions to which the words refer, as well as the words themselves, appear as the marks of acts performed in another grammatical form by the utterance of those very same words. Those social conditions are represented therefore not so much as facts but as *faits accomplis*. The word 'charter'd' bears repetition in the poem because of the force to which it is linked. These performatives are uttered in churches and law courts where their force is inseparable from the fact that they have been said before and will be said again.

Blake's use of these words tends to confirm another of Austin's contentions, that performative utterances depend for their plausibility on at least a tacit acceptance by the interlocutor of the conventions involved in their use. Indeed to describe the situations of their use as conventional implies as much. Most of Austin's examples, and these three words from the poem, are concerned with human power relationships. And the poem's use of these words suggests that to be at the receiving end of performative utterances of this kind is to be more than labelled: it is to take the label to heart, to assume it as one's identity, even unwittingly. The religious and juridical act of christening could be taken as exemplary in this respect. It is an act of labelling imposed arbitrarily on the basis of our father's name and our parents' wishes that we take as the sign of our personal identity. The achievement of the poem is to register such acts as the imposition of arbitrary labels that are nevertheless not external to those who receive them: as marks inscribed by authority that are also signs of an inward condition, marks 'of weakness and of woe'.

There is only one actual performative in Blake's poem, and that is 'I ... mark'. Of course, one sense of the verb *mark* in the poem is 'to observe'. In this sense the word reports on the poet's action as he walks the streets and is not performative. But since the same word used as a noun in 'Marks of weakness, marks of woe' refers to physical alterations of the human body, and since the practice in which the poet is actually engaged involves inscription on paper and the subsequent biting of the copper plate by acid to reveal the letters in relief, then surely there is also a reference in 'I ... mark' to itself. In so far as 'I ... mark' means 'I observe', the relationship established between the marked faces and the poet who marks them is of the fatally reflexive kind that Heather Glen has so accurately described. Blake, she argues, shows us what it means to be both at odds with and yet conditioned by one's cultural ethos:

> The relentless, restricting categorising which stamps the Thames as
> surely as it does the streets is like his own mode of relating to the
> world. He may 'wander' freely enough, but he can only 'mark' one
> repetitive set of 'marks' in all the different faces before him.[8]

And this is still the case if one admits the sense of 'mark' as an act of
perception involving a registering or noting of what is perceived. The
writer and reader implied by that registering are still caught within
the same kind of specular relationship, in a poetic utterance that presents itself as an unmediated survey of the reality it simply repeats.
But in so far as 'I ... mark' refers also to itself as an act of inscription,
all those mirror-relationships are fissured, marked, rendered problematic. The best way to explain this effect is in terms of the different
forms of the present tense that the ways of reading 'I ... mark' imply.
The poem employs a generalising present tense, one that describes
not 'what I am doing' but 'what I do' (repeatedly). But in so far as 'I
... mark' is self-referential, it introduces the present tense of 'what I
am doing', and this has a number of consequences. First, it links the
poetic utterance existentially to the writing self, in a way that can be
associated with the existential link that I have argued for between the
deactivated performatives and the actual performative utterances to
which they refer.[9] But, second, this self is not the unitary entity that
its grammatical name, 'first person singular', suggests; it is not the
anterior source of the utterance. 'I ... mark' is self-referential both in
the sense that it refers to the self and in the sense that it refers to
itself. 'I ... mark' describes me in the act of scription, but it also *is* the
act of scription. Consequently the present it reveals is not a moment
but a movement, and there is no governing subject but a continual
differentiation in which the subject of the act of writing and the
subject of what is written never finally coincide or separate.

The presence in the poem of actual and deactivated performatives is part of its concern with the power of discourse to effect (in
both senses) the development of physical life and human relationships.[10] This power is most strikingly evident in the case of a curse,
which not only performs the act to which it refers but whose action
is the creation of a real future. Moreover, curses are classically, as
they are in the poem, about generation (in both senses). It is families, lineages, 'houses' that are traditionally cursed, to the nth generation. Thus in Sophocles, as Geoffrey Hartman puts it, 'The
oracle takes away, from the outset, any chance of self-development:
Oedipus is redundant, he is his father, and as his father he is

nothing, for he returns to the womb that bore him'.[11] The Oedipus myth does seem peculiarly apposite to Blake's final stanza. So that Hartman's comment that 'the marriage-bed is the death-bed' is another way of saying 'Marriage hearse'. And the last line of the poem is so powerful partly because (to adapt another Hartmanism) we converge on the final word like a Greek tragedy on its recognition scene: 'hearse' appears on the horizon of our expectations simultaneously with the word – 'bed' – whose place it usurps. It represents the reappearance of those blights and plagues that we thought we had left behind at the beginning of the line.

Heather Glen and Edward Thompson, in their comments on Blake's 'charter'd', refer to the significance that charters have for Edmund Burke and Tom Paine.[12] They suggest that Blake uses the word in a bitterly ironic reversal of its laudatory Whig sense, to imply (perhaps following Paine) that charters represent a *licensed* freedom, a freedom that is exclusive and granted by authority, rather than universal and of right. I would only add that it is also characteristic of charters to commit future generations, on both sides of the relationship. Thus James I, in the Third Charter of the Virginia Company (12 March 1612):

> We therefore ... of our royal power and authority, have therefore, and of our special grace, certain knowledge, and mere motion, given, granted, and confirmed, and for us, our heirs, and successors, we do by these presents, give, grant, and confirm, to the said company of adventurers and planters of the city of London for the first colony of Virginia, and to their heirs and successors, for ever, all and singular those islands whatsoever, situate and being in any part of the ocean seas bordering upon the coast of our said first colony of Virginia.[13]

This aspect of chartering is at the forefront of the argument for both Burke and Paine. 'From the Magna Carta to the Declaration of Right,' argues Burke,

> it has been the uniform policy of our constitution to claim and assert our liberties as an *entailed inheritance* derived from our forefathers, and to be transmitted to our posterity.[14]

To which Paine counters:

> I am contending for the rights of the *living*, and against their being willed away, and controlled and contracted for, by the manuscript assumed authority of the dead.[15]

Paine magnificently establishes the authority of the living through performative utterance: 'I am contending... .' I would not want in any way to condescend to Paine's self-confidence, or its proven power to elicit self-confidence in others, but Burke's argument was by and large victorious in practice. *One* reason for that must be that Paine is mistaken in his idea that human generations are autonomous and that manuscript-assumed authority is a paper tiger. Blake, wandering through the London streets, finds everything – 'the man-made streets, the freely flowing Thames', as Glen puts it[16] – always already owned and named, trademarked, an abstract and schematic geography where everything is already (with the help of the *OED*) chart*ed*, marked out. According to one of the passages from Revelation quoted by Thompson and Glen, the 'marks' are anyway both charters and inscribed names:

> And he causeth all, both small and great, rich and poor, free and bond, to receive a mark in their right hand, or in their foreheads:
>   And that no man might buy or sell, save he had the mark or the name of the Beast, or the number of his name.
>
> (Rev. 13.16–17)

All the people are, fatally, sons and daughters of the one Father, bearing his name: Albion and Dombey Incorporated.

The allusion to Revelation is undoubtedly significant, given the radical Protestant context in which Blake moved. But it is sectarian, and an allusion that would have been more generally available is surely to the marks ('x his mark') that many of the people whom Blake sees in the street would have used as their signature, registering their names in, and thereby giving their assent to, legal instruments such as certificates of marriage.[17] Both these allusions to marking as naming are therefore to situations in which one accedes to a kind of freedom, an identity as a human subject and centre of initiative, by virtue of one's subjection to a name.[18] As with the name of the Lord, 'whose service is perfect freedom', so it is by virtue of the inscription of the name of the Beast that individuals are freed to buy and sell themselves and their products in the free market, in weakness and in woe. Thompson concludes his discussion of the poem by arguing that there is

> an ulterior symbolic organisation behind the literal organisation of this street-cry following upon that. ... And the symbolic organisation is within the clearly conceived and developing logic of market

relations. ... 'Charter'd' both grants from on high and licences and it limits and excludes; if we recall Paine it is a 'selling and buying' of freedom. What is bought and sold in 'London' are not only goods and services but human values, affections, and vitalities.[19]

However, 'market relations' is not a sufficiently specific description of the kinds of interchange involved. For instance, charters may represent a 'selling and buying of freedom', but they also represented a deliberate restriction of market relations in the interests of corporation and lineage. Moreover, acts of discourse, of licensing and crying, are fundamental to the character of the social relations that the poem reveals. People who advertise themselves and their wares for sale in the streets, crying their own subjection over and over again, thereby name themselves: 'weep weep weep weep', as Blake puts it in 'The Chimney Sweeper' (*SI*).

The second and third stanzas of the poem are evidently concerned with acts of discourse that in themselves effect material change. The poet hears

> How the Chimney-sweepers cry
> Every blackning Church appalls,
> And the hapless Soldiers sigh
> Runs in blood down Palace walls
> (E 27)

Glen suggests that 'the cries, in two startlingly surrealistic images, have *become* marks'.[20] But it may be said that whereas charters and curses are ritual utterances that can literally effect material change, these are metaphorical, indeed assertively so. As images of almost magical transformation, their effect is to emphasise the vast difference between the charters and bans of authority on the one hand and the powerless voices of the oppressed on the other, the repetitiveness of whose cries signals their impotence. Indeed, there are numerous, often contradictory, implications of these lines, none of which can be completely ruled out. The variety of critical interpretations put upon the lines testifies to their ineradicably unstable and multiple significance, an instability and multiplicity that it has been the ideological function of literary criticism to resolve, conceal, or condemn.[21]

It is the nature of the images themselves, their extraordinary combination of concreteness and abstraction, that makes all single-minded and unequivocal interpretations so inadequate. And this would be true of any interpretation that amounts to a translation of the lines into a hypothetical real-life sequence of cause and effect. On the other hand it is inevitable that one should be drawn into this activity of translation; it is inseparable from the activity of reading, and I have obviously spent hours doing it myself with this poem, helped by the literary critics I have just criticised. But what all these different critical interpretations (with their often startlingly different moral and political implications) testify to is this: it is the same characteristics of Blake's lines that require us to translate them and that so successfully prevent any of us from doing so in a way that carries much conviction for anybody except possibly ourselves.

This impasse has to do with the combination of extreme concreteness and extreme abstraction in the lines. They play in a particular way with the relationships that can be set up in language between the literal and the figurative, between cause and effect, between the material, the less material, and the non-material. The various interpretations essentially involve different decisions about how to read the images in these respects: whether to read them as rather more or rather less figurative, and whether to read the lines of cause and effect between the terms of the action as travelling in one direction rather than in another.

Blake makes 'sigh' and 'blood' immediately and magically correlative in a way that suggests the active exclusion of chains of cause and effect that might *really* link them. This polarisation of a complex set of relationships, excluding intermediate links so as to produce a dramatic condensation of its terminal points, is accomplished by various methods, for instance by the substitution of 'Church' and 'Palace' for the people and relationships that utilise them. The condensation of 'hearse' and implicit 'bed' in the poem's final line is a similar case. The difficulty of course is to know *how far* these are figures of speech. Real blood is very likely involved, and by definition the blood of both the soldiers and their enemies. Yet they are clearly also figures of speech, powerfully condensed 'ways of saying' something else, such that Damon can read the blood flowing down the palace walls as 'a stain upon the state'.[22] What is finally at issue is the relation between such figures of language and modes of substitution intrinsic to non-linguistic forms of social activity. After all, walls *do* stand, and they stand *for* princes and states.

The other image in the stanza, of the chimney sweeper's cry, provides another fascinating example of how we are led to construct incompatible 'real-life' narratives out of the lines. Glen quite reasonably claims that the word 'appalls' suggests, 'in a submerged pun, the pall-like appearance of the blackened walls'.[23] But if that is so we must surely be equally aware, in a splendidly impossible mental perception, of the sense of 'appalls' as 'to go pale' or 'to make pale'. And that radical ambivalence has to do with how the syntax of the lines allows alternative readings of the relations of cause and effect and the degree of figurativeness involved: does the cry appall the blackening church, or does the cry blacken the church?

I have suggested that this third stanza links utterance and material change in a way that is assertively problematic. But perhaps this is true also of 'the youthful Harlots curse'. I am surely wrong to have written of the harlot's curse as if it were really a curse in the theological and oracular (or Muggletonian) sense. It certainly invokes that ancient practice, and that concept, but only by fusing two quite different meanings of the word: on the one hand a blasphemous expletive (one of the cries heard in the streets) and on the other a figure of speech – 'the harlot's curse' – naming venereal disease. Or, to look at it another way, by using the unitary concept in this context Blake produces fission within it (or reactivates a fission that already existed in common usage). The split in the word takes place, what is more, exactly between the two elements whose inseparability is the *differentia specifica* of the ancient curse considered as a method for doing things with words: utterance and physical effect. Finally, what gives the lines their extraordinary power is precisely the fateful combination that sustains the narrative logic of the ancient curse, between aggressive and repetitious utterance deprived of material effect and a physical condition that has all the contagious power, the power to repeat itself through generation/s, of the ancient curse. The very splitting of utterance and physical life gives a new lease of life to the metaphysical violence of the ancient curse, whose unity it bifurcates. Utterance and physical life, like marriage and prostitution, are bound together, but back to back like Bromion and Oothoon. Relations of cause and effect go in both directions, not as a reciprocity but as a moral and epistemological impasse. The 'Marriage hearse', which is part of the 'ancient curse' in 'An Ancient Proverb', is threatened and/or sustained by the 'Harlots curse'. And the internal bifurcation of that 'curse', which 'An Ancient Proverb' uses in its unitary sense, is linked to the problematic redistribution of that poem's terms. The separa-

tion of utterance and physical life that removes the *ancient* curse
is such as to give it a new lease of life.

The Magna Carta (1215) contains passages such as the following:

> Know that we ... in the first place have granted to God and by this
> our present Charter have confirmed, for us and our heirs in perpetu-
> ity, that the English church shall be free, and shall have its rights
> undiminished and its liberties unimpaired; ... And the city of London
> is to have all its ancient liberties and free customs by land and
> water.[24]

In his analysis Austin suggests that the characteristic grammatical
form of the performative is the first-person singular present indicative active: 'I give, grant, and confirm ...', where the grammatical
form in a sense advertises the performative character of the utterance. But the notable thing about the Magna Carta or James I's
charter to the Virginia Company is that elements of the grammatical form that Austin stipulates are mixed with the first-person
plural and the *past* tense, without the utterance being any less performative. Thus 'we ... by this our present Charter have confirmed'
is in fact one man speaking, and his speech is an act of
confirmation. But he uses a certain rhetoric, speaking *as if* he were
the embodiment of an authority larger and less personal than
himself and were reporting on an action that had already taken
place. Emile Benveniste has pointed out that the so-called first-
person plural pronoun is never really a pluralisation of the first-
person singular.[25] It does not name a plurality of 'I''s but is always
a combination of 'I plus you' or 'I plus he (or she, or it, or they)'.
And the fact that a king is addressed to his face as 'your majesty'
suggests that the royal 'we' is in fact a combination of 'I' and 'it',
where 'it' is 'majesty'.[26] I suggested at an earlier stage of this argument that a crucial feature of performative utterance is the internal
differentiation it introduces into the first-person pronoun 'I', as
subject of the act of saying and as subject of what is said. The
significance of the rhetorical form of the performative in the charters is that it gives a degree of explicit embodiment to the elements
of this differentiation that neutralises some of its effects. The royal
'we' and the past tense of 'we ... by this our present Charter have
confirmed' put the speaker together with the reader in position as
spectators of an event in which the speaker is also a participant. In
so far as this can be done, the 'I' that is nothing but the subject of
the utterance in which the word 'I' is uttered is continually

suppressed, appearing as an entity external to the discourse, the spectator of an action in which 'I' figures as the subject. By such a mechanism as this we participate in the production of a state of affairs that has all the character of a given.

But we do not have to go back to the seventeenth century and the royal charters to discover these mechanisms. A characteristic eighteenth-century idiom puts us in position as spectators of our own lives conceived as a kind of third-person narrative. This is not necessarily an external view in the limiting, modern sense of that word. Rather, our capacity to see things as they really are is taken to be the capacity to see our own lives, inner as well as outer, in the same form as we see the lives of others. The idiom could be said to be dominated by the quasi-personal pronoun 'one', considered as a unity of the subject of the narrative and the subject of the act of narration. Correlatively, the tense that contains this idiom is the universal and morally normative present tense of 'what one does', or of 'what is done' in the good-manners sense of the phrase. Of course, a great deal of eighteenth-century writing, notably satirical writing, emphasises the gap between quotidian experience on the one hand and its moral and artistic ordering (Poetic Justice) on the other. But that gap, that distance can also be what is required if we are to see that reality as it *really* is, to get it 'into perspective', as it were. Such writing is able to assert, via the alibi of perspective, both its separation from and its identity with a reality prior to representation.

This idiom is by no means a purely literary matter, even in the wider sense of literature then current. This putting of the self into position as the spectator of a narrative in which the self also figures is akin to the process shown to be at work in charters and which defines the work of performative utterances in the exercise of social power. What we are talking about when we concentrate on the written literature of the eighteenth century, and the character of its language, is not only a certain implicit conception of narrative and character and their ethical function. We are beginning to define the historically specific position that literature may have held among other forms of social relationship, specifically its overwhelmingly, and perhaps crucial, ideological function, its rule in the forging of manacles. We are concerned not just with a certain idea of narrative but, as Martin Golding puts it, with 'a narrative idea of the moral life' in which 'character' as personal identity and 'character' as figure in a narrative are identical meanings.[27]

Blake's poem emerges from this idiom, and it represents a particular testimony to its crisis.[28] The poem's generalised present tense and its generic definite articles suggest its allegiance to that idiom. Yet it is precisely the generic, repetitive character of experience that is at issue ('In *every* cry of *every* Man') even as the poem itself lives within it (*'the* hapless Soldiers', *'the* youthful Harlots').

In Samuel Johnson's *The Vanity of Human Wishes* each one of us is credited simultaneously with the clearsightedness of 'Observation' (which involves the ability to see ourselves in terms of the same categories we are all too willing to acknowledge as applicable to others) and the blindness of Vanity (which involves a systematic misrecognition of the world in the image of our own hopes and fears). That extraordinary simultaneous placement of each of us in the positions of Truth and Vanity is only possible by virtue of the concealed proximity of the epistemological characteristics attributed to each. How that proximity is concealed I cannot properly go into here, though one crucial factor is the availability of an attenuated Heaven. But Blake's poem can be seen as making that latent tension within the inherited mode patent. The complicity of the Observing 'I' in the systematic social estrangement it observes simultaneously substantiates and subverts its Observation. The eighteenth-century alibi is revealed as such, in all its strength, as a fearful hall of mirrors. Johnson's 'Observation' does not distinguish between seeing and the making of statements; Blake's poem makes that relation – the relation between distinct senses of 'I ... mark' – visible and problematic. The process whereby we are put into position as Spectators of ourselves as 'genre-figures' (in Golding's phrase) is revealed, in a liberating movement from offstage, as a work of scription and vocalisation, an inscription of written characters.

From *Unnam'd Forms: Blake and Textuality*, ed. Nelson Hilton and Thomas A. Vogler (Berkeley, CA, 1986), pp. 26–48.

NOTES

[Gavin Edwards' essay originally appeared in a volume taken from the proceedings of a conference called 'Blake and Criticism' held at the University of California, Santa Cruz, in 1982. The present version reproduces only the first half of Edwards' text, the second part of which was concerned with the use and status of 'proverbs' in Blake. The argument here takes as its base the linguistic/philosophical theory of 'performatives' elaborated by

J.L. Austin and others, and tests this approach through a detailed reading of 'London', drawing also upon, and revising, a series of previous accounts of 'London', principally those of Heather Glen and E.P. Thompson. Ed.]

1. Most editors now follow Keynes's edition of copy L and put the 'Conclusion' plate in the [b] series. Blake probably never assembled the loose sheets of *NNR*; in whichever way we choose to assemble them repetition of 'the same dull round' will occur, but of course its significance will be different for each assembly.

2. This is not simply a competition between rival interpretations. Blake would not be able to rouse my faculties to act in this way (making me author of his punctuation) unless it were impossible for me to be sure that this is what he is doing.

3. For another version of this part of the argument, paying more attention to social contexts, see Edwards, 'Mind-Forg'd Manacles: A Contribution to the Discussion of Blake's "London"', *Literature and History*, 5 (1979), 87–105.

4. [Only the first part of the argument is reproduced here – Ed.]

5. J.L. Austin, 'Performative Utterances', in *Philosophical Papers* (Oxford, 1961), p. 223.

6. Barbara Johnson, 'Poetry and Performative Language', *Yale French Studies*, 51 (1977), 146.

7. Austin, *How to Do Things with Words* (Oxford, 1962), p. 63.

8. Heather Glen, 'The Poet in Society: Blake and Wordsworth in London', *Literature and History*, 1:3 (March 1976), 6.

9. In both cases this existential link shifts the poem toward C.S. Peirce's 'indexical' mode of signification. Roman Jakobson discusses the pronoun *I* as an 'indexical symbol' (Jakobson, *Shifters, Verbal Categories, and the Russian Verb* [Cambridge, MA, 1957]). My discussion of subjectivity in language is also indebted to Emile Benveniste. A semiological study of Blake's composite art would also take account of Vincent A. De Luca's insights (in 'A well of Words: The Sublime as Text', in *Unnam'd Forms: Blake and Textuality*, ed. Nelson Hilton and Thomas A. Vogler [Berkeley, CA, 1986], pp. 218–41) into the 'iconic' aspects of the verbal text.

10. In 'The Little Girl Lost' Blake's etched sentence claims the force of a legal sentence, but in a punning process that separates the imperative and the indicative even as it presses them together: '(Grave the sentence deep)'.

11. Geoffrey Hartman, *Beyond Formalism: Literary Essays, 1958–1970* (New Haven, CT, 1970), p. 348.

12. See Glen, 'The Poet in Society', and E.P. Thompson, 'London', in *Interpreting Blake*, ed. Michael Phillips (Cambridge, 1978), pp. 5–31.

13. *English Historical Documents*, ed. M. Jensen, vol. 9 (London, 1955), p. 248.

14. Edmund Burke, *Reflections on the Revolution in France*, ed. C.C. O'Brien (Harmondsworth, 1968), p. 119.

15. Thomas Paine, *The Rights of Man*, ed. Henry Collins (Harmondsworth, 1969), p. 64.

16. Glen, 'The Poet in Society', p. 7.

17. Catherine Boucher/Blake signed her wedding bond with an 'X' (see G.E. Bentley, *Blake Records* [Oxford, 1969], pp. 23–4).

18. See Louis Althusser, *Lenin and Philosophy and Other Essays*, trans. B. Brewster (London, 1971), pp. 123–73.

19. Thompson, 'London', pp. 21–2.

20. Glen, 'The Poet in Society', p. 11.

21. See Edwards, 'Mind-Forg'd Manacles', for a more detailed discussion of the variety of interpretations.

22. S. Foster Damon, *William Blake: His Philosophy and Symbols* (1924; reprinted Gloucester, MA, 1958), p. 283.

23. Glen, 'The Poet in Society', p. 11.

24. J.C. Holt, *Magna Carta* (Cambridge, 1967), pp. 317, 321.

25. Benveniste, *Problems in General Linguistics*, trans. M. Meek (Coral Gables, FA, 1971), pp. 202–3.

26. Benveniste talks about the 'Royal We' in rather different terms from my own.

27. This section of my argument owes a lot to discussions with Martin Golding; the quotation is from an unpublished essay.

28. For other manifestations of the crisis, see Edwards, 'Politics and Characterisation', *Essays in Criticism*, 28:3 (July 1978), 254–9, and Kelvin Everest and Edwards, 'William Godwin's *Caleb Williams*: Truth and Things as They Are', in *1789: Reading Writing Revolution*, ed. Francis Barker et al. (Colchester, 1982), pp. 129–46.

7

Visible Language: Blake's Wond'rous Art of Writing

W.J.T. MITCHELL

> All agree that it is an admirable invention: To paint speech, and speak to the eyes, and by tracing out characters in different forms to give colour and body to thoughts.
>
> (Alexander Cruden)[1]

> But to show still clearer that it was nature and necessity, not choice and artifice, which gave birth and continuance to these several species of hieroglyphic writing, we shall now take a view of the rise and progress of its sister-art, the art of speech; and having set them together and compared them, we shall see with pleasure how great a lustre they mutually reflect upon one another; for as St. Austin elegantly expresses it, *Signa sint VERBA VISIBILIA: verba, SIGNA AUDIBILIA.*
>
> (William Warburton)[2]

'Visible language' is a phrase that has primarily a metaphorical meaning for both art historians and literary critics. In painting we construe 'visible language' in the idiom of Joshua Reynolds or Ernst Gombrich, as the body of conventional syntactic and semantic techniques available to a pictorial artist. Reynolds called these techniques 'the language of art', and Gombrich has provided the outlines of a 'linguistics of the image' that would describe its syntax (schematisms) and its semantics (iconography).[3] In literature, conversely, the notion of 'visible language' imports the discourse of painting and seeing into our understanding of verbal expression: it tempts us to give terms like 'imitation', 'imagination', 'form', and 'figuration' a strong graphic, iconic sense and to conceive of texts as images in a wide variety of ways.[4] If there is a linguistics of the image, there is also an 'iconology of the text' which deals with such matters as the representation of objects, the description of scenes, the construction of figures, likenesses, and allegorical images, and the shaping of texts into determinate formal patterns. An iconology of the text must also consider the problem of reader response, the claim that some readers visualise and that some texts encourage or discourage mental imaging.

Both of these procedures – the 'linguistics of the image' and the 'iconology of the text' – involve a metaphorical treatment of one of the terms in the phrase 'visible language'. The treatment of vision and painting in the lingo of linguistics, even in a strong sense like Bishop Berkeley's 'visual language' of sight, is commonly understood to be metaphoric.[5] Similarly, the 'icons' we find in verbal expressions, whether formal or semantic, are (we suppose) not to be understood literally as pictures or visual spectacles. They are only likenesses of real graphic or visual images – doubly attenuated 'images of images' or what I have elsewhere called 'hypericons'.[6]

But suppose we were to take *both* the terms of 'visible language' literally? We would encounter, I suggest, the point at which seeing and speaking, painting and printing converge in the medium called 'writing'. We would grasp the logic that made it possible to change the name of *The Journal of Typographical Research* to the simpler, more evocative *Visible Language*. 'Writing', as Plato suggested in the *Phaedrus*, 'is very like painting', and painting, in turn, is very like the first form of writing, the pictogram. The history of writing is regularly told as a story of progress from primitive picture-writing and gestural sign-language to hieroglyphics to alphabetic writing 'proper'.[7] Writing is thus the medium in which the interaction of image and text, pictorial and verbal expression, adumbrated in the tropes of *ut pictura poesis* and the 'sisterhood' of the arts, seems to be a literal possibility. Writing makes language (in the literal sense) visible (in the literal sense); it is, as Bishop Warburton noted, not just a supplement to speech, but a 'sister art' to the spoken word, an art of both language and vision.

There is no use pretending that I come innocently from the sister arts to the topic of writing. We live in an era obsessed with 'textuality', when 'writing' is a buzz-word that is not likely to be confused with the sort of writing promoted by textbooks in composition. We even have what sometimes looks like a 'science of writing', a 'grammatology' that concerns itself not only with the graphic representation of speech, but with all marks, traces, and signs in whatever medium.[8] This science includes an interpretive method for deconstructing the complex ruses of writing and for tracing the play of differences that both generates and frustrates the possibility of communication and meaning. What I propose to do in the following pages is to come at the topic of writing from the standpoint of what it seems to exclude or displace. In a sense, of course, this is almost a parody of deconstructive strategies, and I suppose one could think of this as an essay written about and 'for' Blake, and 'against' Derrida, as long as one understands its 'Blake' as a complexly decentred authority figure, and its 'Derrida' as a dialectical background rather than an opponent.

What is it that writing and grammatology exclude or displace? Nothing more or less than the *image* – the picture, likeness, or simulacrum – and the *iconology* that aspires to be its science. If 'différance' is the key term of grammatology, 'similitude' is the central notion of iconology. If writing is the medium of absence and artifice, the image is the medium of presence and nature, sometimes cozening us with illusion, sometimes with powerful recollection and sensory immediacy. Writing is caught between two othernesses, voice and vision, the speaking and the seeing subject. Derrida mainly speaks of the struggle of writing with voice, but the addition of vision and image reveals the writer's dilemma on another flank. How do we say what we see, and how can we make the reader see?

The familiar answer of poets, rhetoricians, and even philosophers has been this: we construct a 'visible language', a form that combines sight and sound, picture and speech – that 'makes us see' with vivid examples, theatrical gestures, clear descriptions, and striking figures. If we are a painter-poet like William Blake we may even construct a 'composite art' of word and image that plays upon all the senses of 'visible language' simultaneously. But alongside this tradition of accommodating language to vision is a countertradition, equally powerful, that expresses a deep ambivalence about the lure of visibility. This tradition urges a respect for the generic boundaries between the arts of eye and ear, space and time, image and word. And its theory of language is characteristically oriented around an aesthetic of invisibility, a conviction that 'the deep truth is imageless', and that language is the best available medium for evoking that unseeable, unpicturable essence.

Both these traditions were alive and well in Blake's time, but I think it is fair to say that the latter, anti-pictorialist position is the dominant one among the major, canonical Romantic poets. For all the talk of 'imagination' in theories of Romantic poetry, it seems clear that images, pictures, and visual perception were highly problematic issues for many Romantic writers. 'Imagination', for the Romantics, is regularly contrasted to, not equated with, mental imaging: the first lesson we give to students of Romanticism is that, for Wordsworth, Coleridge, Shelley, and Keats, 'imagination' is a power of consciousness that transcends mere visualisation.[9] We may even go on to note that pictures and vision frequently play a negative role in Romantic poetic theory. Coleridge dismissed allegory for being a mere 'picture language', Keats worried about the temptations of description, and Wordsworth called the eye 'the most despotic of our senses'.[10] It is a commonplace in intellectual history that the relation of the 'sister arts' of poetry and painting underwent a basic shift in the early nineteenth century, a shift in which poetry abandoned its alliances with painting and found new analogies in music.[11] M.H. Abrams' story of Romantic poetics as a replacement of the 'mirror' (epitomising passive, empirical models of the mind and of art) by the 'lamp' (a type of the active imagination) is simply the most familiar way of schematising this shift.[12] Coleridge's distinctions between symbol and allegory, imagination and fancy, the 'Idea' and the 'eidolon', all employ a similar strategy of associating the disparaged terms with pictures and outward, material visibility, the favoured term with invisible, intangible 'powers' of the mind.

It is in this sort of context that I would like to situate the question of visible language and writing in Blake. I have previously discussed the relation between word and image in his illuminated books in terms of his commitment to a revolutionary religious and aesthetic sensibility based in dialectical transformation through conflict. But the specifically political character of Blake's commitment to making language visible can best be seen by reflecting on his 'graphocentrism', his tendency to treat writing and printing as media capable of full presence, not as mere supplements to speech. These reflections will fall into three sections: first, a look at Blake's 'ideology of writing' in the context of Romantic hostility to the printed word; second, a consideration of some major 'scenes of writing' represented in his art; third, some observations on Blake's calligraphy and typography, the 'wond'rous art of writing' which is his 'visible language' in what he would call 'the litteral sense'.[13]

ROMANTICISM AND THE POLITICS OF WRITING

He who destroys a good booke, kills reason it self, kills the Image of God, as it were, in the eye.

(Milton)[14]

The source of the Romantic animus toward 'visible language' in general and writing in particular is not far to seek. William Hazlitt put it most succinctly when he suggested that 'the French Revolution might be described as a remote but inevitable result of the art of printing'.[15] Modern historians like Peter Gay and Elizabeth Eisenstein have echoed Hazlitt in tracing the intellectual roots of the French Revolution to the philosophes' 'devotion to the art of writing' rather than to any specific philosophical doctrine.[16] The first French Republic, Eisenstein suggests, grew out of a prior 'republic of letters', a polity of unrestrained 'speculation' in both the philosophical and financial senses of the term.[17] Nor was the visual sense of 'speculation' lost on critics of the Revolution. Burke traced revolutionary fanaticism to an excess of 'imagination' (in the visual eighteenth-century sense) and to a deficiency in 'feeling', the blind, untutored habits that make for a stable society.[18] And Coleridge identified this tendency to reify and idolise imaginary conceptions as the peculiar defect of the French people: 'Hence the *idolism* of the French ... even the *conceptions* of a Frenchman, whatever he admits to be conceivable, must be imageable, and the imageable must be fancied tangible.'[19] The materialism of the French Enlightenment, the pictorialist psychology of empiricism and rationalism, and the emergence of an economy of unfettered philosophical and financial speculation all add up to a coherent pathology called 'idolism', the tendency to worship our own created images. Carlyle summarised the iconoclastic English reaction to the French Enlightenment most comprehensively:

> Shall we call it, what all men thought it, the new Age of Gold? Call it at least of Paper; which in many ways, is the succedaneum of Gold. Bank-paper, wherewith you can still buy when there is no gold left; Book-paper, splendent with Theories, Philosophies, Sensibilities,

beautiful art, not only of revealing thought, but also of so beautifully hiding from us the want of Thought! Paper is made from the *rags* of things that did once exist; there are endless excellences in Paper. What wisest Philosophe, in this halcyon uneventful period, could prophesy that there was approaching, big with darkness and confusion, the event of events?[20]

This is the context that makes Wordsworth's notorious ambivalence about books intelligible. In the *Lyrical Ballads* Wordsworth associates printed books with the sterility of 'barren leaves', the lifeless knowledge passed 'from dead men to their kind', and with the 'dull and endless strife' of 'meddling intellects' who 'murder to dissect'.[21] These expressions of bibliophobia have to be taken with some scepticism, of course, coming as they do in a printed book that Wordsworth hoped would be widely read. But no appeals to Wordsworthian 'irony' can explain away his anxiety about the printed word. Wordsworth locates the essence of poetry in speech, song, and silent meditation, and consistently treats writing as a necessary evil, a mere supplement to speech. A book of poetry is a 'poor earthly casket of immortal verse',[22] and true moral or political wisdom is not to be found in books of 'Science and of Art', but in the 'natural lore' of oral tradition.

The battle lines between the conservative oral tradition and the radical faith in the demotic power of printing and 'visible language' had been clearly drawn in the famous debate between Thomas Paine and Edmund Burke about the nature of the English constitution. For Burke, the essence of law is to be found in the *unwritten* customs and traditions of a people; writing is only a supplement for 'polishing' what has been established by immemorial practice. Thus, 'the constitution on paper is one thing, and in fact and experience is another'.[23] For Burke, the Enlightenment faith in the unlicensed printing of speculative theories and speculative paper currency was bound to produce a host of speculative constitutions. The National Assembly's Declaration of the Rights of Man was, in Burke's view, nothing more than 'paltry blurred shreds of paper' in contrast to the immemorial, invisible sinews of the English constitution.[24] Paine's reply was to insist on the primacy of a written, *visible* constitution: 'Can Mr Burke produce the English Constitution? If he cannot, we may fairly conclude, that although it has been so much talked about, no such thing as a constitution exists. ... A constitution is not a thing in name only, but in fact. It has not an ideal, but a real existence; and wherever it cannot be produced in visible form, there is none.'[25]

Where did Blake stand in this dispute over the political significance of writing and 'visible language'? In so far as Blake was a professed ally of radical intellectuals in the 1790s, we expect him to be on the side of Paine, quite apart from his professional self-interest as a printer, engraver, and painter – a technician of 'visible languages' in every sense of the phrase. One way of defining Blake's difference from the other Romantics is to see his lifelong struggle to unite these languages in a 'composite art' of poetry and painting as the aesthetic symptom of his die-hard fidelity to the Revolution. Blake would have agreed with Wordsworth's claim that books are an 'endless strife', but (like Hazlitt) he thought of this strife as anything but dull. On the contrary, he regarded the battles of books, the 'fierce contentions' fostered by a free, independent press, as the very condition of human freedom. While Coleridge and Wordsworth found themselves arguing for censorship of the 'rank and unweeded press'[26] that encouraged the excesses of the Revolution, Blake was busy planting new seeds in the fields of unlicensed printing. Blake never forsook the 'republic of letters' for the tranquillity of the oral tradition. The underground printshop or 'Printing House in Hell' that turned out subversive illuminated books in the 1790s expands into the 'Wine Press of Los' in the 1800s, becoming the scene of the 'Mental Warfare' that Blake hoped would replace the 'Corporeal Warfare' ravaging Europe throughout his maturity. Blake continued, in short, to think of writing as a 'wond'rous art' when many of his contemporaries were blaming it for all the evils attendant on modernity.

This contrast between radical writers and reactionary speakers is, of course, a vast oversimplification; I present it as a way of foregrounding a subtle tendency in the rhetorical stances taken by intellectuals in the aftermath of the Revolution (my claim is *not*, obviously, that radicals refused oratory, or that conservatives eschewed the written word). There is a kind of writing (call it 'natural hieroglyphics') that Wordsworth regularly celebrates, and Blake's encomia on writing are frequently 'stained' by irony:

> Piper sit thee down and write
> In a book that all may read.
> So he vanish'd from my sight
> And I plucked a hollow reed.
>
> And I made a rural pen
> And I stain'd the water clear

And I wrote my happy songs
Every child may joy to hear.
(E 7)

The celebratory emphasis on writing is obvious: Blake's version of the pastoral refuses to keep it in the realm of oral transmission. The hollow reed is not plucked to make the expected flute, but a pen, and the act of writing is immediately identified with the process of publication: 'all may read' the books written with this rural pen, and without any loss of the original presence of the speaker: 'every child may joy to hear' the voice transmitted in the visible language of writing.

No critical reader of this poem, however, has been able to avoid the ironic undertones. The moment of writing is also the moment when the inspiring child vanishes; the hollow reed and the stained water suggest that a kind of emptiness, darkness, and loss of innocence accompanies the very attempt to spread the message of innocence. What makes this a song of *innocence*, then, is the speaker's unawareness of these sinister connotations. Indeed, we might say that the most literal version of this innocence is the speaker's blithe assumption that the mere act of writing is equivalent to publication and a universally appreciative readership, a bit of wish-fulfilment that every writer will recognise. The piper sees no difference between the creation of a unique, hand-written manuscript and the creation of a text that can be universally disseminated. He is unaware of both the problems and the possibilities of print culture, the culture of mechanical reproduction, what Blake would later call 'the Machine of Art'.[27]

Blake's struggles with the fearful symmetry of this machine are evident throughout his writings. From his earliest projects for books in illuminated printing we see a man obsessed with the idea of having it both ways – that is, by producing unique, personal texts that would be widely distributed through a new technology combining the arts of poet, printer, and painter. We see his awareness of how easily this dream could become a nightmare in the title page to *The Book of Urizen*, an image that might be labelled 'textual man'. This image is usually read as a satire on Blake's enemies, as a figure of political, religious, and psychological tyranny – king, priest, and rational censor of the liberating energies of the Revolution. When Urizen is given a more particular historical identity, he is usually equated with English tyrants and reactionaries such as George III, Pitt, or Burke.[28]

But suppose we were to look at this image as a self-portrait of the artist as a solitary reader and writer of texts, a figure of the textual solipsist who insists on doing everything at once – writing his poems with one hand, for instance, while he illustrates them with the other? Or reading the classics and writing commentaries at the same time? Suppose we were to see this, in other words, as a self-parody in which Blake has a bit of fun at his own expense, expressing in a pictorial joke what he cannot quite bring himself to say in print? This reading of the image would also help us, I think, to make a more precise historical identification of the sort of figure Urizen represents in the literary-political battles of the revolutionary era. Instead of representing English reactionaries, Urizen might be seen as a certain kind of French radical, an elder statesman in the republic of letters, a paragon of the 'age of paper'.

While I know it is heresy to suggest that Blake could have held any reactionary opinions or agreed with Edmund Burke about anything, it seems to me that certain features of the Urizen figure have to be faced in their historical context.[29] Urizen is no doubt sometimes employed as a figure of English reaction in the late 1790s, but it is also clear that in *The Book of Urizen* (1794) Blake represents him as a revolutionary, utopian reformer who brings new laws, new philosophies, and a new religion of reason. The general prototype for Urizen's 'dividing and measuring' is, of course, Edmund Burke's characterisation of the 'geometrical and arithmetical constitution' of the new French Republic.[30] But Urizen may be identified even more specifically as a composite figure for two French philosophes who were much in the news in the early 1790s. The first is Rousseau, the universally acknowledged intellectual father of the Revolution, whose confessions of self-absorption, onanism, and obsession with 'pity' must remind us of the drama of Blake's Urizen.[31] The second is Condorcet, who spent much of his life in attempting to reduce moral and political questions to problems in mathematics, and who was the principal author of the 'Principles of the Constitutional Plan' presented to the National Convention in 1793.[32] Condorcet's constitution, like Urizen's 'books of brass', attempted to promulgate one rational law to govern France (his scheme to abolish the traditional geographical divisions of France in favour of a geometrical grid became one of Burke's favourite figures of ridicule). Condorcet's Girondin constitution, like Urizen's 'iron laws', immediately produced a reaction: Condorcet was ousted by the

Jacobins under the leadership of Robespierre and died in prison; Urizen's 'laws of peace, love & unity' are spurned by the fiery eternals, and we last see him imprisoned in the web of his own creation. The new leader of the 'sons of Urizen' is a fiery rebel named Fuzon who attempts to kill Urizen and is eventually killed by his own 'hungry beam' (the guillotine). David Erdman's suggestion that Fuzon represents Robespierre (who deposed the Girondins and pulled down their statue of Reason in 1794) makes even more sense if Urizen is a figure of Condorcet.[33]

We need not see Urizen as a political cartoon, unequivocally linked to Rousseau and Condorcet, to see that he makes considerable sense as a neo-Burkean caricature of revolutionary rationalism and the ethos of letters. But even this interpretation tells us only half the story. It helps us see something of Blake's anxieties about the Revolution and his own role in it as technician of 'visible languages'; it shows a world in which the 'wond'rous art of writing' has become grotesque and obsessive. But seeing this is not quite the same as understanding the position from which Blake could mount his self-parodic critique of writing. The pure negativity in Blake's attack on rationalist writing is scarcely distinguishable from that of Burke, Coleridge, or Carlyle. We still need to ask, then, how Blake could sustain his faith in the printed word, the visible language that seemed to have brought him and his generation into Urizen's abyss.

The answer, I think, is that Blake never did buy into the rationalist version of the Revolution with the same fervour that Coleridge and Wordsworth did.[34] His understanding of it seems to have been mediated, from very early on, by the typology of seventeenth-century English Puritanism rather than the eighteenth-century French Enlightenment. His faith in writing is grounded not in the brilliance of the modern 'republic of letters', but in the tradition of a free English press to be traced back to the English Revolution, Milton's *Aereopagitica*, and beyond that, to the religious reformation fostered by Wyclif's vernacular Bible. More specifically, I suspect that Blake identified himself with the urban guilds of radical printers and engravers whose pamphlets and broadsides helped to bring down Charles I.[35] Blake was, in short, an *English* revolutionary, a radical throwback to the 'Good Old Cause' of Cromwell who was incapable of separating politics from religion, reason from feeling or imagination.[36] That is why, no matter how mercilessly Blake satirises the rationalist corruption of writing, he is still able to maintain the sort of faith in it that he expresses in the 'Introduction' to *Songs of Innocence*, and in the much later introduction to his long song of experience, *Jerusalem*:

> Reader! lover of books! lover of heaven,
> And of that God from whom all books are given,
> Who in mysterious Sinais awful cave
> To Man the wond'rous art of writing gave,
> Again he speaks in thunder and in fire!
> Thunder of Thought, & flames of fierce desire:
> Even from the depths of Hell his voice I hear,
> Within the unfathomd caverns of my Ear.
> Therefore I print; nor vain my types shall be:
> Heaven, Earth & Hell, henceforth shall live in harmony
>
> (E 145)

Blake's affirmation that writing is a divine gift must be understood here in opposition to two contrary ideologies of writing. Blake counters the conservative hostility to the free press and provides an answer to poets like Wordsworth who sought an escape from the 'dull and endless strife' of print culture in the traditionalism of oral, rural culture. If Coleridge could argue that the popular press, especially in the hands of French writers, was producing a sort of 'idolism', Blake's reply is that there are some kinds of printing (his own, for example) that generate not vain, hollow signifiers or 'idols', but efficacious 'types' that are anything but vain.

On the other hand, the die-hard radical would have to read Blake's account of the divine origin of writing as a direct contradiction of the rationalist position. When Enlightenment philosophes like Warburton, Rousseau, Condillac, and Condorcet reflected (as they invariably did) on the progress of writing as an index to the progress of mankind, they unanimously debunked the notion of divine origin as an outmoded superstition. Bishop Warburton even went so far as to deny that writing had a *human* origin: 'it was nature and necessity, not choice and artifice' that produced the evolution of writing from pictogram to hieroglyph to phonetic script.[37]

It is easy to see why Blake, an engraver-printer in the tradition of radical English millenarianism, would want to treat the invention of writing as a divine gift. It is also easy to see why this position could be so readily dismissed as superstition, self-interest, and vanity. Benjamin Disraeli suggested that it was a superstition 'peculiar' to English calligraphers:

> I suspect that this maniacal vanity is peculiar to the writing masters in England; ... writing masters or calligraphers, have had their engraved 'effigies', with a Fame in flourishes, a pen in one hand, and a trumpet in the other; and fine verses inscribed and their very lives written! They have compared 'The nimbly-turning of their silver quill' to the beautiful in art and the sublime in invention; nor is this wonderful since they discover the art of writing, like the invention of language, in a divine original; and from the tablets of stone which the deity himself delivered, they traced their German broad text or their running hand.[38]

Actually, Blake's 'maniacal vanity' goes even further, for he is not just claiming a divine origin for writing in the mythic past, but is affirming that his own art of printing, as well as the message it conveys, has been given directly to him as a divine gift in the histor-ical present. Taken literally, Blake's claim is that the writing of *Jerusalem* is on the same level as the writing of the Ten Commandments on Mt Sinai!

Blake would no doubt answer the charge of vanity by claiming that he, unlike the vain English writing masters, has something important to say. He is not merely playing with empty, ornamental signifiers, but recording a prophecy – that is, speaking his mind on public and private matters. He might answer the charge of supersti-tion by pointing out that the divine origin of writing is synonymous with a *human* origin, since 'All deities reside in the human breast' (*MHH* 11: E 38). Blake claims for his writing no more and no less authority than that of Moses – the authority of the human imagina-tion. What he disputes is the rationalist reduction of writing to 'nature and necessity' on the one hand, and the phobia about idola-trous writing (and its attendant fetishiration of orality and invisibil-ity) on the other.

Blake criticises both the radical and conservative views of writing from a position which looks irrational and even fetishistic from either flank, but which from his own point of view offers a possibil-ity of dialectical struggle and even harmony. He does not single out his own books for unique authority. His writings, like those of Moses (and, presumably, of Warburton, Rousseau, Wordsworth, and even Burke) are gifts of 'that God from whom all books are given'.[39] And the particular text in question, *Jerusalem*, is presented as a 'writing' that unravels all the oppositions that have made books a 'dull and endless strife' in Blake's time. 'Heaven, Earth & Hell, henceforth shall live in harmony.' God speaks in both 'thunder' and 'fire', a double voice that marries the contraries of thought and desire, reason and energy. This voice is heard both in the 'depths of Hell', the underground printshop that produced Blake's radical prophecies of the 1790s, and from the mountaintop, the heaven of Urizenic invention that designs the massive symmetries of *Jerusalem*.

We must notice, finally, that Blake's encomium on writing undoes all the semiotic oppositions that were reified by the political conflicts of his time. Writing and speech, for instance, are not at odds in Blake's scenario of imaginative creation. God speaks to Moses, and in the act of speaking also gives man a new art of alphabetic writing. God (the human imagination) speaks to Blake, and in that speaking gives him symbolic or poetic 'types' that will transform the invisible voice and message into a visible language of graphic and typographic signifiers. If Blake's visible language heals the split between speech and writing, it is also designed to undo certain oppositions within the world of textuality, most notably the gap between the pictorial and the linguistic use of graphic figures. Perhaps less obvious is the fact that Blake's composite art is an attempt to fulfil the piper's fantasy of a 'writing' that would preserve the uniqueness of the hand-inscribed manuscript and yet be reproducible so that 'all may read' and 'joy to hear' the poet's message. Blake is perhaps hinting at this marriage of the values of print and manuscript culture when he has God give Moses a 'wond'rous art of *writing*' while reserving for himself an art of printed '*types*'.

It is one thing to project the goal of an idealised writing that will harmonise all the conflicts an artist may feel; it is quite another actually to achieve such a goal or even to recognise what would count as its realisation. In the remainder of this essay I want to examine the way Blake's ideology of writing, his commitment to a divinely given 'visible language' that would fulfil the piper's fantasy of full presence, expresses itself in 'scenes of writing' and in his concrete practice as a calligraphic and typographic designer.

THE SCRIBAL SCENE : BOOK AND SCROLL

> And all the host of heaven shall be dissolved, and the heavens shall be rolled together as a scroll.
>
> (Isaiah 34:4)

If it is accurate to view Blake the way he regarded himself, as a traditional 'History Painter' who depicts (contra Reynolds) 'The Hero, & not Man in General' (E 652), then it seems clear that the writer is one of Blake's particular heroes. The moment of writing is, for Blake, a primal scene, a moment of traumatic origin and irrevocable commitment. Inspiration does not come to him from a disembodied spirit into an evanescent voice, later to be recorded in script, but comes directly 'into my hand / ... descending down the Nerves of my right arm / From out the portals of my Brain' (*M* 2: 4–6: E 96). And the 'Hand' that wields the pen, burin, or paintbrush is as capable of becoming a rebellious demon as a dutiful servant.[40] Writing, consequently, is not just the means of recording epic action: it is itself an activity of world historical significance, worthy of representation in its own right.

The treatment of writing as an epic activity is hardly original with Blake, of course. Ceremonial scenes of writing (the signing of the Declaration of Independence or the Magna Carta) and scenes involving the transmission of sacred texts (the Ten Commandments, the Book of Revelation) were the frequent subjects of history painting, and Blake produced his own versions of these themes. Probably the most important model for his image of the 'scribe as hero' was Michelangelo's series of prophets and sibyls in the Sistine Chapel.[41] Blake made pencil copies of engravings after these figures, and employed their postures frequently in his own art – so frequently that the image of writing takes on a heavily elaborated, obsessively repetitious character in his iconography. His illustrations of Milton, Dante, the Book of Job, Young's *Night Thoughts*, and the Bible regularly feature the figure of the reader or scribe. And his choices of unusual subjects (Newton inscribing his mathematical diagrams, the Angel writing the sevenfold 'P' on Dante's forehead with his sword, Christ writing on the ground to confound the scribes and pharisees) suggest that the moment of inscription tended to stand out for him as a principal subject for illustration in any narrative. The prominence of these 'scribal scenes' is such that it is hard to think of them as metaphors or symbols for something else. We have to say of Blake what Derrida says of Freud: he 'is not manipulating metaphors, if to manipulate a metaphor means to make of the known an allusion to the unknown. On the contrary, through the insistence of his metaphoric investment he makes what we believe we know under the name of writing enigmatic.'[42]

The clearest indication that writing imposes itself on Blake as enigma rather than simply being deployed as an instrument is its inflationary, universal character. For Blake, anything is capable of becoming a text, that is, of bearing significant marks. The earth, the sky, the elements, natural objects, the human body and its garments, the mind itself are all spaces of inscription, sites in which the imagination renders or receives meaning, marking and being marked. This 'pantextualism' looks, at first glance, rather like the medieval notion of the universe as God's text and seems quite alien to the modern sense of universal semiosis as an abyss of indefinitely regressive signifiers. But Blake's consistent identification of God with the human imagination makes this abyss an ever-present possibility. 'Writing' makes its appearance in Blake's work both as imaginative plenitude and presence and as the void of doubt and nihilism; his pantextualism stands right at the hinge between the ancient and modern view of semiosis. (A similar division was, of course, already latent in the medieval division of the universal text into the Book of Nature and the Book of Scripture.[43])

This hinge in the textual universe is represented emblematically in Blake's art by a formal differentiation between what I will call, for simplicity's sake, the 'book' and the 'scroll'. In the context of Romantic textual ideology, the book is the symbol of modern rationalist writing and the cultural economy of mechanical reproduction, while the scroll is the emblem of ancient revealed wisdom, imagination, and the cultural economy of hand-crafted, individually expressive artifacts. We might summarise this contrast as the difference between print culture and manuscript culture.[44] Alongside these quasi-historical differentiations, however, Blake treats book and scroll as synchronic emblems of an abiding division within the world of sacred or 'revealed' writing. The book represents writing as *law*: it is usually associated with patriarchal figures like Urizen and Jehovah, and Blake regularly uses the rectangular shape of the closed book and the arch shape of the open book to suggest formal rhymes with more primitive textual objects like gravestones, altars, gateways, and tablets. The scroll represents writing as *prophecy*: it is associated with youthful figures of energy, imagination, and rebellion, and its spiralling shape associates it formally with the vortex, the Blakean form of transformation and dialectic.

In the illuminated books Blake's most monolithic presentation of the book motif is, as we would expect, *The Book of Urizen*, which completely excludes the image of the scroll. The only relief from the cave- and grid-like shapes of *Urizen* is the scroll-like posture of the guiding sibyl in 'The Preludium' plate. The scroll, by contrast, never seems to dominate any of Blake's illuminated books as an explicit motif the way the book does *Urizen*. It appears in the marginal designs, as a scarcely perceptible extra-textual activity, occasionally to be 'blown up' into monumental proportions, as in *Jerusalem* 41. Here Blake depicts himself as an elfin scribe writing what Erdman calls a 'merry proverb' in reversed engraver's writing. The Giant Albion (England/Mankind) is too deeply asleep to notice, much less decipher the prophetic message, but Blake's joke seems to be having its effect nonetheless. The scroll is beginning to 'grow' on Albion, becoming one with his garments. The picture cannot tell us whether this is a good or bad thing, but even without Blake's puckish intervention, it is hard to imagine this sleeping giant staying that way indefinitely. His head is buried so deeply in the centre of his book that it seems about to break through the spine (as his flowing locks already have) and wake the sleeper with a jolt.

The most systematic use of the book-scroll opposition in Blake's art occurs in his illustrations to the Book of Job, where it serves as a kind of emblematic gauge of Job's spiritual condition. Blake's opening plate shows Job and his family in a scene of rational, legalistic piety, praying from their books while their musical instruments (several of them shaped like scrolls) hang idle in the tree above their heads. The accompanying text tells us that Job is 'perfect & upright' – he conforms to the letter of the law – but it also issues a warning (carved on the stone base of a sacrificial altar) about this sort of perfection: 'The letter Killeth The Spirit giveth Life.' In the final plate of the Job illustrations all these emblematic signals are reversed: the books have been replaced by scrolls,[45] the musical instruments are being played, reading has been replaced by song, and the inscription on the altar repudiates the altar's function: 'In burnt Offerings for Sin thou hast no Pleasure.' The stress on oral performance in this final plate is, of course, quite in keeping with Blake's consistent association of the scroll/vortex form with the structure of the ear.[46]

The emblematic opposition of book and scroll settles quite easily, then, into an allegory of good and evil, a code which could be schematised in the following table of binary oppositions:

Book	Scroll
mechanical	hand-crafted
reason	energy, imagination
judgement	forgiveness
law	prophecy
modern	ancient
science	art
death	life
sleep	wakefulness
literal	spiritual
writing	speech/song

The interesting thing about Blake's use of this iconographic code, however, is not just its symmetrical clarity, but the way it disrupts the very certainties it seems to offer. We have to note, for instance, that the final plate of Job has not completely banished the bad sort of text: one of his daughters seems to be holding a book (albeit a rather limp, flexible one).[47] And what are we to make of Blake's depiction of Newton inscribing mathematical diagrams on a parchment scroll? Everything we know about the 'doctrinal' Blake would lead us to expect the great codifier of Natural Law and Reason to be presented as a patriarch with his writings inscribed on books and tablets. Blake presents him instead as a youthful, energetic scribe whose writings take the form (perhaps unintentionally) of a prophecy. This is the Newton, not of 'single vision' and 'sleep', but the 'mighty Spirit from the land of Albion, / Nam'd Newton' who 'seiz'd the Trump, & blow'd the enormous blast!' (*E* 13:4–5:E 65) that awakes the dead to judgement. Or perhaps, more accurately, it is the Newton whose 'single vision' is so intensely concentrated that it opens a vortex in his own closed universe, a figure of reason finding its own limit and awakening into imagination.

A similar dialectical reversal occurs in Blake's association of books with sleep, scrolls with wakefulness. We have already remarked on the way the elfin scribe with his prophetic scroll in *Jerusalem* 41 insinuates his message into the garments of the sleeping giant with his Urizenic law book. Blake disrupts the stability of this opposition even further in *Jerusalem* 64 where the sleeping patriarch has become a scribe pillowing his head on a scroll, and the wakeful figure is poring over a book. The joke is further complicated when we notice that the wakeful reader has been distracted from his text by the lively erotic dream of his sleeping colleague, so much so that he makes a gesture of shielding his book from the tempting vision above him. In that vision, a pair of sylphs soar amid a blast of pollen, unrolling a minia-ture sexual heaven in the form of a scroll. What is the point of this scene? Are we to take the sleeping writer as a figure of superior imag-inative status whose fertile dreams contrast with the barren wakeful-ness of the inferior reader? (Their position on the page sustains this interpretation, the reader looking up wistfully to the writer, across the gulf of Blake's text.) Or should we take it as a satire on writerly wish-fulfilment, the idle pen of the sleeping writer ironically contrast-ing with his dream of infinite, pleasurable dissemination of the text, of intellectual radiance (note the aureole around the sleeper's head) combined with sensuous enjoyment (the dream of the unrolling scroll emanates like a giant phallus from the sleeper's loins)? Either way the viewer is confronted with the dilemma of the reader's relation to Blake's authority: Is his work a vision or merely a dream? A prophe-cy or an idle fantasy? Is his authority, as he claims, on a par with Moses? Or was he a harmless eccentric who had too many ideas and too little talent?

Blake dramatises the whole issue of scribal authority in Plate 10 of *The Marriage of Heaven and Hell*, a scene which brings the emblems of book and scroll into direct contact. The design shows a naked devil kneeling on the ground, dictating from a scroll to two clothed scribes who are copying his words down in books. The devil is looking up from his scroll, keeping his place with his finger while he checks on the progress of the scribe at his right. The scribe on his left (who appears slightly feminine in most copies) seems to have finished her secretarial duties, and joins the devil in peering over at the dili-gent copyist on the other side. When viewed in the context of Michelangelo's prophetic and sibylline scribes in the Sistine Chapel, the image reveals itself as a kind of blasphemous joke. Michelangelo placed naked figures or *ignudi* above his prophets and sibyls to repre-sent the inspiring angels who bring them heavenly wisdom. Blake places his naked devil *below* his angelic scribes, a transformation one can read as a parody of Michelangelo or as an appropriation of angelic authority for Blake's 'Infernal Wisdom'. The basic point of the design seems to be a conversion of the dialectics of *The Marriage of Heaven and Hell* (Prolific/Devourer; Active/Passive; Energy/Reason; Devil/Angel) into a scene of textual transmission. The devil is the authority figure: he and his scroll represent the primitive original, the 'Prolific' source of prophetic sayings like the 'Proverbs of

Hell' that Blake has been recording in Plates 7 through 10. The clothed scribes (whom we are tempted to call 'angelic' in their modest, dutiful passivity) are, by contrast, the textual 'Devourers', mere middle-men (and women) who copy and perhaps interpret the 'original derivations of Poetic Genius'. In this reading of the image, all scribal authority is reserved for the prophetic scroll and 'the voice of the Devil'. The scene may be read, then, as a kind of warning against the transformation of prophetic 'sayings' (scroll-writing again associated with oral performance) into the dead, silent form of derivative book-learning.

And yet the image refuses to settle quietly into this 'doctrinal' reading of its oppositions. For one thing, the two bookish scribes are themselves divided by an emblematic contrast. Erdman calls them the fast learner and the slow learner, but the sexual differentiation also suggests an allusion to and condensation of Michelangelo's seven (male) prophets and five (female) sibyls, symbols of the distinction between canonical Jewish prophecy and non-canonical 'gentile' prophecy.[48] The quick study on the devil's left (a female Daniel, in Michelangelo's idiom) is the figure of un-authorised, non-canonical textual transmission, and she seems to get the prophetic message sooner than her more reputable brother. But a second moment of unsettling occurs when we notice that even the authority of the Devil's voice (and scroll) will not survive extended contemplation. He, after all, is no 'author', but merely a reciter, reading off 'Proverbs of Hell' which, by definition, can have no author, no individual source. They are impersonal, authorless sayings whose authority comes from their repetition, their efficacy in articulating a collective national 'character' ('I collected some of their Proverbs: thinking that as the sayings used in a nation, mark its character, so the Proverbs of Hell, shew the nature of Infernal wisdom better than any description of buildings or garments': *MHH* 6: E 35).

We may say, of course, that this guise of impersonality is a transparent fiction, and we know very well that Blake the historical individual was the author of the Proverbs of Hell. And yet we also have to acknowledge that, for Blake, the claim of individual expressive authority and the disclaimer of authority ('I dare not pretend to be any other than the Secretary the Authors are in Eternity': E 730) involves no contradiction, for the universal poetic genius that is God acts only through individuals. That is why Blake can seem to be both the author of original writings and merely a conduit through which innumerable writings (tradition, historical reality, textual and pictorial influence) transmit themselves. All writings, both books and scrolls, are best described by Blake's oxymoron of 'original derivation'. The attempt to settle the question of origin and authority, to stabilise it in the voice of the Devil, the writing of the Blakean scroll, or the voice of the historical individual William Blake, is precisely what reifies prophecy into law, the bounding lines of the scroll into the closed gates of the book.

Blake's vision of a synthetic text that would reconcile the claims of book and scroll is most directly expressed in the illustrations to the Book of Job. If the first and last plates tell the story of Job as a direct movement from legalistic, bookish religion to the musical, celebratory religion associated with the scroll, the intervening plates treat this movement as a complex struggle between these contrary kinds of writing. The second plate in the Job series is the opening engagement in this battle of books, every figure in the design except Satan holding some sort of text. As it happens, this textual war is being conducted on two fronts simultaneously, one on earth, the other in 'heaven' (generally taken by commentators to be Job's mind). The war on earth seems to follow directly from the scene of Plate 1. Job's allegiance to the letter of his law-books is being challenged by two angels who appear on his right offering their scrolls as an alternative to Job's books. Job resists this offer by facing his open book toward the angels, as if projecting the power of its message toward them. It appears that his allegiance to the book and resistance to the scroll is supported by all his family except his eldest son, whose offered scroll is rejected by Job's turned back. Meanwhile, in heaven, the same event is being played out as a scene of judgement. God, presented as Job's spiritual double, is besieged by six petitioning angels who cast down scrolls at his feet (S. Foster Damon suggests that these are lists of Job's good deeds).[49] Below these petitioners are two more angels, one holding a book open before Jehovah, the other *withholding* a closed scroll. Presumably these two figures symbolise the balance of mercy and justice one looks for in representations of the Last Judgement; if so, the open book and closed, withdrawn scroll depict the upsetting of this balance, as does the figure of God himself, who ignores the petitioners' scrolls, consults only his book, and issues the condemning judgement on Job. Amid all these textual battles the figure of Satan intrudes as the voice of accusation from beyond the world of writing, disrupting the dialectic between book and scroll, insisting on the unalloyed rule of law. This disruption of the balanced dialectic between book and scroll is re-enacted in Plate 5, where Blake shows God himself torn between the two alternatives. Instead of a serene, assured judge, we find God writhing on his throne, his left side and upper body (anchored by the book in his left hand) recoiling from the scene of Job's affliction, his right side drawn down in sympathy by the scroll that trails from his right hand.

These scenes of textual warfare are answered in later plates by images of reconciliation. Blake frames his illustration of the Lord blessing Job and his wife with marginal ornaments that show verses from the Gospel stressing the unity of father and son, the Lord and his people, printed in a display of open books flanking a central scroll. The point here seems to be that the messages of law and prophecy, letter and script, book and scroll have been harmonised in the Gospel, and this reconciliation extends even to the 'senses' in which the world and texts are interpreted. Job has previously *heard* a great deal of advice (from his wife and comforters) about God's ways, but what he has *seen* has not been consistent with that advice. Now he says, 'I have heard with the hearing of the Ear but now my Eye seeth thee', an experience which, at the level of reading and writing, is something like that of seeing an illuminated book – language made visible – for the first time.

Blake further develops this association between sensory, spiritual, and textual synthesis in his depiction of Job telling his story to his daughters. In the engraved version of this scene, Job instructs his daughters in a room lined with murals showing scenes from his own story. The priority of word and image here is strictly undecidable: Job may be using the pictures to illustrate and embellish his narrative, or he may be using the pictures as the starting point and telling a story by way of interpretation. In his earlier watercolour of the same scene, Blake made these priorities even more complex: here Job gestures, not toward a series of wall-paintings, but toward a cloud-encircled vision that emanates from his head. His daughters do not simply listen passively, but are busy taking down (or taking in) the story in a variety of ways (reading, listening, drawing, or writing) and in a variety of media (book, scroll, and a text or image) which will make the mental images of Job's story into a visible language in the 'litteral sense'.

Two things should be clear about the motif of book and scroll in Blake's scenes of writing. One is that it forms a fairly consistent iconographic code, expressing in emblematic form the basic contradictions – voice versus print, ancient versus modern textuality, and imaginative versus rational authority – that wracked the Romantic ideology of writing; the second is that Blake consistently uses this code in ways that unsettle its authority and frustrate the straightforward judgements it seems to offer. For Blake, writing does not move in a straight line toward a single version (or vision) of the story. It traces the clash of contraries and subverts the tendency to settle into the fixed oppositions he calls 'Negations', whether these are the moral antitheses of law and prophecy, the sensory divide between eye and ear, or the aesthetic gulf between word and image.

From *Romanticism and Contemporary Criticism*, ed. Morris Eaves and Michael Fischer (Ithaca, NY, 1986), pp. 46–95.

NOTES

[The original version of W.J.T. Mitchell's essay contained a further section on Blake's calligraphy, 'Human Letters', and leads into a lengthy and fascinating question and answer session reproduced from the conference which gave rise to the Eaves and Fischer volume. The essay situates Blake's work in a context of romantic attitudes to 'writing', and then proceeds to detail Blake's own approach to verbal and visual textuality and, especially, to the politics of the image; Mitchell describes it as 'an essay written about and "for" Blake, and "against" Derrida, as long as one understands its "Blake" as a complexly de-centred authority figure, and its "Derrida" as a dialectical background rather than an opponent'. Ed.]

1. Alexander Cruden, *Concordance to the Old and New Testament* (1738).

2. William Warburton, *The Divine Legation of Moses Demonstrated* (1740).

3. See Discourse V of Reynolds' *Discourses on Art* (1797): 'This first degree of proficiency is, in painting, what grammar is in literature. ... The power of drawing, modelling, and using colours, is very properly called the Language of the art' (ed. Robert Wark [New Haven, CT, 1975], p. 26). Gombrich discusses the 'linguistics of the visual image' in *Art and Illusion* (Princeton, NJ, 1956), p. 9.

4. See the *Princeton Encyclopaedia of Poetry and Poetics* (Princeton, NJ, 1974), s.v. 'Imagery'. For further discussion of the notion of 'text as image', see W.J.T. Mitchell, 'Spatial Form in Literature', in *The Language of Images*, ed. Mitchell (Chicago, 1980), and 'What Is an Image?', *New Literary History*, 15:3 (Spring 1984), 503–37.

5. See Berkeley, *The Theory of Vision or Visual Language* (1733).

6. In *Iconology: Image, Text, Ideology* (Chicago, 1986).

7. See, e.g., I.J. Gelb's *A Study of Writing* (Chicago, 1952; revised edn, 1963), which characterises 'writing in its evolution from the earliest stages of *semasiography*, in which pictures convey the desired meaning, to the later stage of *phonography*, in which writing expresses language' (p. 190).

8. Although Jacques Derrida is usually regarded as the founder of grammatology, it may be worth noting that the first book to employ the notion systematically was Gelb, cited above.

9. I take as exemplary here Coleridge's famous definition of the primary imagination as the 'living power and prime agent of all human perception'. See *Biographia Literaria*, ch. 13.

10. Coleridge's comments on allegory as a private language appear in *The Statesman's Manual* (1816), quoted here from *The Collected Works*, vol. 6: *Lay Sermons*, ed. R.J. White (Princeton, NJ, 1972), p. 30. Keats's claim that 'descriptions are bad at all times' occurs in his letter to Tom Keats, 25–27 June 1818. Wordsworth's remark on the despotism of the eye comes up in *The Prelude*, both in 1805 (11. 174) and in 1850 (12. 129). For further discussion of Wordsworth's ambivalence about imagery, see W.J.T. Mitchell, 'Diagrammatology', *Critical Inquiry*, 7:3 (Spring 1981), 622–33.

11. See Roy Park, '"Ut Pictura Poesis": The Nineteenth-Century Aftermath', *Journal of Aesthetics and Art Criticism*, 28:2 (Winter 1969), 155–64.

12. M.H. Abrams, *The Mirror and the Lamp* (New York, 1953).

13. [Only the first and second sections are reproduced here: see context note above – Ed.]

14. Milton, *Areopagitica* (1644).

15. Hazlitt, *The Life of Napoleon* (1828, 1830).

16. The phrase is used by Peter Gay in his essay, 'The Unity of the French Enlightenment', in *The Poetry of Humanity* (New York, 1964), p. 117.

17. See Elizabeth Eisenstein, *The Printing Press as an Agent of Change* (Cambridge, 1979; one-vol. edn 1980), pp. 136–8.

18. See Burke, 'Appeal from the New to Old Whigs' (1791): 'There is a boundary to men's passions when they act from feeling; none when they are under the influence of imagination', in *The Works of Edmund Burke*, ed. George Nichols (12 vols, Boston, 1865–67), vol. 4, p. 192.

19. Coleridge, *The Friend*, in *Collected Works*, vol. 6:1, p. 422.

20. Carlyle, *The French Revolution* (1837; New York, 1859), pp. 28–9.

21. I quote here from 'Expostulation and Reply' and 'The Tables Turned', Wordsworth's famous dialogue poems on the merits of 'natural lore' versus books. It is worth noting that Matthew, the defender of books, is commonly identified as William Hazlitt, whose claim that the French Revolution was caused by the invention of printing was so widely influential.

22. See Wordsworth, *The Prelude* (1850), 5. 160–5, where he describes the 'maniac's fond anxiety' that entrances him when he holds a volume (i.e. 'casket') of Milton or Shakespeare in his hand.

23. Burke, 'Speech on a Bill for Shortening the Duration of Parliament', in *Works*, vol. 7, p. 77.

24. Burke, *Reflections on the Revolution in France* (1790), quoted from Doubleday edition of the Burke/Paine debate (New York, 1961), pp. 98–9.

25. Paine, *The Rights of Man* (1791–2), Doubleday edn, p. 309.

26. The phrase is Coleridge's. See *A Lay Sermon* (1817), in *Collected Works*, vol. 6, p. 151.

27. See Morris Eaves, 'Blake and the Artistic Machine: An Essay in Decorum and Technology', *PMLA*, 92:5 (October 1977), 907. While Eaves stresses Blake's opposition to mechanical reproduction, my emphasis will be on the evidence for his incorporation of mechanical means into his own expressive project.

28. David Erdman equates Urizen with Britain and Luvah/Orc with France in *Blake: Prophet against Empire* (3rd edn, New York, 1969), p. 309.

29. The orthodox view of Blake's political position is that he remained loyal to the ideals and ideology of the French Revolution throughout his life, and criticised France only when it departed from those ideals. Thus Erdman: 'When Blake reports deteriorative changes in Orc-Luvah he is criticising not "the French Revolution" but the Bonapartism that followed and in a sense negated it' (ibid., p. 313).

30. Burke, *Reflections*, p. 67.

31. Urizen must also remind us of Derrida's Rousseau. See Derrida, *Of Grammatology* (Baltimore, MD, 1976), pp. 142–52, for Derrida's discussion of Rousseau and writing.

32. Condorcet's most famous publications in this line were his *Essay on the Application of Mathematics to the Theory of Decision-Making* (1785) and *A General View of Social Mathematics* (1793). See *Condorcet: Selected Writings*, ed. Keith Baker (Indianapolis, 1976).

33. Erdman, *Prophet against Empire*, p. 314. I must add, however, that Erdman has expressed strong reservations about my claim that Urizen has a 'French connection'.

34. In the early days of the Revolution Blake sympathised with Voltaire and Rousseau as presiding spirits in the awakening of France to liberty (see *The French Revolution* [1791], E 298–9). But Blake's early suspicion of rationalism is expressed clearly in the *No Natural Religion* tracts (1788) and *The Marriage of Heaven and Hell*, and by the 1800s that suspicion had become explicitly linked with Rousseau and Voltaire's attacks on revealed religion (see the address 'To the Deists', which introduces chapter 3 of *Jerusalem*). A good index of Blake's ambivalence about the rationalist ideology of the Revolution is his willingness to find Tom Paine 'a better Christian' than Bishop Watson (whose attack on Paine in his *Apology for the Bible* Blake annotated), at the same time that he notes that neither the bishop nor his radical deist opponent quite measures up to Blake's 'Everlasting Gospel', the tradition of Puritan radicalism (see Annotations to an Apology for the Bible, E 619: 'The Bishop never saw the Everlasting Gospel any more than Tom Paine').

35. For the connection between printing and Puritanism in the English Revolution, see Christopher Hill, *The World Turned Upside Down: Radical Ideas during the English Revolution* (Harmondsworth, 1972), pp. 161–2.

36. The basic study of Blake's ties to the Dissenters is still A.L. Morton's classic *The Everlasting Gospel* (London, 1958).

37. Warburton, *The Divine Legation*, vol. 4, section 4.

38. Benjamin Disraeli, quoted in Donald M. Anderson, *The Art of Written Forms: The Theory and Practice of Calligraphy* (New York, 1969), p. 148.

39. It has to be noted, however, that the crucial phrase, 'all books are given', was etched on Plate 3 of *Jerusalem* but never printed. This particular message now comes to us 'under erasure', thanks to Erdman's textual reconstructions.

40. See my discussion of Blake's rebellious 'Hand' in *Blake's Composite Art* (Princeton, NJ, 1978), p. 202.

41. For a discussion of Blake's use of these figures, see Jenijoy La Belle, 'Blake's Visions and Re-visions of Michelangelo', in *Blake in his Time*, ed. Robert Essick and Donald Pearce (Bloomington, IN, 1978), pp. 13–22.

42. Derrida, 'Freud and the Scene of Writing', in *Writing and Difference* (Chicago, 1969), p. 199.

43. The classic discussion of medieval pantextualism is Ernst Robert Curtius's chapter, 'The Book as Symbol', in his *European Literature and the Latin Middle Ages* (1st German edn, Bern, 1948; 1st English edn, New York, 1953).

44. For a stimulating discussion of this difference, see Gerald Beury's essay, 'The Originality of Texts in a Manuscript Culture', in *Inventions: Writing, Textuality and Understanding in Literary History* (New Haven, CT, 1982).

45. In the engraved version one of Job's daughters is holding a book; in the watercolour version, the scroll has completely taken over. See Martin Butlin, *The Paintings and Drawings of William Blake* (New Haven, CT, 1981), cat. 551, 21.

46. See Mitchell, *Blake's Composite Art*, pp. 62–4, for a discussion of Blake's links between graphic form and sensory structure.

47. In the engraving, that is. In the watercolour version of this scene, all the texts are scrolls.

48. See Edgar Wind, 'Michelangelo's Prophets and Sibyls', *Proceedings of the British Academy*, 51 (1966), 74.

49. S. Foster Damon, *Blake's Job* (New York, 1966), p. 14.

8

Reading Blake and Derrida – Our Caesars neither Praised nor Buried

DAVID SIMPSON

The Blake conference of May 1982 was largely carried on in speech rather than in writing, or perhaps in a mixed genre of speaking from writing.[1] Critics always have been and always will be divided over the gains and losses accruing when the piper, however humble, sits him down to write. One might lament the laying aside of the raised eyebrow and the prospective elation of the successful joke, seeing in the passage from the spoken to the written a kind of fall, a loss of a community of immediately confirming imaginations. A second might applaud the same movement as bringing about the rule of reason over passion, taking on with pleasure the 'arrows ready drawn' of footnotes and acknowledgments. A third might try to turn the printed back into the spoken word, reinscribing into the *text*, as far as possible, the plays and possibilities of *voice*, whose introduction therein brings with it a series of problems, syndromes, and satisfactions familiar to all who are engaged in the interpretations of literature, and particularly Romantic literature.

This third option has become a familiar one among the exponents of the various literary criticisms founded upon the texts of Derrida. It is a heady and beguiling mode in which analysis is replaced, both stylistically and theoretically, by some form of reiteration. The two papers, now become essays, to which I had the pleasure of responding (by Paul Mann and V.A. De Luca), have been very helpful in focusing the issues raised by such a criticism.[2] I would like here to pursue the implications of a Derridean reading of Blake, and to relate them to some questions about the operations of the sublime as it can be posited in Blake's writings. The speech-like flippancy of my title alludes to the possibility that both Blake and Derrida, who have gone through cycles in which they have been defiled and then deified, may now be due for a more reasoned reception in which, among other things, their common history might be explored and explained. It is time to address both as something other than oracles of truth and destroyers of shabby metaphysics. And Blake, who is sturdier and has stood the test of time, can help us with the later man, whose obscurities are worshipped or dismissed but seldom clearly challenged.

I shall not be casting aspersions of madness, for on such issues we should be happy to follow James Joyce in disavowing the word as 'a medical term that can claim no more notice from the objective critic than he grants the charge of heresy raised by the theologian, or the charge of immorality raised by the police'.[3] But I do think it worth pondering whether the gesture of celebration, so often required in the defence of Blake against common sense and its complex assumptions, might not also be blinding us to some significant questions about his writing. And in a fortunate sense some of the initiatives of modern literary criticism are freeing us to ask these questions without risking the demolition of Blake as a worthwhile writer, for in their de-emphasis of the model of a unitary subject 'William Blake' they allow the texts and designs to touch upon a wider range of historical and discursive options and allusions than would have been reached by methods using the traditional yardsticks of, for example, biographical reference or meanings demonstrably produced out of conscious free will. In this respect I take the case of Blake to be crucial for our whole construction of Romanticism, making as he does the severest of all demands upon his readership, occupying, particularly, the other extreme of the axis of private and public from Wordsworth. Basically, I shall try to suggest that some of the oppositions we tend to work with – good and bad, radical and reactionary, for and against women, and so on – operate, in part by way of an overly exclusive attention to language in an ahistorical space, to reify Blake and others in ways that they need not be. So:

BLAKE AND DERRIDA

Of all the major writers I know Blake is, along with Smart (in 'Jubilate Agno') and Joyce, who himself thought of Blake as 'the most enlightened of Western poets',[4] the most open to analysis in terms set forth by Derrida. To my knowledge, and with the notable exception of the essay by Paul Mann, this analysis has not been widely rehearsed, as it has been for Joyce.[5] I shall take, for reasons that will become clear, *Of Grammatology* as my version of 'Derrida', and will seek to sketch out some of the ways in which Blake both perpetrates and subverts the mythology of the primacy of speech over writing, and its inferable consequences, as Derrida takes Rousseau to do.

Of Grammatology is Derrida's most conventionally historical book. His translator, Gayatri Spivak, notes that he 'never again devotes himself to this sort of textual scholarship',[6] and her own introduction to his thought indeed presupposes this move away from Derrida as the explicator of significant eighteenth-century texts toward Derrida the successor of Nietzsche and Heidegger, operating in original ways upon modern philosophy and criticism. I am especially anxious to recover the historical foundation for Derrida in the writings of Rousseau – though I thereby risk the accusation of an outmoded concern for origins – because I want to ask some questions about his common *history* with Blake, and because I sense that this relation to the past is not much attended to by those most active in employing his arguments in contemporary literary criticism. Thus Rousseau has been eliminated, so to speak, in favour of Derrida, who makes all things new.

One could speculate usefully about the reasons for this, and we badly need some sort of sociology of the critical divisions and quarrels that are associated with Derrida. Such an inquiry might well include some reflections on the strangely short life of a structuralist criticism in America (if it ever had one), when compared with the more rapid and pervasive popularity of deconstruction and its attack on the forms of objectivity that structuralism promised to revitalise. But I shall not do that here, except with the obligatory degree of implicitness. Rather I shall lay out three interlocking themes that can be seen in common between Blake and Derrida-Rousseau. I shall myself leave out the presences of Saussure and Lévi-Strauss in Derrida's account.

Writing and Speech

We can trace clearly in Blake the importance of a model or myth of primary articulation and its fall into writing, or even into language itself. In the 'Introduction' to *Songs of Innocence*, for example, the passage from sound to song to writing accompanies the disappearance of the child, who might be thought to stand in the role of an inspiration or immediate audience. And writing is the rule of law in most of the adventures of Urizen. Conversely, we can also identify in Blake (as Derrida does in Rousseau) the other side of the case, where the extreme suspicion of external form is balanced, as it is for most Romantic Protestants, by the recognition that such form is the only means of publicity, survival, and communication, and indeed a gesture demanded of us by our saviour: 'God becomes as we are, that we may be as he is' (E 3). Every child *may* joy to hear, if given the opportunity by being read to, or if so inclined by the free will that is imagination. Albion Blake giantly mediates this potentially rigid paradox, as does Finnegan Joyce, by the deliberate inscription of the traces of writing, as Derrida calls them – those features of the written word that cannot be rendered in speech and therefore signal a plenitude beyond that of the spoken. This mutability of the written word leads us to a whole range of potential etymologies for Urizen, Los, Urthona, and so on, and a variety of possible syntaxes for Blake's protonarrative lines. Such dramatisations of Blake's composition are surely appropriate to his method, in which the painstaking disassembly and reassembly of words and sentences is part of the very technique of relief etching. Perhaps we can even see Blake writing *sous rature*, or 'under erasure', in the newly observed features of *The Ghost of Abel* reported by David Erdman in his revised edition:

> A device impossible to reproduce and explain simultaneously is Blake's etching of delete signs fitted to the tops of certain letters in a line in *The Ghost of Abel*, inviting the reader to read the line and immediately revise it.
>
> (E xxv)

The use of overpainting in some copies of the illuminated works, in which letters and words are highlighted by different colours as if to create a text within a text, also appears in this light.[7]

Similarly, but on a larger scale, the text of *The Book of Urizen* incorporates allusions to analogous myths of law and origination –

those of Lear, Prometheus, Moses, Abraham, Oedipus, Milton, and so forth – which, in order to be apprehended, depend upon a reading rather than a 'being heard spoken', even as they seem to add up perversely to a catalogue of the ways that reading imprisons. Thus, if we are of a scholarly bent, we joyfully discover in Blake's text the traces of the cultural traditions that compose our oppression. The act of reading *Urizen* subverts the closure of the reading theory being described in it. And this move beyond the usefulness of a notion of subjectivity – 'Writing can never be thought under the character of the subject', writes Derrida[8] – is not a move into an abstract play of linguistic slippage but into a rather precise series of decisions about the status of those cultural traces. Compare Blake's 'Mark well my words! they are of your eternal salvation' (E 96) and his notice of 'Marks of weakness, marks of woe' (E 26). The marking is not just that of noticing or observing but that of rewriting, of annotation, of wielding the pen. Which leads us to:

Writing and Onanism

While Milton speaks messianically of 'vital fluid infused, and vital warmth/Throughout the fluid mass' (*Paradise Lost* 7.236–7), Blake interpolates another series of pagan creation myths, infusing Urizen with himself:

> the eternal Prophet howl'd
> Beating still on his rivets of iron
> Pouring sodor of iron; dividing
> The horrible night into watches.
>
> 2. And Urizen (so his eternal name)
> His prolific delight obscurd more & more
> In dark secresy hiding in surgeing
> Sulphureous fluid his phantasies.
>
> (E 75)

At least, we may assume Urizen as agent, for as copulation is suspended so too is the security of the syntactic copula; this passage could also be read as describing Los hiding Urizen in his (Los') phantasies, or Los hiding Urizen's phantasies ... or all at once.

This figure compounds with Rousseau, more famous as a masturbator even than Leopold Bloom, with the folds of his curtains and silent pillows drawn back for public inspection first by himself and then again by Derrida.[9] Derrida's reassembly of the key moments in Rousseau's ethic of civil society further suggests the point of the connection between writing and masturbation. If writing is a fallen form of public *speaking*, then it is a replacement of the speaker's actual and present *demos* by an absent or at best phantasised public, one that may or may not come into being as the author decides to release his book, and as they decide to take it up. Thus the author–reader relation can never be directly reciprocal in the way that it would be in the more democratic speech relation in a public forum, involving an (ideal) symmetry of speech and civic identity. This myth of immediate reciprocity can never have a place in writing, which is always private (enacted behind the curtain) and deferred in its effect.

As well as finding a confirmation of this model in the figure of Urizen, we can also implant its converse, seeing a counter-mythology in Blake's writing in which the dictatorial or irrational power of direct speech is implicit – for every Demosthenes a Burke – and according to which the democracy of writing is asserted through its being meditated at a pace chosen by one's own reason or imagination. The sin of privacy is then also a requirement of the Protestant ethos, for it is there that one finds the privacy to be with God, though risking always his being supplanted by selfhood. Extreme forms of Protestant self-consciousness even celebrate the distance provided by writing, by which we gain distance also from the confusions and false tendencies of the immediate. Friedrich Schleiermacher comments:

> What takes the place of miracles for our time is our historical knowl-edge of the character, as well as of the scope and the duration, of Christ's spiritual achievements. In this we have an advantage over the contemporaries of the Redeemer, and a witness whose power increases exactly in proportion as the impressiveness of the miracles is lost.[10]

Again Blake contains both admission and refutation (or qualification) of privacy and solipsism, which is why the both posi-tive and negative estimation of Urizen is so hard to get convincingly right. In the Rousseau-Derrida version of these notions, one can sense the importance of the model of small, self-sufficient communi-ties that may be credibly described as marked by the immediate conversion of word into deed without the necessity of the mediation of writing (compare to Wordsworth here) – a show of hands in the *agora*. Which leads us to:

North and South

Here we are introduced to Urizen:

> Of the primeval Priests assum'd power,
> When Eternals spurn'd back his religion;
> And gave him a place in the north,
> Obscure, shadowy, void, solitary.
> (E 70)

Urizen properly belongs in the south, but it seems to be his task in life to conquer the north, and the trouble starts when he does so (see *M* 19:15ff.: E 112). It is interesting to see Urizen's displacement in the tradition of Grecian versus Gothic, a polarity that runs right through eighteenth-century thinking about the origins and ideals of civil society.[11] Here again is Derrida on Rousseau:

> Rousseau would like the absolute origin to be an absolute south ... the place of origin or the cradle of languages ... closer to childhood, nonlanguage, and nature, ... purer, more alive, more animated. ... In [the northern languages] one can follow the progress of death and coldness.[12]

South is to north as passion to need, love to law, energy to clarity, desire to work, song-speech to writing.[13] The north is the place of Blake's books of brass. But once again Blake is complicated. We know how he elsewhere resolved the polarity: 'Gothic is Living Form' and the place of the imagination, against the mathematic ratios of the Greeks (E 270). The return of analytical reason to the south, if that is what Blake aims at, would in terms of Derrida-Rousseau be the introduction of a writing tradition where it is supposed to have had no place, and correspondingly an insistence upon the abolition of a potent polarity in Blake's intellectual environment.

One could go on with parallels between Blake and Derrida. Derrida's citation of Rousseau's notion of the ideal originary language – in which there is variation of sound, accent, rhythm, and a use of composite words and aphorisms[14] – sounds at least in part close to the declaration of stylistic perversity with which Blake

opens *Jerusalem* (E 145–6). Derrida's remarks on the implicit relation in Rousseau between the incest prohibition and the alienation
of the 'father' by the letter of the law invite renewed attention to
the terms of the Los–Enitharmon–Orc–Urizen relation, and so on.

The point is that Derrida's Rousseau opens up a series of avenues
for the reading of Blake, for example in the areas of the relations
between writing and speech, writing and masturbation, north and
south, and in so doing simultaneously raises the question of a
common *history* against which Blake's specific deviations may be
plotted. This history might be expanded to contain Joyce, Pound, or
perhaps others, but it would remain a history and not a critical
'theory' or 'method'. Such terms seem to signify approaches created
by our institutional eagerness to deprive Derrida of his own historical coordinates, to subsume Rousseau and others into the original
and radical presence that is 'Derrida'. The real reasons for this are
not to the point here, but the effects tend to be the creation of more
north–south polarisations, both between deconstruction and the
rest of the trade, and within deconstruction itself. Thus, in the first
instance, Derrida has come to be identified with a critique of all
forms of historicism (this is ironic since that very gesture itself has a
history) so that he can thus be invoked to remove all possible medi-
ations between the 'new' and the 'old' ways of doing things. In the
second instance, deconstruction itself can sometimes seem to hold
within itself an unmediated oscillation between omnipotence and
impotence. The will to power, which is conscious, consists in the
invocation of a language that is outside institutionally repressive
norms and *therefore*, it is said, subversive of those norms (more of
this later, in relation to Blake); the will to impotence, sometimes
but not always conscious, consists in the reciprocal suspicion that in
the adoption of such a language, a verbal sublime, we conspire in
our own supersession by the very powers we purport to be fighting.
These things, needless to say, need not be as opposed in fact as they
seem to be in theory. Their profiles may be traced in two elements
of Derridean thought that often seem particularly popular. The first
is the selective encoding of play, and the second is the rhetoric of
self-implication.

On the matter of play, I cite Gayatri Spivak's shrewd observation
that it is 'curious that, although Derrida often speaks of Nietzsche's
explosive and affirmative and open play, he speaks rarely of Freud's
own analysis of play as a restrictive gesture of power'.[15] She goes on
to qualify this point, but let us register here the comparative lack of

encouragement that Derrida offers for a consideration of the negative or falsely conscious play. Play is for him rather a pleasure, a joyous perversity, a standing outside the limits of order. This may be a making virtue of necessity in that the second element, the rhetoric of self-implication, tells us that we *have no* place to stand, no alternative form of order that is not itself undercut. Thus Derrida writes that

> operating necessarily from the inside, borrowing all the strategic and economic resources of subversion from the old structure, borrowing them structurally, that is to say without being able to isolate their elements or atoms, the enterprise of deconstruction always in a certain way falls prey to its own work.[16]

This moment of confession and others like it (for it is of course built into the method) tempts forth a whole litany of self-underminings; I take, almost at random, Stefano Agosti's introduction to Derrida's *Spurs: Nietzsche's Styles*, which refers to itself as 'a bit of magnetised and commemorative jetsam, tossing in the wake of a ship', speaks of a 'textual and semantic drift' that renders us 'powerless to fix or seize hold of it', and intimates that the reader of Derrida might 'with his own eyes, touch ... and be blinded'.[17] Play thus becomes the random play of incapacity, embracing the idea of total psychic contamination and finding relief only in a moment in which self-intelligibility may be put aside. This is what Paul Mann refers to, eloquently, precisely, and perhaps a little too celebratively, at the end of his essay as an 'after-life of the selfhood' produced perhaps by 'accident, by counter-error, by an involuntary twitch that leaves one suddenly writing blindly in the rough basement'. Beyond ideology, beyond system, beyond the figurative umbrella known as the 'book', the ear is closed to its own destruction because it operates at random. In the twitch we are free, but the price of freedom is the isolation of linguistic effect per se as the single place of a merely celebrative play.

BLAKE AND THE POLITICS OF THE SUBLIME

I begin with Burke, whose *A Philosophical Enquiry into the Origin of Our Ideas of the Sublime and Beautiful* (1757) has been aptly discussed by Stephen Land.[18] If I may summarise his emphases: Burke denies the need for the calling up of referential images in the mind's eye, or for the decomposition of complex ideas into their constitutive simple parts, to ensure the success of the verbal sublime. The sublime plays on the relation between language and the mind, and reference to nature has no part in it. Poetry might lose much of its effect if it made such reference, moreover, for 'we find by experience that eloquence and poetry are capable, nay indeed much more capable of making deep and lively impressions than the other arts, and even than nature itself in very many cases'.[19] Blake and Burke in many ways must seem an infamous coalition, and it may be doubted that Blake would have placed eloquence and poetry in the same category as Burke does here. Nevertheless, we are reminded of how Blake saw Wordsworth to be fettering himself, poetry, and the human race: 'Natural Objects always did & now do Weaken deaden & obliterate Imagination in Me' (E 665). This is an astute insight into the complications Wordsworth necessarily invokes by employing natural objects as the vehicles of the essential human imagination, compelled as he then is to agonise over the fetishistic possibilities latent in such a decision.[20] But for the moment we may note simply that Blake's comment, and indeed his practice, is in line with Burke's idea that the proper place of the sublime is the mind itself. This supersession of a reference to an outside world of natural objects that might be thought to be held in common between poet-speaker and audience entails a risk or choice. On the one hand (let us call it the pole of eloquence, in Blakean terms), we register the potential for deceit implicit in such a sublimity. The famous passage in *King Lear* (IV. iv) that pretends to look down from the cliffs of Dover is of course a *lie*. The blind Gloucester is deceived by *language* ('Methinks the ground is even') into thinking that he stands at the top of a cliff. There are no crows, no choughs, no midway air, except in the rhetorical abundance of the verbal sublime. Blake cannot be accused, I think, of choosing this pole; rather we find him occupying the pole of imagination, in which the excision of the natural object is designed to stimulate the powers within. But there is a very narrow category of self-election into this imaginative society – though we should never forget that the softening first appeal of Blake's designs is an inducement to a relaxation of the Protestant intensity of true vision. Generally, however, the poet takes risks with his audience in such a cutting off from what they habitually recognise as nature; moreover, it is part of his purpose that he does so. W.S. Walker, reviewing in 1821 Shelley's *Prometheus Unbound*, by Blakean standards a rather accessible poem, comments as follows:

All is brilliance, vacuity and confusion. We are dazzled by the multitude of words which sound as if they denoted something very grand
or splendid: fragments of images pass in crowds before us; but when
the procession has gone by, and the tumult of it is over, not a trace of
it remains upon the memory. The mind, fatigued and perplexed, is
mortified by the consciousness that its labour has not been rewarded
by the acquisition of a single distinct conception.[21]

Here is the same critic again:

They argue in criticism, as those men do in morals, who think
debauchery and dissipation an excellent proof of a good heart. The
want of meaning is called sublimity, absurdity becomes venerable
under the name of originality, the jumble of metaphor is the richness
of imagination, and even the rough, clumsy, confused structure of
the style, with not unfrequent violation of the rules of grammar, is,
forsooth, the sign and effect of a bold, overflowing genius, that dis-
dains to walk in common trammels.[22]

I would not wish to be seen to be siding with the rotten rags of
memory and the rules of grammar against either Shelley or Blake,
but I want to make the point that such contemporary criticism
ought to make us wary of reposing in the myth that the single function of Blake's texts 'is' (and the present tense tells all) to make us
joyously aware of the usefulness of difficulty in the achievement of
valuable forms of self-consciousness. Such modern critical recupera-
tion misses a whole series of questions about the politics and indeed
the theology (for we are dealing with the literature of self-election)
of the sublime. Kant, among others, stressed that the sublime is
always a cultivated taste; to the ordinary consciousness it is merely
terrifying.[23] Not only might Blake's books have terrified many
readers, if he had had them, it is part of his very *purpose* that he did
not. As with Blake, so for Derrida?

We know that times were hard in England after 1794, and that it
was dangerous to say anything in public that could even be interpreted as democratic. Working as we now can with a 'Blake' who is
free from the chains of a unitary or monolithic subjectivity and its
existential dichotomies (this being as I have said the most valuable
contribution of the Derridean movement, though not unique to it),
we can understand the obscurity of Blake's writings without any
accusation of bad faith. My sense is, however, that we tend to go to
the opposite extreme, making Blake the yardstick of right thinking
in an age when so many others can be seen to be making compro-

mises with the establishment. Because his *text* is radical, sublime in the aesthetic sense, we move, in a gesture that surreptitiously inscribes the importance of our own discipline of exegesis, to a radical Blake. The radical text was very possibly written on the assumption that it would not be read, and indeed it was produced in such a form that it could *never* have had mass circulation or radical effect (unless we make an argument for the policy of changing the minds of the rich and powerful). Even today we seldom read Blake but have to make do with variously inadequate facsimiles, a subject on which Essick's and Carr's essays in [the conference] volume comment in detail.[24] The real Blake is locked away in museums, a prey to the very social tendencies we assume that he opposed. Or did he? For Blake was never 'there' for the taking, ignored by a merely ignorant or prejudiced public. Most of his books were incapable of being mass-produced, given the colouring process, and they were too expensive for most potential readers.

Perhaps I am labouring the point, but the radical Blake, as we know him, may be a consequence of our allowing the space vacated by the old-fashioned subject 'William Blake' to be reoccupied by text or language *alone*, imaged as an autonomous organism generating a self-engaging play, rather than language as the repository of the play of *powers* in the *structuring* of the *historical* psyche (which may indeed take the *form* of a self-engaging play) – a language allowing in, in other words, the play of politics, history, sexuality, and all the things that give language a content in the traditional sense of the term – a play that might bear the question of a false consciousness. This cannot be good for Blake, for Romanticism, or for criticism. We must work to complicate the reified contrast, which still appears, between Blake and Wordsworth as radical and reactionary. It is not enough to say that Blake is 'radical' because his *text* is so, while Wordsworth is somehow reactionary because he writes a language more nearly approximating to that of ordinary social intercourse, or because his poems are in some unanalysed aesthetic sense 'unachieved'. These confusions may embody their own meanings, their burdens of political and imaginative crisis or alienation; in our myth of Blake's aesthetic wholeness there may be something we should suspect.[25]

Derrida and many of his disciples seem to offer precious little in the way of incentives to move the analysis beyond the surface of the text, back into the historical powers that constitute its play. Such a movement is indeed usually dismissed by Derrida's disciples as metaphysically improper, a social blunder in the direction of the old beliefs in 'substance'. This dismissal confuses subjectivity with the powers that constitute and pass through subjectivity. The former is certainly to be posited as fluent, but the latter are very substantial; they are the historical constituents of identity. Only when this is admitted can there be any *rapprochement* between critical Marxism and deconstruction, whose ossified popular forms are certainly incompatible (is that the logic of the profession?) but whose theoretical, mutual exclusion is unnecessary once language is recognised as one of the areas in which the powers identified by Marx make their (often secret) appearance.

Blake, I think, offers more incentives for the move *behind* the text, and invites reference to a substantial archive to which the text may be related. Like many Romantics, and unlike many moderns, he insists always on the existential seriousness of superficiality when it does occur. Blake, like Kierkegaard, sees despair *and* joy, and a great many implications for both, where many a deconstructionist would tend to rest comfortably with a demonstration of the infinite artificiality of text. In particular, Blake and many of his contemporaries write a language through which a highly sophisticated political energy may be discovered to be latent, and occasionally obvious. The recovery of this energy of course takes *research*, in the old-fashioned sense; it cannot be expected to emanate from a mere exercise in 'reading the poem', however ingenious. Putting the case simply and crudely, we may demonstrate the question of Blake's *textuality* in the form of a paradox, the elucidation and specification of which would entail a sophisticated and extensive historical inquiry. On the one hand, the irrationalist movements in whose orbits Blake can be situated can be read as democratic, taking the creation of significant meaning out of the control of established institutions (Parliament and the Church of England). On the other hand they can seem to reinforce the status quo by focusing all oppositional energies in a language so deflected and esoteric that it only registers as a fringe phenomenon (if at all), a Hobbesian nightmare or scrambling of all sociable codes.

[The conference] volume entertains various speculations about the future of Blake criticism. No one seems to see Blake as a future Dryden, now alas all too often a stranded whale on the beach of literary history. I have enough of the celebrative impulse in me to hope that this will never happen. Perhaps I have been guilty of stating the obvious in outlining a move away from celebration, and many will feel that they have already made that move. It is a truism to all of us that undergraduates no longer read on library walls that the tigers of wrath are wiser than the horses of instruction, and it is a further truism that we are as the times are. But this matter of celebration (along with its opposite, serious historical self-consciousness) does pertain to the presence of Derrida in contemporary criticism, and the reasons for and consequences of this are worth pondering. Perhaps there will come a time when our successors, if they ever come into being, will look back with scholarly disinterest on the period now ending, or beginning, or continuing. I quote from an imaginary *PMLA*, say the May issue of the year 2125, now electronically flashed up on the wall (is this 'writing'?) of every subscriber's home or office:

> The English Christian radical William Blake proved irresistibly attractive to a generation of critics interested, by virtue of apprenticeship in mid-century liberationist movements, in an aesthetic of fertile indeterminacy, irreverence for the past, and the possibilities of a macrocosmic dance to the tune of an exemplary subjectivity. The more imaginative members of the profession found him an infinite provider of epiphanies. ...

Perhaps this colleague-to-be may also conclude that 'signs of change could be seen emerging at the Santa Cruz conference of May 1982, and in the volume of essays emanating from it'.

From *Unnam'd Forms: Blake and Textuality*, ed. Nelson Hilton and Thomas A. Vogler (Berkeley, CA, 1986), pp. 11–25.

NOTES

[Like Gavin Edwards' essay above, David Simpson's essay originally appeared in a volume taken from the proceedings of a conference called 'Blake and Criticism', and it is based on responses to other papers delivered at the conference. And like W.J.T. Mitchell's essay, it focuses on the issue of 'writing' in Blake, which Simpson situates in terms of Derrida, Rousseau and 'Derrida's Rousseau' before going on to raise a series of important questions about the 'radicalism' of Blake's text in its historical context, a context which crucially includes the sublime, the natural and the imaginative, all categories which are seen as under contemporary critical revision. Ed.]

1. [See context note above – Ed.]
2. See Paul Mann, '*The Book of Urizen* and the Horizon of the Book' and Vincent A. De Luca, 'A Wall of Words: The Sublime as Text',

both in *Unnam'd Forms: Blake and Textuality*, ed. Nelson Hilton and Thomas A. Vogler (Berkeley, CA, 1986), pp. 49–68 and 218–41.

3. *James Joyce: The Critical Writings*, ed. Ellsworth Mason and Richard Ellmann (New York, 1964), p. 220.

4. Ibid., pp. 74–5.

5. See, for example, *James Joyce: New Perspectives*, ed. Colin MacCabe (Bloomington, IN, 1982), and the other work to which this valuable collection of essays refers.

6. Derrida, *Of Grammatology*, trans. G.C. Spivak (Baltimore, MD, 1981), p. lxxxv.

7. For a description of this technique at work in copy W of 'The Little Boy lost', see Simpson, *Irony and Authority in Romantic Poetry* (London, 1979), pp. 214–15. It can of course be observed elsewhere in Blake's books.

8. Derrida, *Of Grammatology*, p. 68.

9. Ibid., pp. 165ff.

10. Friedrich Schleiermacher, *The Christian Faith*, ed. H.R. Mackintosh and J.S. Steward (Edinburgh, 1928), pp. 448–9. Compare the arguments in Kierkegaard's *Philosophical Fragments*, trans. David F. Swenson (Princeton, NJ, 1962).

11. Its nineteenth-century continuation is incisively delineated by Marilyn Butler in *Romantics, Rebels and Reactionaries: English Literature and its Background, 1760–1830* (New York, 1982), pp. 113–37.

12. Derrida, *Of Grammatology*, pp. 217–18.

13. Ibid., pp. 224–6.

14. Ibid., p. 243.

15. Ibid., p. xlv.

16. Ibid., p. 24.

17. Derrida, *Spurs: Nietzsche's Styles*, trans. Barbara Harlow (Chicago, 1978), pp. 25, 9, 3.

18. See Stephen K. Land, *From Signs to Propositions: The Concept of Form in Eighteenth-Century Semantic Theory* (London, 1974), pp. 36–50.

19. Burke, *A Philosophical Enquiry into the Origin of Our Ideas of the Sublime and Beautiful* (2nd edn, London, 1759), p. 334.

20. However, this emphatically does not mean that he simply repeats or endorses such a deadness. Often the Wordsworthian speaker is presented dramatically as the perpetrator of misunderstandings that the

argument of the poem as a whole is meant to expose. I have tried to show Wordsworth's sense of this, in its relation to his theory of mind and his views of the human and natural environment most proper to it, in David Simpson, *Wordsworth and the Figurings of the Real* (London, 1982).

21. *Shelley: The Critical Heritage*, ed. James E. Barcus (London, 1975), p. 254.

22. Ibid., pp. 263–4.

23. Kant, *Critique of Judgement*, trans. J.H. Bernard (London, 1914), section 29.

24. See Robert N. Essick, 'How Blake's Body Means' and Stephen Leo Carr, 'Illuminated Printing: Toward a Logic of Difference', in *Unnam'd Forms*, ed. Hilton and Vogler, pp. 197–217 and 177–96.

25. See, for example, David Aers, Jonathan Cook and David Punter, *Romanticism and Ideology: Studies in English Writing, 1765–1830* (London, 1981). This important series of essays is organised around a Blake–Wordsworth opposition, very much along the lines I am here questioning (apart from some arguments for Blake's assimilation of some of the mythologies he opposes in the sphere of sexuality and patriarchy). Wordsworth is made unitary in his tendency to 'dissolve the social and political dimension of individual life and to lead the reader towards affirmative and reconciliatory attitudes to current modes of social control' (Aers, Cook and Punter, p. 5). Again: 'Unlike Blake, Wordsworth is not concerned with the creation of a poetic form which can imaginatively convey the reader into the reality of contradictory perceptions of the social world' (ibid., p. 59). What this really says is that Blake's text is more apparently complex than Wordsworth's; at least, it misses the signs of alienation in Wordsworth's apparently more easeful manner. When Blake is the stick with which Wordsworth is beaten, we do neither poet much of a service. Similar and greater problems arise in Heather Glen, *Vision and Disenchantment: Blake's 'Songs' and Wordsworth's 'Lyrical Ballads'* (Cambridge, 1983), where the inexplicit category of the 'imaginative' and the language of 'embodiment' are wielded to show Blake the better (or more moral, human, imaginative) poet. Until such terms are traded in once and for all for humbler goals such as more historical documentation and more critical sophistication, one reader's man of property will always be another reader's rick burner.

9

Representations of Revolution: From *The French Revolution* to *The Four Zoas*

DAVID AERS

This essay offers a critical account of the ways in which Blake represents the processes of radical social transformation in the prophetic books up to and including *The Four Zoas*. Although it draws attention to serious problems and even contradictions in Blake's writing about revolution, the essay meets the poems on grounds they themselves have chosen, sharing their view that the issues involved are fundamental to all projects of human emancipation.

However my reading of Blake differs from Leopold Damrosch's, his recent book voices the kind of involvement Blake's longer poems seek: 'As a prophet Blake claims to announce the truth' and it is 'important to consider how his poems might be perceived as true by modern readers'. 'Blake's prodigious genius is evident in the daring with which he attacks the most fundamental problems, and we read him only half-heartedly if we do not respond as human beings to his prophetic demands'.[1] Increasingly uncommon as such moral and metaphysical language is in advanced academic criticism, it is appropriate to the claims made by Blake's writings. Their seriousness calls for a critical dialogue; their range, depth, and scope continually raise issues with which many people are still struggling. The subject of the present essay is one of these issues.

My intention is to shift critical preoccupation and mode, a shift in terrain. My own preoccupations, however congruent with some of Blake's, inevitably set out the grounds of the present inquiry. Nevertheless I hope that this critical mode avoids that theoretical imperialism in which the very possibility of hearing the other is denied. In Bakhtin's terms, I hope that the commentary encourages a 'dialogic' engagement with a writer whose own texts are so rarely 'monologic' and whose work contributes a major critique of 'monologism'.[2] This is, of course, hardly an unproblematic hope. Even the seemingly anarchic poststructuralism favoured in the United States, a display of gamesome signifiers always lacking an 'original' or 'transcendental signified', even this obsessive linguistic revel habitually manifests a narcissistic imperialism in which the historical moment of the text's production is simply dissolved, the specific questions that moment posed to different individuals, social groups, and ideological formations, solipsistically ignored. Of course, a critical method committed to such systematic amnesia concerning the history of social formations and their political culture is not without its own contemporary political and historical meanings.

Whatever the theoretical and practical difficulties involved in my own method, I would describe its aspirations in the following way, aspirations that are part of a recognisable if loosely defined tradition. It seeks to approach the literary text as a social text created in specific circumstances. These circumstances are not 'background', a remote reference point comprising a separate domain of study that can be left to 'historians'. On the contrary, because these contexts are carried in language they are inscribed in the minute particulars of the texts: they permeate them. No static dualism of literature and 'background' can help us understand this situation. Here Bakhtin/Vološinov offers us some relevant reflections as we try to press beyond such dualistic assumptions and the related dualistic construction of 'individual' over against 'society': 'Each person's inner world and thought has its stabilised *social audience* that comprises the environment in which reasons, motives, values and so on are fashioned. ... In point of fact, *word is a two-sided act*. It is determined equally by *whose* word it is and *for whom* it is meant. As word, it is precisely *the product of the reciprocal relationship between speaker and listener, addresser and addressee*. ... I give myself verbal shape from another's point of view, ultimately from the point of view of the community to which I belong.'[3] In this model language, the construction of social subjects, social experience and politics are indissolubly bound together: 'The structure of experience is just as social as is the structure of outward objectification. The degree to which an experience is perceptible, distinct, and formulated is directly proportional to the degree to which it is socially oriented.'[4]

The very generation of meaning is bound up with structures of power and control in the community. So is 'literature', 'criticism', and teaching. Bakhtin/Vološinov's approach transcends the misleading dualisms of literature and background, individual and society, public and private. In the writings we study, the world is mediated, prevalent perceptions reinforced or challenged, contemporary values and problems represented and worked over, a web of discourses engaged with.[5] They were made by actual people in living and complexly diversified relationships created within determinate circumstances and systems (of production, of political order, of sexual organisation, of ideology). Any effort to understand a text should include an attempt to re-place it in the web of discourses and social practices where it was made. This helps us pick up the implications of its different voices and modes, helps us grasp what Bakhtin, in *The Dialogic Imagination*, calls their 'socio-ideological meaning' in terms of a 'knowledge of the social distribution and ordering of all the other ideological voices in the era'.[6] A daunting ideal, certainly, but one we should, in my view, at least strive toward.

The method I pursue also seeks to encourage self-reflexivity: an awareness of the theoretical and political premises of our reading, teaching, and scholarly production; an awareness of the ways in which our own moment and the choices we make within it shape our perceptions. All attempts to recover a specific web of discourses and practices in the past take place within our own ideological horizons, which can never be that of the texts we read. We must try to include a reflexivity about our own horizons (not to say Urizen's) in our critical work, articulating as clearly as possible the evaluative criteria and premises of our approaches. In doing this we are less likely to foster a critical imperialism than if we naturalise our approaches. And if the aims of the method I have sketched can exist only in tension, it is an inescapable tension. All our knowing, whether of past or present others, is produced in contingent, social, political, and gender-specific circumstances.

The fact that the talented community of Blake scholars have not spent much time worrying at the substantial problems considered in

this essay is itself an example of how ideological and political paradigms shape the critical discourses cultivated in the institutions of
higher education. Our institutions are privileged parts of capitalist
social formations – ones so highly militarised and accustomed to
such massive levels of aggression, violence, and fear that they live in
perpetual readiness to launch weapons of mass slaughter across the
globe. The daily threat of genocide, of holocaust, has become natu-
ralised, celebrated, and multiplied, at unimaginable cost, as a sign
of freedom and civilisation's strength. Radical social transformation is hardly an issue in Britain and even less so in the United
States – except when it rears its rebellious head in countries over
which the metropolitan power has a proprietorial interest, economic and military (Nicaragua, Chile). The community of professional
critics flourish within, not above, this situation. Our paradigms
(selecting basic questions, fields, and methods of inquiry) are affected by their position in such a culture. Our reading of Blake will
inevitably bear the mark of that culture, in what is ignored as well
as in what is addressed. Recent works like those by Baldick and
Lentricchia ought to increase awareness of just how politically and
socially determined academic criticism has been, whether in its New
Critical, archetypal, structuralist, or deconstructionist phases.[7]
Blake's admirers might be especially open to such accounts, for his
poetry brings out the political dimensions of writing and reading, of
literature and hermeneutics. It encourages a self-reflexivity about
the presence of institutional, gender, ideological, and class positions
shaping our own outlook and discourse. And it cultivates this self-
reflexivity within a revolutionary perspective, an overall commitment to the radical transformation of dominant forms of human
social existence as Blake saw them.

In Blake's poetry the development of the human subject depends
on a texture of interactions with others, a process quite alien to the
dichotomising categories 'individual' and 'society' normalised
within our traditions of various individualisms. At their happiest, as
in the *Songs of Innocence*, human interactions create the mutual
trust and security essential to open and responsible people living in
peaceful community. In an outstanding book, Heather Glen has
recently shown how these *Songs* confront a grimly oppressive
reality while simultaneously showing alternative possibilities of
being 'rooted in some of our actual experiences, yet threatened
most immediately by much that we ourselves do'.[8] Unless such trust
and acknowledgement of mutual dependency can be maintained,

we are likely to evolve versions of identity like those Blake figures in *Urizen*, 'Where self sustaining I may view all things beneath my feet' (*FZ* VI:72:24:E 349). The sad consequences of this domineering and individualistic form of autonomy Blake explored around Urizen in *The Four Zoas* and returned to in *Jerusalem*.[9]

But the prophetic books become increasingly preoccupied with a possibility not envisaged in the *Songs*. What if the relations within which the human being grows up are not only systematically exploitative but also ones where the ruling class's values have gained such control that they pervade all areas of being? If something like this were to happen then the existing social organisation, its institutionalised violence, its cruel forms of work (so powerfully described by Blake), its massive inequalities in access to the resources of material and mental life, its legitimising ideologies, all this might seem so 'natural' as to preclude alternative possibilities of living. If such were the case, leading social groups would have attained a 'hegemonic' control.[10] The very construction of subjectivity would be assimilated to this and the most intimate relations between even the exploited would be incorporated.[11] So the relations between chimney sweepers, marvellously described by Heather Glen, might be far more disastrously affected than the *Songs of Innocence* allow. No longer would they include prefigurations of an 'alternative possibility' grounded in a 'mutually satisfying actuality' within the exploitative violence Blake characterises so memorably.[12] If, as Blake suggests in *Milton*, 'Human Thought is crushd beneath the iron hand of Power' (*M* 25:4:E 121), and if this state seems pervasive, then Blake would be left with at least three massive problems. First, what relationships can offer the necessary prefigurations for the transformed world? Without such contemporary prefigurations a revolutionary must write the most abstract utopianism, a frivolous activity in itself but dangerous to self and others if it affects consciousness and practice. Second, how can the existing hegemony be dissolved or overthrown, and by whom? This is a crucial question about agency and resources. Third, what explains the revolutionary's genesis if such a hegemony really exists? I will now concentrate on Blake's engagement with these substantial issues in his representations of revolution up to *The Four Zoas*.

In *The French Revolution* Blake projects a fairly simple two-class model. A neo-feudal aristocracy (with a liberal fraction) rules over 'the Commons'. The poem does refer to cities and villages, to ploughmen, peasants, shepherds, husbandmen, soldiers, officers, and bourgeois leaders; it also refers to women and children who seem to constitute a separate domain of decorous passivity. Yet none of these references to people inhabiting thoroughly different situations in the social formation leads to any differentiation of the third estate. Blake settles for the homogenising language of 'the Commons', 'the people', and 'the Nation'.[13] This language enforces the dual-class model and a perception of those in opposition to the traditional ruling class as united bearers of a universal liberation. In doing this Blake swallowed the ideology of one revolutionary group, the bourgeois Jacobins.[14] This encouraged a dissolution of the very different life experiences and politics of peasants, urban artisanate, casual labourers, rioting Parisian women, lawyers, and bureaucrats (key groups in the composition of Jacobinism) and merchants. The consequences were the risk that the text would present experience that no one ever lived, or could live, and ideas no one ever thought, even while it proclaims itself to be a meditation on historical processes and experience.[15]

Perhaps the most troubling difficulties for the revolutionary project the poem espouses can be seen in the oration from the spokesman of 'the voice of the people' (*FR* 11:206–12; 204: E 295–6). Sieyès presents an unequivocally political version of the Fall. Most humans are apparently 'bound' in the ruined world, 'To wander inslav'd'. They are thoroughly passivised: physically intimidated, they are also 'deprest in dark ignorance' by their rulers. Such total control would seem fatal to any revolutionary project. The oppressed come 'To worship terrors, bred from the blood of revenge and breath of desire', to worship 'beastial forms' and 'more terrible men'. The very forms of desire are incorporated, the energies of the oppressed 'madden'd with slavery' and bound into the dominating religious ideology and institutions (*FR* 11:211–16, 12:227–8:E 295–6). There seem to be no resources within present human relations from which alternative forms of social life might be created. But if this is so, there are no grounds for constructing revolutionary visions and peering beyond the fragments.

The French Revolution, however, moves swiftly from this dismal vision of an 'inslav'd' humanity to one of gentle collaboration in which the vicious past is totally transcended (*FR* 11:217–12:240: E 295–7). Of course, the poem's sharp and witty critique of aristocratic power and religious ideology carries an energy that promises us the traditional state of affairs is not 'natural', that things could, surely, be otherwise. But the crucial transition itself is negotiated simply by deploying images from the natural cycle of day succeeding night (*FR* 11:217–12:219:E 295–6). 'Then' comes the revolutionary transformation (*FR* 13:220, 223:E 296). But in the contexts Blake has evoked, if the army abandoned the rulers and 'blood ran down the ancient pillars' (*FR* 13:246:E 297), one would have no reason to connect such events with the forms of human emancipation celebrated in Blake's work (as here, *FR* 12:220–34:E 296). Yet the poem does just this. It figures forth a human regeneration in which 'the bottoms of the world were open'd, and the graves of the arch-angels unseal'd', while 'the Senate in peace, sat beneath morning's beam' (*FR* 16:300–6:E 299–300). The use of the passive ('were open'd', 'unseal'd') deletes the key agents and contributes to the text's evasion of profoundly troubling questions about revolution it has raised.

Visions of the Daughters of Albion engages with these unresolved issues. The poem opens and closes with the 'Enslavd' daughters totally passivised, their contexts unchanged by the revolutionary Oothoon.[16] In Blake's presentation there is no sign of interaction between the daughters. The slave-owning rapist's claim, picking up an idea noted in *The French Revolution* (*FR* 11:215:E 296), becomes plausible: the oppressed, 'stampt with my signet ... worship terrors and obey the violent' (*VDA* 1:21–3:E 46). Oothoon herself appears in peculiar isolation from any reciprocal, sustaining relationships, a version of consciousness that could only foster myths of independent autonomy whose inadequacies Blake's poems have already superseded.[17] It is hardly surprising that the poem offers no way out of the disastrous states it depicts – revolutionary rhetoric in such contexts is both inadequate and inexplicable.

But Blake does not abandon the problems set by the revolutionary social dimensions of his vision. In *America* he figures revolutionary forces in Orc. Those commentators who have emphasised the destructive and dehumanised aspects of Orc in his earliest appearances are certainly correct. He enters with an act of masculine violence that looks much like the rape opening the *Visions*, only now it is glossed with the all-too-familiar male cant that the female really 'joy'd' in such violence (*A* 2:4:E 52). Nothing could be farther from the delicate images of mutuality and trust cultivated in the *Songs of Innocence*. Nor is this observation a naïve failure to observe the difference between the world of innocence and experience: it points, rather, to the fact that the 'end' is prefigured in the 'means'. Contrary to some scholars' impressions, it is not merely Urizen who sees Orc as a dehumanised terror. He describes himself as an 'eagle screaming in the sky', 'a lion / Stalking upon the mountains', a whale lashing the abyss, 'a serpent folding' around the female's limbs while he 'siez'd' her in his 'fierce embrace'; the female sees him as a serpent, eagle, lion, whale, fire, and lightning (*A* 1,2). All these figure domineering, predatory, violently coercive action. They all exclude mutuality, care, and reciprocity, exhibiting a thoroughly macho version of revolutionary force such as Shelley criticised in *Laon and Cythna*. Out of such a process only disaster can emerge.

This the conclusion of *America* seeks to deny. Instead of using the vision of the *Songs* to explore the fatal limitations of the Orc mentality, its *un*revolutionary and very traditional devotion to 'masculine' violence, the poem claims that at least the Orcian revolution achieves sexual liberation and gratification (*A* 15:19–26:E 57). In context, however, this is far from plausible. To proclaim that Orcian 'fierce desire', echoing the 'fierce embrace' of the early rape (*A* 1:10, 2:1–3:E 51–2), unproblematically frees the 'desires' of females, leaving them 'naked and glowing with the lusts of youth', would seem likely only to those enjoying the sexual fantasies analysed in Andrea Dworkin's *Pornography: Men Possessing Women*.[18] The revolutionary (or revolutionised!) women have no voices. Although there is expression of pleasure in the body and sexuality, this is defined *for* women by revolutionary man: women exist solely in the domain of masculine (Orcian) sexual desire. Nor should we overlook another peculiarly male feature in this definition, namely, the tendency to treat sexual desire, masculine and feminine, as an autonomous force abstracted from the full human being and the matrix of relationships within which meaningful life can alone be sustained. The concomitant version of human freedom is similarly distorted. It lacks images of relationship, reciprocity, affection, mutual recognition. Others cannot be perceived as subjects or listened to as different voices with whom dialogue is possible. Such considerations help us see the folly of thinking that the violently masculine and traditional-enough forms of desire figured in Orc could contribute to human liberation and joy.[19] *America* actually figures an ominous collusion between Orc and Urizen, the values of masculine, violent revolutionary and masculine, violent conservative. Orc's 'cloudy terrors', his 'fierce flames' giving 'heat but not light' converge with the Urizen depicted in fires, 'But no light from the fires' (*U* 5:17:E 73). The flames burning round the thrones and abodes of men at the poem's conclusion cannot figure forth any transcendence of Urizenic forms of life. They can only confirm them.

In *Europe* Blake again concludes with 'red' Orc in his 'terrible' fury, now joined by the new figure Los who summons 'all his sons to the strife of blood' (*E* 14:37, 15:2, 11:E 66). The scene is replete with the violence of war. The only interaction is that in which people reduce each other to threatening objects, things which must be destroyed (*E* 14:32–15:12:E 66). Coming from the writer of the *Songs* this is a peculiar version of radical human transformation, although we recognise its affinity with the end of *America*. It is worth pausing over the contexts of *Europe's* conclusion, for they increase our understanding of the difficulties now overwhelming Blake's thinking about revolutionary transformations.

The poem offers a strikingly one-dimensional image of the social contexts of the desired revolution. The citizens' senses are 'petrify'd against the infinite' (*E* 10:15:E 63). And their thought systematically 'Shut up' within the categories of the present order. This generates a religion in which 'man became an Angel; / Heaven a mighty circle turning; God a tyrant crown'd' (*E* 10:1–23:E 63). True enough, the youth of England curse the Urizenic order and the ideology of Kings and Priests (*E* 11:1–5:E 64). Nevertheless, they are educated, socialised into this order:

> The youth of England hid in gloom curse the paind heavens; compell'd
> Into the deadly night to see the form of Albions Angel
> Their parents brought them forth & aged ignorance preaches canting,
> On a vast rock, perciev'd by those senses that are clos'd from thought:
>
> (*E* 12:5–8:E 64)

The last phrase may imply other 'senses', but the text shows us no alternatives among the citizens. On the contrary, even when 'the flames of Orc' drive 'The Guardian of secret codes' from Westminster the author writes this of the citizens:

> Every house a den, every man bound; the shadows are filld
> With spectres, and the windows wove over with curses of iron:

Over the doors Thou shalt not; & over the chimneys Fear is written:
With bands of iron round their necks fasten'd into the walls
The citizens: in leaden gyves the inhabitants of suburbs
Walk heavy: soft and bent are bones of villagers

(*E* 12:26–31:E 64)

This completes a moving and particularised image of a desolately one-dimensional society in which Urizen's codes and practices dominate all domains of life. But once again it evokes the question emerging from *The French Revolution*: if this is anything like an adequate representation of people's experience, practices, and relations, then should not Blake abandon his vision of revolution and his model of humanity, which assumes possibilities of major transformation from the present reality? For the account leaves no spaces in which a counterculture can be created, no agents who might make alternative forms of relations and ideas, and certainly no prefigurations of the regenerate society. Without these it was perhaps inevitable that Blake's representations of revolutionary processes should become as undifferentiated and desocialised as those concluding *Europe* (*E* 14:37–15:11:E 66).

I will now move to *The Four Zoas*, a poem that opens by emphasising the inseparability of human identity and fulfilment from community and active relationship (*FZ* I:3:4–6:E 300–1). In such a perspective as that of the *Songs*, individual development and morality depend on human interdependence, the interplay of self and others, trust, cooperation. Yet the long poem concentrates on psychic fragmentation and the interlockings of many kinds of exploitation, mutual fear, and violence in a recognisably capitalist society dominated by Urizen's values. It focuses on the appalling 'torments of Love & Jealousy' (*E* 300), evoking a world in which sexual and family relations are a site of destructive conflict. Human cruelty and fiercely defended ideological delusions that encourage it are presented with great depth and connectedness. The resulting range of human suffering is sharply and compassionately realised. But the very power of this achievement and the nightmarishly totalising effect of Blake's vision foregrounds fundamental problems we encountered in the earlier prophetic books.

To recapitulate the basic problem: if humans have produced a world such as Blake describes, where are the sources of radical transformation intrinsic to the projects of all reformers, let alone revolutionaries? No more do we meet the models of benevolent interaction generated in the *Songs* than we did in *America* and *Europe*. Indeed, echoes of those lyrics in *The Four Zoas* seem to yield up their vision as the product of 'the shadows of Tharmas & of Enion in Valas world', as the compensatory, desocialised, and almost solipsistic fantasies of 'sleepers entertaind upon the Couches of Beulah / When Luvah & Vala were closd up in their world of shadowy forms' (*FZ* IX:131:19–22:E 400).[20] As for Orc, Blake is now totally clear that the forms of life he figures do not offer any resources for breaking through the disastrous present.[21] On the contrary his energetic activity merely makes Babylon stronger (*FZ* VII[a]:80:30, 44–8:E 356). The poem now acknowledges explicitly that Orcian rebellion involves profound collusion with the dominant Urizenic reality, its assumptions, values, and practices.

Nor does the poem present the sphere of work as prefiguring human liberation, whether in development of material forces promising an end to the reign of scarcity over the majority of people or in the forms of organisation working people might evolve in the face of their employers. Unlike many pre-Marxist and Marxist radical traditions, Blake's poem does not see the forces and relations of production as decisive areas in the desired transformation of the social formation and the forms of human life it makes possible.[22] Night II does, of course, concentrate on the labour processes with the kinds of pain and domination they incorporate. But they are represented in a way that denies the existence of significant working-class struggles and their potential for change. The 'Human Imagination' is apparently turned to stone (*FZ* II:25:6:E 314), while 'Multitudes without number work incessant'. The poetry evokes a state of dehumanising labour under the 'care & power & severity' of Urizen, 'the great Work master' (*FZ* II:28–32:E 318–21).[23] As we are shown 'many a net / Spread & many a Spirit caught, innumerable the nets / Innumerable the gins & traps', the poetry invites us to trace the weave of the nets (*FZ* II:29:16–30:2:E 319). We are led to connect the destructive processes of labour with the possessive individualism fostered in the capitalist society Blake inhabited, with the forms of education, with ruling scientific ideology, with militarism, with orthodox Christianity and the 'moral' framework it supported. For the workers, the nets, gins, and traps seem to define existence. The famous passage on alienated labour, which Blake liked well enough to write into *Jerusalem* (Plate 65), confirms the sense of how closed the system is, how lacking in the potential for emancipatory change:

They forgd the sword the chariot of war the battle ax
The trumpet fitted to the battle & the flute of summer
And all the arts of life they changd into the arts of death
The hour glass contemnd because its simple workmanship
Was as the workmanship of the plowman & the water wheel
That raises water into Cisterns broken & burnd in fire
Because its workmanship was like the workmanship of the Shepherd
And in their stead intricate wheels invented Wheel without wheel
To perplex youth in their outgoings & to bind to labours
Of day & night the myriads of Eternity. that they might file
And polish brass & iron hour after hour laborious workmanship
Kept ignorant of the use that they might spend the days of wisdom
In sorrowful drudgery to obtain a scanty pittance of bread
In ignorance to view a small portion & think that All
And call it Demonstration blind to all the simple rules of life

(FZ VII[b]:92:19–33:E 364)

Characteristic of Blake's writing about labour in the prophetic books, this offers no grounds for cultivating ideas about a revolutionary working class, the privileged bearers of human emancipatory potential. Far from it, the vision here is of a working class assimilated to evolving capitalist production processes. The workers are represented as quietly accepting the degrading specialisation imposed on them, accepting the new industrial discipline and its control of human time,[24] they accept the constitution of themselves and their labour power as a commodity for exchange on a market structured according to the employers' interests. The production processes become 'arts of death' (foreshadowing our own industrial-military fusion), but such is the workers' assimilation that they can be persuaded to abandon all concern with the nature of the products they themselves make. Such incorporation in the system negates any possibility that the workers might grasp the totality within which they are exploited and that they actually construct. Even more starkly does it negate hope that the producers might create forms of association through which they can take control of the means, modes, and ends of production, reorganising them to benefit the physical and mental life of all rather than of the privileged, powerful minority, Urizen's sons. Indeed, the working people are figured as not even offering *any* resistance.

Los too mostly internalises the dominant practices and ideologies in the culture.[25] For example, in Night IV Blake reworks the *Book of Urizen* showing the attempts of the 'Prophet of Eternity' to control Urizen:

> Pale terror siezd the Eyes of Los as he beat round
> The hurtling Demon. terrifid at the shapes
> Enslavd humanity put on he became what he beheld
> He became what he was doing he was himself transformd
> (*FZ* IV:55:20–4:E 338)

As Blake had emphasised earlier in Night IV (*FZ* IV:53:23–4: E 336), Los assimilates his Urizenic contexts and pays the penalty of fighting Urizen on his own ground, in his own modes. The defensive rage and fear, the frenetic attempt to bind down Urizen by force, involves a collusion with Urizen's fundamental assumptions. In this collusion Los's potential for creating alternative possibilities is 'transformd', assimilated to the culture he would oppose and change. Aggressive practices, grounded in well-justified fear of the threatening other, transform consciousness and potential. We have seen how Orc's activity is represented within a similar configuration, one the poem continually repeats, fascinated at the way opposition to Babylon is so often mounted in forms that share much with its basic foundations and actually perpetuate it. We are pushed to agree with the narrator that the 'fetters' of humans in Urizen's world 'grew from the soul' (*FZ* VI:71:11:E 348). Once more we encounter the citizens bound with mind-forged manacles in a manner that negates the qualifying dialectic of voices and interactions so movingly created in the *Songs*. Now, the text insists, Urizen gains 'a New Dominion over all his sons & Daughters / & over the Sons & daughters of Luvah' (*FZ* VI:73:24–5:E 350).

Perhaps this is what makes even Urizen a pitiful ruler. He too is seen as victim of the disastrous hegemony he has done so much to produce, a hegemony that joins rulers, would-be revolutionaries or prophets, and productive workers (*FZ* VI:70:39–45:E 347; *FZ* VI:71:13–14:E 348; *FZ* VI:72:22–39:E 349). Urizen is himself subject to his own cruel web:

> Travelling thro darkness & whereever he traveld a dire Web
> Followd behind him as the Web of a Spider dusky & cold
> Shivering across from Vortex to Vortex drawn out from his mantle
> of years
> A living Mantle adjoind to his life & growing from his Soul
> (*FZ* VI:73:31–4:E 350)

Toward the end of *The Book of Urizen* this web is described as made of twisted cords, knotted meshes, 'twisted like to the human brain', and it is called, 'The Net of Religion' (*U* 25:21–2:E 82). The depiction in the later poem also makes clear that the web figures the way Urizen naturalises the dominant practices and ideologies of the culture he rules: they take on an existence autonomous of his will and, like his workers, he becomes the victim of his own product (*FZ* VIII:100:30–4:E 373). The web also symbolises the disastrous transformation of human interconnectedness, interdependence, without which none can survive, into traps, a predatory world.

Once more we reach the impasse described earlier in my discussions of *The French Revolution* and *Europe*. If such a hegemonic order exists, if human work, imagination and relationships are as deformed as *The Four Zoas* suggests, then we have no hopes for the radical transformation of what is recognisably Blake's society and recognisably ours, one launched on a genocidal and suicidal path.[26] Blake's own revolutionary project, his continuing call to build Jerusalem, 'called Liberty', now and 'in hope', his prophetic and visionary stance, becomes a self-deceptive irrelevance (*J* 54:5: E 203; *J* 12:43–4:E 156).

The Four Zoas, however, does not acknowledge the corner into which humanity has painted itself, by the poem's own account. Instead, the long final Night reaffirms the revolutionary project of human liberation. It denies the consequences entailed by the poem's version of hegemonic order, the consequences of victims' propensity to internalise its values and become resigned, incorporated. In itself, Night IX has received great scholarly admiration. According to the immensely influential Northrop Frye, 'There is nothing like the colossal explosion of creative power in the ninth night of *The Four Zoas* anywhere else in English poetry'; while to the almost as influential Harold Bloom, this Night is 'the most poetically success-ful section of *The Four Zoas*, and taken by itself is one of Blake's most remarkable achievements'.[27] High claims. Yet writers differ over the basic issue of what is being figured in Night IX. Some have claimed that it celebrates the 'spiritual resurrection after death', a turning away from history to an 'otherworldly fulfilment'.[28] More have more wisely attended to the 'startlingly literal ... realistic scenes ... in which the oppressed take vengeance on their dethroned oppressor', although some of these, perhaps anticipating the emphasis of the later *Jerusalem*, have found the vengeance 'out of keeping with the theme of spiritual regeneration predicated on for-giveness', or even as a mark of Blake's 'sadistic fantasy'.[29] Most, however, have seen such features as inevitable revolutionary means to achieve the desired social transformation: 'the whole groaning Universe bursts its chains and explodes, releasing all the oppressed ... Now is unchained the terrible democracy of Blake's apocalypse against Kings, Warriors, Priests and Merchants, ... a brief but violent dictatorship not only of the child-bearers (proletariat) but the children themselves, the child labourers of street and mill' establishing a 'thoroughgoing democracy'.[30] Similarly, 'the emphasis on work, brotherhood and cooperation in Night IX links up with the rise of utopian socialism during the period; and hence with more practical, if no less utopian attempts at making such millenarian visions a reality.'[31] Or, in a more psychologising but congruent mode: 'Night IX shows us an expansion of consciousness beyond the limits of the self and of orthodox reality, its commitment to the discovery and the building of a new age for all men, the restoration of its connections with loins, emotions, what we would call the unconscious.'[32] A grand vision, certainly, but as one scans the scholarly industry on Blake it seems increasingly implausible to assert that 'to anyone who has read through the preceding Nights of this marvellous poem with sympathetic understanding, the events of the apocalypse will perhaps be clear enough'.[33] One of my aims here is to show how the different kinds of 'clarity' proposed by scholars involve critical oversight of problems in Blake's poem, oversight that is, as so often, not without its ideological and political dimensions.

Night IX has several revolutionary surges, making use of the apocalyptic language traditionally deployed by Christians working and hoping for radical change in their cultures. As much recent work has amply illustrated, both in relation to the seventeenth century and to Blake's period, this language is replete with political meanings in a culture where religious discourse was pervasive.[34] In the first surge:

> The thrones of Kings are shaken they have lost their robes & crowns
> The poor smite their opressors they awake up to the harvest
> The naked warriors rush together down to the sea shore
> Trembling before the multitudes of slaves now set at liberty
> They are become like wintry flocks like forests stripd of leaves
> The opressed pursue like the wind there is no room for escape
> (FZ IX:117:18–23:E 387)

We earlier recalled that in the *Songs* Blake discloses how human fulfilment depends on mutual trust, security, and kind reciprocity.

In *The Four Zoas* he substitutes an oppressively one-dimensional version of Urizenic hegemony for the possibilities found within the 'fallen' world of the *Songs*. Now he represents the transcendence of this hegemony through the extremely violent collective action of the 'oppressed'. Only in such revolutionary practice will the 'living flames winged with intellect', the 'mental fire' and the 'bright visions of Eternity' burst forth (*FZ* IX:119:19:E 388):

> And all the while the trumpet sounds from the clotted gore & from
> the hollow den
> Start forth the trembling millions into flames of mental fire
> Bathing their limbs in the bright visions of Eternity
>
> (*FZ* IX:118:17–19:E 387)

Again the retributory violence is stressed: 'Their opressors are falln they have Stricken them' (*FZ* IX:118:24:E 387). The young Marx too thought that 'The coincidence of the changing of circumstances and of human activity or self-changing can only be grasped and rationally understood as revolutionary *practice*', and classical Marxism argues that the ruling class apparatus of violent oppression means that, in the end, 'revolutionary *practice*' entails armed struggle.[35]

I will conclude by suggesting that *The Four Zoas does* very briefly evoke possibilities of revolutionary transformation that break with these myths and evokes entirely different models to the ones found in Night IX. The pity is, however, these possibilities are not explored in the poem and are simply ignored in the final Night. The location I have in mind is the conclusion to Night VII.[36] Here Blake concentrates on the antagonistic relations between Los, Enitharmon, and his Spectre. Despite the antagonisms, human experience is not represented as locked within a closed hegemonic order. In the torments of love, jealousy, delusory ideologies and the nightmare of past conflicts, Los comes to feel pity (*FZ* VII:85:28:E 367). This also involves accepting his Spectre, the 'ravening devouring lust continually / Creating & devouring' (*FZ* VII:84:37–8:E 360), as his own self, not a vicious other he can hold responsible for evil:

> Los embracd the Spectre first as a brother
> Then as another Self; astonishd humanizing & in tears
> In Self abasement Giving up his Domineering lust
>
> (*FZ* VII:85:29–31:E 367)

This is an extraordinarily moving moment and it challenges the very framework of the terrible conflicts and states (social and psychic) refracted in the poem. No longer colluding with Urizen and his methods, Los now feels 'a World within / Opening its gates' and determines to 'quell my fury & teach / Peace to the Soul of dark revenge & repentance to Cruelty' (*FZ* VII:86:4–12:E 368). The contrast with the supposedly revolutionary processes and assumptions informing Night IX could not be starker. Nor does Blake sentimentally pretend that Los's radical change of feeling and orientation guarantees anything. At first Enitharmon, not surprisingly, rejects his move as a delusory one in a Urizenic (Hobbesian) world where:

> Life lives upon Death & by devouring appetite
> All things subsist on one another thenceforth in Despair
> (*FZ* VII:87:19–20:E 369)

But Los, renouncing his earlier violence against her, perseveres, and Enitharmon joins in collaborative work, striving to 'fabricate embodied semblances' that will suggest alternative possibilities of life for those in a world dominated by the collusion between Orc and Urizen.[37]

Blake's model here rejoins the vision of the *Songs of Innocence*: within Urizen's world even more affective, caring forms of life actually exist (and not only in fetishised textual play, self-referential linguistic revels) and it is these that hold the potential for the revolutionary transformations at the centre of Blake's projects. Revolutionary values are grounded and cherished in the most intimate and trusting personal relations:

> But Los loved them & refusd to Sacrifice their infant limbs
> And Enitharmons smiles & tears prevaild over self protection
> They rather chose to meet Eternal death than to destroy
> The offspring of their Care & Pity
> (*FZ* VII:90:50–4:E 371)

Nothing could be farther from the representations of revolution in Night IX *or* from the representations of culture and society as closed one-dimensional systems that we encounter so often in the prophetic books of the 1790s. The parent-labourers bring the values and emotional experiences of the *Songs of Innocence* into the world of Urizenic experience as they evoke and enact an ethic of care and affection. Once again Blake stresses there is no guarantee that this will permeate and transform human reality. Los and Enitharmon have to abandon 'self protection' to *risk* everything. Yet the risk is not taken at the dictate of some abstract moral system, not with an eye on the orders and rewards of the deity. Grounded on particular desires for nurturing relationships within Urizen's world, the activity is quite alien to the 'impersonal' commandments of Urizenic law. Blake's hope here is that through such practice the terrible destruction of human life, made inevitable by Urizenic assumptions (whether in their leftist or rightist modalities), can be checked and superseded. He imagines an outcome in which Los finds his enemy in his hands:

> he wonderd that he felt love & not hate
> His whole soul loved him he beheld him an infant
> Lovely breathd from Enitharmon he trembled within himself
> (*FZ* VII:90:65–7:E 371)

Blake writes not that Urizen becomes an infant, but that Los beheld him so – perhaps sharing the vision that every criminal was once an infant love,[38] the perception of potential in others cherished by the Quakers in our culture, by Gandhian traditions in Hindu culture. The forms of perception here are truly revolutionary: they avoid both the profoundly misleading figuration of society as a one-dimensional homogeneous mass, *and* they avoid the related contradictions of Night IX traced in this essay, contradictions all too familiar within radical politics.

The espousal of violence in Night IX is bound up with the despairing sense of Urizenic hegemony and mass passivisation I have outlined. It is part of an abstract utopianism that falsifies the diversity of the problematic, dismal-enough present, and surrenders it to some putative future to be won by the violent processes just described. This utopianism participates in the mentality allegedly abandoned by the converted Urizen, a mentality that fails to grasp that the desired 'futurity is in this moment', or probably not at all (*FZ* IX:121:3–22:E 390). Perhaps another way of writing about the differences between the vision and assumptions at the close of Night VIII[a] and the representation of revolution in Night IX might be in the terms of Carol Gilligan's wonderful study, *In a Different Voice*. Night IX, with the version of society, power and relationships it assumes, lacks what Gilligan describes as 'contextual particularity'. This alone allows us: 'the understanding of

cause and consequence which engages the compassion and toler-
ance repeatedly noted to distinguish the moral judgements of
women. Only when substance is given to the skeletal lives of hypothetical people is it possible to consider the social injustice that their
moral problems may reflect and to imagine the individual suffering
their occurrence may signify or their resolution engender.'[39]

The representation of revolution in Night IX, and the associated
contexts discussed in this essay, is characterised by an absence of
such 'contextual particularity', such human 'substance'. This
involves a failure that is imaginative, moral, and, profoundly so,
political. It contrasts with the achievement of the *Songs*, the close of
Night VII and much in Blake's writing,[40] writing that at its best
helps us give 'substance' and social scope to Gilligan's claim: 'The
truths of relationship, however, return in the rediscovery of connection, in the realisation that self and other are interdependent and
that life, however valuable in itself, can only be sustained by care
and relationships.'[41] The dynamics she describes, fostered elsewhere
in Blake, are crushed in Night IX and the representations of revolution and society analysed above. Their crushing gives the lie to all
claims that we are reading a vision of revolutionary regeneration. It
is the close of Night VII that figures a radical transformation of
subjectivity and social practice, a transformation without which the
survival of our species is now barely imaginable. There Blake
figures an ethic of care, a commitment to evolve a trust of the other,
an abandonment of domination in the quest for a community that
will overcome destructive aggression, and equally destructive passivisation, by creating mutual security. This will foster individuality
in connection with others rather than in antagonistic competition
and hostile separateness. It is there the revolution resides, not in the
long representations of revolution in Night IX or its antecedents.

From *Critical Paths: Blake and the Argument of Method*, ed. Dan
Miller, Mark Bracher and Donald Ault (Durham and London,
1987), pp. 244–70.

NOTES

[David Aers' essay was originally a much longer piece, and I have had to
omit some important material on *Vala, or, The Four Zoas*. The argument
as it stands approaches *The Four Zoas* by way of *The French Revolution*
and *Europe*, and constitutes a strongly worded reassertion of a historical

and materialist approach as against what Aers terms the 'anarchic post-structuralism' which relies upon a 'display of gamesome signifiers'. Ed.]

1. Leopold Damrosch, *Symbol and Truth in Blake's Myth* (Princeton, NJ, 1980), p. 9.

2. Mikhail Bakhtin, *The Dialogic Imagination* (Austin, TX, 1981).

3. Bakhtin/Vološinov, *Marxism and the Philosophy of Language* (Cambridge, MA, 1986), p. 86.

4. Ibid., p. 87.

5. Some forms of contemporary sociolinguistics are helpful here: see Bob Hodge and Gunther Kress, *Language as Ideology* (London, 1979), and Roger Fowler, Bob Hodge, Gunther Kress and Tony Trew, *Language and Control* (London, 1979). The approach here is used and extended in David Aers, Bob Hodge and Gunther Kress, *Literature, Language and Society in England 1580–1680* (Dublin, 1981).

6. Bakhtin, *The Dialogic Imagination*, p. 417.

7. Works I have in mind here include Chris Baldick, *The Social Mission of English Criticism* (London, 1983); Tony Bennett, *Formalism and Marxism* (London, 1979); Terry Eagleton, *Literary Theory* (Oxford, 1983); John Fekete, *The Critical Twilight* (London, 1977); Jerome J. McGann, *The Romantic Ideology* (Chicago, 1983); Francis Mulhern, *The Moment of Scrutiny* (London, 1979); *Re-Reading English*, ed. Peter Widdowson (London, 1982); Frank Lentricchia, *After the New Criticism* (London, 1982) and *Criticism and Social Change* (Chicago, 1983); Raman Selden, *Criticism and Objectivity* (London, 1984).

8. Heather Glen, *Vision and Disenchantment: Blake's 'Songs' and Wordsworth's 'Lyrical Ballads'* (Cambridge, 1983), p. 344.

9. Here his work converges with important developments in feminism still marginalised by the academic left, which, for reasons that cannot be unpacked here, are preoccupied with Lacanian traditions of psychoanalysis. See, for example, Carol Gilligan, *In a Different Voice* (Cambridge, MA, 1982); Dorothy Dinnerstein, *The Rocking of the Cradle and the Ruling of the World* (London, 1978); Louise Eichenbaum and Susie Orbach, *What Do Women Want?* (London, 1984).

10. On hegemony, see Antonio Gramsci, 'Notes on Italian History', 'The Modern Prince' and 'State and Civil Society', in *Selections from the Prison Notebooks* (London, 1971), esp. pp. 243–53; also contrast Raymond Williams' account in *Marxism and Literature* (London, 1977), with what I see as Blake's more static version – cf. esp. pp. 112–13.

11. For a haunting account of how such a society could be, see Colin Turnbull, *The Mountain People* (London, 1973).

12. Glen, *Vision and Disenchantment*, pp. 95–109, 345.

13. For example, *FR* 4:54; 10:186; 11:204, 206; 4:62; 15:286: E 288–99.

14. On the Jacobins and the contexts, see Albert Soboul, *The French Revolution* (London, 1974), parts 2 and 3; see Edmund Burke's extremely shrewd comments on English Jacobins in *Letters on the Proposals for Peace* ... [1796–7] in *The Works*, vol. 6 (London, 1907), pp. 129–31, 148–9, 203–9, 362–70, 375, 383–5.

15. I write 'risk' because it is not inevitable: in grasping the key structures of any social formation, abstractions (class, modes, and forces of production) are essential: the problematic issue is how such abstractions are controlled and tested out against the empirical world. See E.P. Thompson, *The Poverty of Theory* (London, 1978) and Perry Anderson's responses in *Arguments within English Marxism* (London, 1980). It should also be noted that in *The French Revolution* Blake does direct attention toward realities of political power and institutions (unlike *The Four Zoas*, Night IX and the merry endings of *Milton* and *Jerusalem*).

16. For contradictions and problems in this figure, see David Aers, 'Blake: Sex, Society and Ideology', in Aers, Jonathan Cook and David Punter, *Romanticism and Ideology* (London, 1981).

17. See Glen, *Vision and Disenchantment*, chs 4 and 5.

18. Andrea Dworkin, *Pornography: Men Possessing Women* (London, 1981). Against Blake's texts should be set the approaches to desire in Mary Wollstonecraft, *Vindication of the Rights of Woman* and *Mary: A Fiction and the Wrongs of Women*, ed. Gary Kelly (London, 1976).

19. Despite marvellously sharp criticism of political economy and its moralising, *The Song of Los* concludes with a version of revolution like *America*'s: see *SL* 7:31–40: E 69–70. This reflects the abstraction of sexuality discussed in the text here and perpetuates the same macho model of revolution and sex: revolution is a cosmic fuck, allegedly liberated sexuality an activity isolated from care, affection, reciprocity.

20. See also *FZ* IX: 126–31: E 395–400 passim. On the 'pastoral' in Night IX, see David Wagenknecht, *Blake's Night* (Cambridge, MA, 1973), pp. 214–15.

21. See Morton D. Paley, *Energy and the Imagination* (London, 1970), p. 154.

22. The pre-Marxist traditions that emphasise the decisive nature of the sphere of production in social change would include the peasantry of 1381 (see R. Hilton, *Bond Men Made Free* [London, 1973], ch. 9),

Winstanley in the seventeenth century, Spence and Owen in Blake's own time.

23. On work in Blake, see Punter, 'Blake: Creative and Uncreative Labour', *Studies in Romanticism*, 16 (1977), 535–61.

24. Thompson, 'Time, Work-Discipline and Industrial Capitalism', *Past and Present*, 38 (1967).

25. The exception in Night VII[a], I discuss below. See *FZ* VI: 70:39–45: E 347; *FZ* VI: 71:13–14: E 348.

26. On the exterminist course of our culture, see Thompson, 'The Logic of Exterminism', *New Left Review*, 121 (1980), 3–31; and Ronald Aronson, *Technological Madness: Towards a Theory of Impending Nuclear Holocaust* (London, 1983).

27. Northrop Frye, *Fearful Symmetry* (Boston, 1962), p. 303; Harold Bloom, 'Commentary', E 964.

28. A.K. Mellor, *Blake's Human Form Divine* (Berkeley, CA, 1974), p. 190; Paley, *Energy and the Imagination*, p. 164. Contrast Paley's views in his recent study *The Continuing City* (London, 1983), pp. 132, 136, 234: here the millennium is *this* worldly, although apparently confined to an autonomous aesthetic dimension.

29. B. Wilkie and M.L. Johnson, *Blake's Four Zoas* (Cambridge, MA, 1978), p. 213; Brenda Webster, *Blake's Prophetic Psychology* (London, 1983), p. 244.

30. David V. Erdman, *Blake: Prophet against Empire* (Garden City, NY, 1969), pp. 352–3.

31. S. Crehan, *Blake in Context* (Dublin, 1984), p. 314.

32. T.R. Frosch, *The Awakening of Albion* (Ithaca, NY, 1974), p. 141.

33. M.K. Nurmi, *Blake* (London, 1975), pp. 144–5.

34. This language has nothing to do with critical talk of 'supreme fictions' or ahistorical archetypes. On Blake's period see Thompson, *The Making of the English Working Class* (London, 1963), especially chs 2 and 5; Clarke Garrett, *Respectable Folly* (Baltimore, MD, 1975), chs 6–9; J.F.C. Harrison, *The Second Coming: Popular Millenarianism 1750–1850* (London, 1979).

35. The quotation comes from the fifth thesis on Feuerbach. On Marx's ideas about revolution an excellent starting place is John Elster's outstanding study, *Making Sense of Marx* (Cambridge, 1985), pp. 428–9.

36. The question of the order of composition of the parts of Nights VII [a] and [b] is not crucial here.

37. In my view even Blake's admirable ideal of collaborative male and female labour reproduces patriarchal power and sexual inequality of a rather traditional kind.

38. 'Every Harlot was once a Virgin: every Criminal an Infant Love!' (*J* 61: 52: E 212).

39. Gilligan, *In a Different Voice*, p. 100.

40. In the project of which this essay is part, *Milton* and *Jerusalem* should be studied in this context.

41. Gilligan, *In a Different Voice*, p. 127.

10

Blake, Women, and Sexuality

BRENDA S. WEBSTER

One eighteenth-century contemporary of Blake's described him as an 'insane and erratic genius'.[1] In their efforts to normalise Blake and to find shared historical and religious meanings later critics not only shy away from the bizarre or disturbing elements of his work but generally ignore its personal emotional components, its combat with 'The torments of Love & Jealousy' (*FZ* title: E 300).

In particular, Blake's attitude toward sexuality creates a variety of problems for critics. Liberated sexuality seems a source of high value for Blake – he links it with vision and art – but sexuality also elicits his most hostile, negative, and regressive images. Critics take several approaches to Blake's contradictions. Early critics like S. Foster Damon, who sees Blake as a pure mystic, simply deny the importance of his preoccupation with sex and fantasies of sexual freedom. Damon urges the reader not to take seriously Blake's apparent justification of 'illicit ways' and assures us that Blake didn't follow his teachings himself, citing as evidence his ideal marriage to a submissive wife.[2] Other critics are reluctant to think about Blake's bizarre or explicit sexual illustrations and what these imply about his personality or his attitudes toward women. They see him as portraying degradations of erotic life only so that error may be clarified and redemption achieved.[3]

More recently, commentators instead see Blake celebrating unrepressed sexuality. But here, too, the full force of Blake's sexuality creates problems, and some critics deny its emotional implications.

Forty years after his classic book, Damon now remarks, as though it is an emotionally neutral issue, that Blake, like Shelley, thinks incest is innocent and 'the very root of marriage'.[4] Even such a sophisticated critic as Diana Hume George praises Blake for articulating a non-selfish, non-aggressive sexuality. She regards him in this respect as freer and more advanced than Freud but does not see that Freud is simply more self-aware.[5] Blake's rhetoric often serves as a cloak or defence that distracts the reader, and Blake himself, from seeing the aggressive or selfish nature of the sexual fantasies he is portraying.

Idealisation isn't the only way of dealing with Blake's emotional dynamite. Some critics do not have to mobilise defences to avoid perceiving Blake's negative attitudes. They may consciously agree with them. Before it was taboo to say such things, a male critic – I don't think it is an accident that most of the Blake critics until recently have been male – could admit satisfaction with Blake's views of women.[6] Bernard Blackstone's misogynistic remarks are embarrassing in their forthrightness but I think he has correctly caught Blake's anger at women's power and his wish that they be properly subservient. Male critics who are consciously more benign toward women may still respond to Blake's underlying fantasies without being quite aware of it. This creates a subtler kind of distortion – a not seeing what might be uncomfortable. One critic, Jean Hagstrum, misreads the line 'In Beulah every female delights to give her maiden to her husband', noting that 'maiden' means maidenhead.[7] The point of the line is that Blake's ideal female freely provides her husband with other women like Oothoon in *Visions* (VDA 7:26:E 50). At the end of his essay, Hagstrum's funny tone of mixed apology and male congratulation suggests that at some level he understands very well what Blake is talking about. He concludes that 'some modern women may have much to object to in Blake's latest thought about the relation of the sexes. But it's hard to believe that *l'homme moyen sensual* would reject the hearty bread and full bodied wine the late Blake is offering him'.[8] Erdman, as I will show later, similarly fails to see the male sexual fantasy in *Visions*.

Women critics have parallel difficulties with Blake's sexuality. Early feminist critics generally see Blake as much more favourable to women than he actually is.[9] These writers respond positively to Blake's struggle against the patriarchal system and its paternal oppressors, which suggests that he wishes to free women to be equal partners of men. Also seductive to feminists is Blake's de-emphasis of the penis in favour of a total body sensuality, seemingly more in tune with, and more accepting of, woman's sexuality. Unfortunately, as a poet-prophet Blake is not any more interested in redefining sexuality to give a more equal place to women than as a husband he was interested in giving equal status to his wife. In his own marriage, when his wife offended his brother, he made her kneel down and beg his forgiveness, or, he told her, she would never see his face more.

In general, earlier critics ignore Blake's radical sexual ideas and fantasies; and later critics, while acknowledging them, ignore their regressive and aggressive content and Blake's guilt over them. The limitation of conventional criticism, including feminist criticism, is that it tends either to ignore these fantasies (or this fantasy world) or to recast them in terms of official theologies or ideologies and so misses the special energy of the fantasies and their unconscious origins. The power in Blake's work derives from his recognition and description of demonic forces (the eighteenth-century equivalent of unconscious drives) that influence every aspect of human relationships, but particularly sexuality.

Critics who ignore Blake's radical sexual ideas and fantasies do so partly because of a feeling that to acknowledge them would be to diminish or interfere with his religious or moral authority and return him to the status of eccentric genius. Because Blake's work embodies religious values that point to transcendence, it seems particularly offensive to relate his cosmic speculations to his fantasies or to his personal biography. One critic argues, for instance, that to accept a biographical interpretation of a major prophecy (*Milton*) would be to see Blake as 'mad Blake indeed'.[10] This feeling of incompatibility between any kind of cherished meaning and the fantasies or personal motives of the poet is one of the main blocks to understanding between psychoanalytic critics and other sorts. Conversely, if one values Blake as a prophet of sexual revolution, pointing out his guilt and conflict diminishes him as a type of Übermensch just as much as pointing out his underlying sexual fantasies diminishes his visionary claims. But to understand Blake adequately, both sides (sexuality and guilt) have to be recognised. The history of desire frozen in his images and dramatic situations has to be connected with his transcendent vision, and his conflicts of conscience with his expressions of sexuality. When this is done, we see a radically different Blake.

If we accept at least as a working assumption the importance of psychosexual issues in Blake's work, and if we are to go beyond impressionism or commonsense psychology, we need a theory of mental functioning to serve both as a framework for clarifying our responses to Blake and as a technique for exploring his psychic preoccupations and the ways in which they, paradoxically, both energise and limit his poetry.

Of the available psychologies, Freudian psychoanalysis is most productive for studying Blake. The psychoanalytic emphasis on Oedipal conflict and motives of 'Love & Jealousy' is in many ways similar to Blake's own. Freudianism is unique in its emphasis on the problems caused by man's long dependency and the psychic cost involved in the taming of his sexual and aggressive impulses. The early stages of development are crucial to Freud because the fantasies and modes of experience associated with them are outgrown only imperfectly. Stress in the adult can awaken them. Blake's diffusive narratives are given what coherence they have by a linked series of fantasies made familiar by psychoanalysis. Particularly in his late work, Blake's manifest emphasis begs to be described as Freudian. In works like *Vala*, he not only deals exhaustively with the mutual entanglements of parents and children but he literally depicts the staples of the Freudian view of the psyche: he illustrates acts of incest, he shows children watching adults copulate and he presents a woman with a penis (the Freudian phallic woman) and a man without one. It is not surprising then, that a psychoanalytic approach can reveal aspects of Blake's attitudes toward women and sexuality that are not available to other methods. This in turn opens up other important related topics for investigation; for instance, his development toward a male-centred creative world and his growing sympathy with paternal figures makes sense as part of a reaction against the female.

As Paul Ricoeur has argued, psychoanalysis need not be considered as the enemy of religious meaning[11] (or of other meanings); instead it should be considered a useful tool for clarifying religious values. Blake himself performs this kind of analysis on traditional religious structures, values, and on the concept of an authoritarian God (old Nobodaddy). Blake's most brilliant analysis goes into the repressed and repressive character of Urizen. Blake acutely observes the distortions induced by Urizen's anxiety – his need for sadistic and total control, his terror of sexuality. This kind of insight into the role of anxiety or suppressed sexuality is essential to evaluating the religious vision. But Blake's insight into Urizenic values and personality doesn't necessarily mean that he himself is free of similar anxiety-caused distortions.

Fantasies in a text offer the literary critic a way into unconscious preoccupations. They give him an opportunity to see elements from the past re-experienced (much as the analyst observes the past re-enacted in the transference). The artist replays the early patterns of conflict and desire through character and image rather than by projecting them onto the person of the therapist. Through creative reorganisation similar to the reorganisation of the self that takes place in therapy, the artist integrates fantasy material into a meaningful world.[12] If integration of fantasy, dream, or childhood memories is successful the work elaborates them in ways that illuminate their meaning.

Though the artist is not necessarily conscious of his fantasies as he integrates them into his larger design, he has to let them come near enough to the surface to allow their expression without being too threatened by them. His success may have something to do with being able to allow the fantasies to proliferate freely and then to elaborate or play with them in different textual contexts without being overcome. If he fails to balance the relative claims of his conscious design and the fantasy material (with its own logic and unity), his failure should be clear in a text that doesn't work aesthetically – is confused, dull or highly contradictory. The fantasies, instead of adding intensity and depth to the text, may be narrowed down to a single repetitive form, or if themes are being used primarily as a defence to control fantasies that are too frightening, then these fantasies may subvert or undercut the writer's conscious concerns (as in Blake's late prophecies). There are as many varieties of failure as there are of success. Analysing the fantasy content in its relation to the text helps isolate the areas in which integration has succeeded or where it has failed and unconscious motives overwhelmed the text.

In Blake perhaps more than in most writers the fantasies are not difficult to spot. The difficulty is in knowing what to do with them when we do see them. Perhaps the first task is to determine the extent of the fantasy in the body of the text and also its degree of primitiveness. (Like a disease in the body, it may change forms, move around, have different patterns in different places.) Fantasies are not such simple entities as has been assumed (Frederick Crews ironically comments on the monotony of certain standard ones[13]);

they are elusive in that they perpetually shift, expressing first wish, then fear, first from one person's viewpoint, then another, changing who does what to whom with no regard for ordinary logic. A fantasy is not just an idea or wish; it reflects a totally different, archaic way of seeing and experiencing things that has its own kind of logic, expressing a wholly different way of perceiving and experiencing the world. Depending on what stage of development it derives from, it can be extremely primitive or very far removed from its archaic sources, perhaps no more than a faint verbal echo. Seeing evidence of a fantasy is only a first step. Only a full reading of the text can tell us the dimensions of the fantasy and its effect on this particular text.

For instance, in *Tiriel* a father accuses his sons of causing their mother's death. Tiriel could have made his accusation in a variety of ways. He could have said 'she died gnawed by grief'. The verb gnawed here has a nuance that Freudians would relate to the oral stage but any orality in the statement as I have formulated it is far removed from primitive fantasy; it is only a verbal echo, a half-dead metaphor. But Tiriel instead accuses his sons of devouring their parents' flesh and draining their mother dry. Later Tiriel reverses the situation and asks Pestilence to poison his sons (*Tir* 5:8–10:E 282). This is slightly less literal; he doesn't threaten to eat them as does the witch in Hansel and Gretel, but his acts still have the extreme and reversible quality characteristic of early fantasies. We don't need Freud to relate this to oral needs. Blake does it himself when he has Tiriel explain his own murderous greed as due to maternal deprivation and a harsh weaning (*Tir* 8:14–23:E 285). The point is, again, not labelling the fantasy but experiencing through it the issues that are vital in the text – questions of love, separation, and conflict. Once these issues are experienced, it is possible to see the ways in which the fantasy is given special resonance in the text. Does the fantasy enrich or limit? Is it integrated or invasive?

In order to explore these issues more fully, I am going to consider Blake's attitudes toward sexuality and women. To follow Blake's development, I divide his attitude toward women into two stages with a transition. In the first, roughly the stage of the revolutionary prophecies, he sees women (and sexuality) as a source of salvation and continually imagines his heroes liberating females from paternal tyrants. But even in the early work where he has a more positive use for women there is a strong undercurrent of hostility and fear, which is important to recognise if you want to understand his later attitudes. In mid-life during the decade-long writing of *Vala* he goes through a transitional stage during which he becomes increasingly negative toward sexuality. As he Christianises the work in rewriting, he comes to see woman as responsible for the Fall. What he is coming to think of as the 'Female Will' is blamed for war and all the world's evils (*J* 30:30:E 176). His negative images of women become ever more extreme and bizarre. The only positive images of women are totally weak females sequestered in a separate realm called Beulah. Finally, in his late Christian prophecies, *Milton* and *Jerusalem*, he suggests that the female should cease even to exist independently and become reabsorbed into the body of man where she belongs.

One of the main reasons for Blake's increasing negativity is that he isn't talking about adult love at all. Instead he constantly recreates Oedipal dramas in which his heroes experience the emotions – rage, deprivation, desire – of an adolescent or younger boy caught in dreams of competition with his father for his mother's love. In the early work you have to interpret to see this, but one need not worry about reading it dogmatically into Blake's material, because in his late work he makes it perfectly clear in the illustrations and the text – showing us, for instance, a naked adolescent first embracing his mother then chained to a rock by his jealous and fearful father.

Blake's obsession with incest has an unfortunate effect on his attitude toward women. Because he is obsessed with the overthrow of paternal rivals, he feels guilty and begins to blame women for causing trouble between fathers and sons. Another reason for Blake's increasingly negative attitude is that his demands on women as nurturers and lovers are so total – it wouldn't be unfair to call them infantile – that he can't help imagining them as being enraged and wanting revenge. So his ambivalence toward women is inherent in his harbouring these kinds of pre-Oedipal and Oedipal fantasies.

Blake's attitudes are expressed in various ways in his poems. His early poems *Thel* and *Visions of the Daughters of Albion* suggest the absolutism of his ideal of the totally giving woman and how it brings with it even in his early work a countering image of woman as murderous. For ease of understanding the layers of Blake's fantasy, I present his views of women developmentally, starting with what he expected and feared from woman as nurturer, then moving on to what he hoped from her at a later stage as sexual gratifier.

In *Thel*, an early lyric, Blake presents what at first seems simply a benign model of a good nurturing mother. In a pastoral setting, he creates fairy-tale creatures – a Lily, a Cloud, and a Clod of dirt who instruct the reluctant heroine Thel how to care for others. However, when looked at more closely what Blake is expressing is the wish for a mother's unlimited giving, even if it means her death. Both Lily and Clod give their lives in the act of nourishment. A lamb crops the Lily's blossoms; the Clod exhales her life in 'milky fondness' over the infant worm (*Thel* 4:9:E 5). The heroine is enjoined to think with satisfaction that at her death her own body will be food for worms. 'If thou art the food of worms. O virgin of the skies, / How great thy use. how great thy blessing' (*Thel* 3:25–6:E 5). Critics preach at Thel and criticise her for her selfishness. They do not appreciate that the prospect of being eaten by worms – death as being devoured – might be terrifying, nor do they perceive behind Blake's moral tone the implicit degradation and forced submission of the woman. The implications of the imagery are much clearer in a poem by another poet. In Andrew Marvell's famous 'To his Coy Mistress', the speaker reminds the woman he is trying to seduce that she can be as coy as she likes to him but eventually worms shall try her 'long-preserved virginity' – there the threat is plain enough.

At the end of *Thel* after describing the ideal of maternal sacrifice, Blake goes on in a coda, seemingly out of keeping with the mood of the piece, to describe the dangers of sexuality and the hatred between men and women. The language of courtly love evokes the deadly woman with 'poison' smile who will be prominent in Blake's later work. In *Tiriel*, a narrative poem written just before *Thel*, there is another such image. She is called Pestilence (and is here clearly imagined as a punishment for infant greed). She is invoked by the tyrant Tiriel to punish his sons who he says have killed their mother by greedily draining her life ('Nourishd with milk ye serpents. nourishd with mothers tears & cares / ... [you] have draind her dry as this' [*Tir* 1:26–31:E 277]). It is striking that the invocation of Pestilence contrasts line by line with the Lily in *Thel*. This is Tiriel's invocation of Pestilence:

> Where art thou Pestilence that bathest in fogs & standing lakes
> Rise up thy sluggish limbs. & let the loathsomest of poisons
> Drop from thy garments as thou walkest. wrapt in yellow clouds
> Here take thy seat. in this wide court. Let it be strown with dead
> And sit & smile upon these cursed sons of Tiriel
>
> (*Tir* 5:8–12:E 282)

And here is the Lily:

> Thy breath doth nourish the innocent lamb, he smells thy milky
>   garments,
> He crops thy flowers. while thou sittest smiling in his face,
> Wiping his mild and meekin mouth from all contagious taints.
>
> *(Thel* 2:4–7:E 4)

In each line the Lily replaces Pestilence's noxious qualities with beneficent ones. Even the Lily's beauty, whiteness, and perfume are prized not for themselves but for the pleasure they give the infant lamb who smells her 'milky garments' before he crops her blossoms. Most important is the Lily's relation to the lamb as contrasted with Pestilence's to the sons. The Lily welcomes the lamb's greedy feeding with a loving smile even though it means her death. In what constitutes a final contrast between the two figures, the cropped Lily wipes the lamb's mouth of all contagious taints.

The contrasting images of Pestilence and Lily are perhaps Blake's earliest portrayal of the two types of feminine nature that became so important in his myth. We can see now that the ambivalent double image is self-perpetuating. Guilt over greed creates the punishing image of Pestilence, so Blake creates an ideal image to cancel out or compensate for imagined murderousness: his Lily reverses Pestilence's attributes. But then new guilt over the idea of devouring the mother creates the idea expressed in Thel's coda that woman is sexually threatening. In fact, Blake's efforts to create an ideally satisfying figure have to be continually renewed. The paradoxically smiling Pestilence develops in later poems into a series of wicked females whose smiles promise love but proffer death.

Going back even further in the self-perpetuating cycle of crime and punishments, Blake gives psychological reasons for the extreme greed of his characters. They feel deprived. He imagines them as so needy that they become either monstrous or depressed if the ideal mother doesn't offer herself.

Another important aspect of the ideal woman is her aspect as sexual gratifier. *Visions of the Daughters of Albion* presents a nurturing woman who unlike the Lily offers not food but total sexual gratification to the male hero who is seen as quite helpless and hopeless without her. The poem is particularly interesting to feminists because the chief woman character, Oothoon, is very strong and preaches what appears to be a doctrine of reciprocally free love to the male character. However, what is really involved is a male fantasy of having a harem of beautiful women. Oothoon in one of her final speeches offers to net girls of 'mild silver' and 'furious gold' for her lover and watch him while he enjoys them 'In lovely copulation bliss on bliss' (*VDA* 7:26:E 50). There is no reciprocity. Theotormon, the semi-impotent hero, is furiously jealous and rages at Oothoon abusively after she has been raped. Generosity is all on one side: hers.

Still critics persist in seeing the poem as somehow in favour of women's rights. David Erdman suggests, following Schorer, that it is a versification of Mary Wollstonecraft's *The Rights of Women*.[14] This is oddly off the mark. Blake pictures Oothoon as totally benevolent and totally available. Wollstonecraft feels that woman's first duty is to develop her mind and particularly her reason. Far from seeing woman as devoted to 'Happy, happy love', she wants to substitute equality based on reason for women's sexual character as gratifier of man.

Blake's fantasy of sexual gratification in *Visions* has another level that is vital to understanding his attitude toward women. On this level, the sexually gratifying woman is imagined as a sexually permissive mother. This is important not in order to prove a Freudian point but because Blake's attitude toward women is so saturated with his conflicting feelings toward the mother. He is interested in his female characters primarily in so far as they can be placed in triangular situations that remind him of the Oedipal triangle of mother, father, and son. In *Visions'* triangle, the heroine Oothoon is raped by an older man named Bromion while she is on her way to give herself to her young lover, Theotormon, who then spends the rest of the poem lamenting. Though she is not literally Theotormon's mother or sister, Blake suggests that this is a mother–son relationship in several ways. One of the clearest of these is his opening illustrations.

The opening illustration of Oothoon is developed from an engraving by Vien showing a procuress holding onto a small cupid by his wings. Blake adapts the figures but gives them an opposite meaning. His naked woman lifting full breasts and kissing a small male figure leaping from a flower suggests both the maternal nature and the special non-possessive quality of Oothoon's love, which combines generosity and lack of restraint. The next illustrations replace the idealised view of mother and child with sexual fantasies. The mother–son theme continues in the image of a small naked male angel standing in the lap of a woman riding a cloud horse. The sexual nature of the embrace between woman and small angel is clearly shown by the penis and testicles Blake has drawn emerging between the woman's legs where we should expect the neck and head of her cloud mount. In some versions, Blake has added a beak or bill to the penis, which seems equivalent to biting teeth in its potential to injure the maternal body.

In the illustration Blake's images of mother and child are untroubled by any hint of a rival. The fantasy is of undisputed possession of the mother. Blake's description of Oothoon raped by a paternal tyrant fits such a fantasy's assumption of the mother's resistance to the father – her loyalty to the child. However, what Theotormon struggles with in the poem is that Oothoon doesn't regret the rape. Moreover, she is aroused by it. Her arousal represents the side of parental lovemaking that the child denies because it signifies the mother's unfaithfulness to him. This idea of unfaithfulness makes emotional sense of Theotormon's extreme jealousy and his angry wish to punish Oothoon which is expressed in sexualised imagery. Blake makes Oothoon collaborate in Theotormon's ambivalent wish to punish and possess her by having her writhe naked calling on his eagles to penetrate her flesh.

Blake doesn't use just visual imagery to suggest the young boy's fantasies about his mother and sexuality. In presenting Theotormon's reaction to the rape, Blake uses imagery that evokes a young child's possible reaction to a situation that arouses impotent rage. Theotormon's first act is to surround Oothoon and Bromion with 'black jealous waters' (*VDA* 2:4:E 46). If the image isn't quite clear in context, it becomes clearer when we remember a previous character of Blake's, the serpent Envy, who expresses its jealousy by discharging a river of filth ('then She bore Pale desire' [E 446]). Using faeces as a weapon is characteristic of very young children. Melanie Klein, for example, cites cases of children who react to observations of parental intercourse with angry soiling.[15] From Blake's imagery one might infer his own repressed memory of such a reaction, but whatever the source of his insight, as artist Blake is able to connect Theotormon's childishly ineffectual rage with the body imagery that best expresses it.

Blake's imagery not only evokes a young child's reactions to parental sex at a time when his only weapon is his own excrement, but he also connects this reaction with other psychological themes typical of the child's perceptions. For instance, the rape's violent sadism suggests a child's perception of intercourse. Blake depicts Theotormon as being caught in the emotions of this stage (hating the sadistic Bromion) but unable to fight back successfully, Theotormon turns his anger against himself (in one illustration he whips himself) and against Oothoon. In another illustration his eagles approach Oothoon to rip her naked body – an image of sexualised violence. Oothoon urges Theotormon to give up his anger and his masochism and enjoy her. She reminds him that she, like a mother choosing her son's wife, would gladly supply other women for his pleasure. In a series of monologues, she acts like a psychoanalyst encouraging him to dredge up his forbidden sexual desires – the forbidden 'joys of old' (*VDA* 4:4:E 48); here again the imagery turns to childhood as she reminds him of 'Infancy, ... lustful, happy! nestling for delight / In laps of pleasure' (*VDA* 6:4–5:E 49). But unlike a psychoanalyst, instead of helping him give up his incestuous wishes, she urges him to act on them and free himself from his sense of failure.

What Blake seems to be doing is evoking a set of early experiences of despair and rivalry and then imagining the woman – in the past, the mother – who could by her total generosity make up for what he had suffered. When this is understood, it is easy to see how far Blake is from portraying equality between the sexes. His male characters are no more capable of mature love than a man jealously fixated on his mother is in real life.

Subsequent prophecies reinforce the interpretation of Oedipal drama in *Visions* and show what a pervasive and haunting theme it was for Blake. In the next prophecy, *America*, the hero Orc, furious about earlier deprivation, rapes his sister – committing the incest that Theotormon failed to do – while the young patriots overthrow the paternal tyrant.

In still later prophecies, we read in more detail how Orc was originally chained to a rock by his father, Los, who was furiously jealous of the boy's closeness to his mother, Enitharmon.

> But when fourteen summers & winters had revolved over
> Their solemn habitation Los beheld the ruddy boy
> Embracing his bright mother & beheld malignant fires
> In his young eyes discerning plain that Orc plotted his death
> Grief rose upon his ruddy brows. a tightening girdle grew
> Around his bosom like a bloody cord. ... [He]
> Calld it the chain of Jealousy.
>
> (*FZ* 60:6–22:E 340–1)

In an illustration Blake pictures Orc as a naked adolescent embracing his mother while his father watches angrily, a red chain of jealousy around his neck. Throughout this whole series of poems Blake is depicting Oedipal dramas in which father and son are alternately dominant.

In discussing Blake's gratifying females, the Lily in *Thel* and Oothoon, it is important to realise that imagining them and their satisfaction of his most forbidden desires was uphill work against guilt. Not only are they mother figures and so taboo, but there is also guilt in imagining the death of paternal rivals. Coping with this guilt is apparently too much for Blake. Even in *America* the hero's triumph doesn't last long. The poem ends with the father god's vengeful cold mists descending on the rebels. The dangers of woman's retaliatory anger for the incestuous and greedy impulses are even more severe. In thinking himself further and further back into the experiences of childhood, Blake becomes more angry and fearful.

By the time he finishes *Vala*, a transitional work of his middle years that he worked on for over a decade, Blake's images of women have taken on a preponderantly negative tone. Though he still keeps a formal split between good and bad women, the good ones never again capture his imagination, but his fantasies about what bad women do to males get more and more violent and bizarre. *Vala* is fascinating because it shows his changing attitude toward women as well as how the change is connected with his shift from revolutionary to Christian. In its early drafts we see him giving way totally to negative fantasies: women destroy men's bodies, unweave them on their looms, drain them in sex, appropriate their penises – these are just a few of the horrors he expresses. Blake becomes increasingly certain that any attempt to satisfy basic needs for food and sex is bound to have horrible consequences. Rather than being satisfied, the characters receive a destructive version of the need itself: if they want food, they are eaten; if they want sex, they are castrated. Blake views essential needs as dangerous not only because they leave the individual vulnerable to painful deprivation, but also because they are too excessive and too mixed with aggression, thus damaging those chosen to satisfy them.

An episode at the beginning of *Vala* exemplifies the mutually destructive activities of male and female. Enion, a type of earth mother, initiates the pattern by destroying Tharmas in retaliation for his jealous possessiveness. Enion literally takes him apart. She draws out and manipulates his nerves, 'every vein & lacteal' (*FZ* 5:17:E 302). She then gives birth to him again by reweaving him on her loom. Her woven child soon becomes a self-glorying, righteous bully who addresses her as 'my slave' and revenges himself for her earlier treatment of him by raping her.

Tharmas's body fuses with Enion's during intercourse, creating a monstrous woman-serpent. This is a variation of an earlier fragment describing the even more bizarre mating of a woman with a penis and a man without one. Here, though, Blake seems to be suggesting that sexuality is horribly dangerous because the woman appropriates or absorbs the man's penis in intercourse. She also seems to appropriate the creativity that Blake associates with male sexuality. She acquires a poetic voice. Enion's first act after the rape is to sing. In a later revision, Blake gives her a serpent's voice whose complaints suggest that the absorbed male is protesting within her.

Having imagined himself into a corner where the male is threatened with either feminisation or death or both, Blake tries through revisions to lessen the female's power or to transfer it to the male. His most successful strategy is his concept of an outside will, Christ, directing events. This seems to be a strong internal reason for his shift from revolutionary to radical Christian. He needs Christ to help him control his imagined women and his impulses. With Christ there, retaliatory acts become a necessary if painful part of a benign pattern of redemption. Within the protection of a Christian framework, Blake is able to reintroduce his idea of the totally giving woman to counter his fears of the murderous mother. In extensive additions to *Vala* he works up the concept of a realm called Beulah, the married land, inhabited by benign females. He first introduces them right after the Enion–Tharmas episode, and their self-abnegating actions soften or deny woman's power to mutilate or kill men. Blake contrasts Enion's cruel treatment of Tharmas with an ideal state where Beulah's 'Females sleep the winter in soft silken veils / Woven by their own hands to hide them in the darksom grave / But Males immortal live renewd by female deaths' (*FZ* 5:1–3:E 302). Although the males do not actually kill these females who reportedly delight in self-immolation, this Eden seems created out of fear, not love.

Blake continues to build up his countering idea of Beulah. In *Milton*, Beulians nourish the sleeping hero feeding 'His lips with food of Eden' (*M* 15:14–15:E 109). In addition, in *Milton* Blake imagines the poet Los totally recreating time so that the satisfaction of basic needs will be central. Los's time is defined by satisfaction of hunger. In between each moment of time stands a daughter of Beulah 'To feed the Sleepers on their Couches with maternal care' (*M* 28:49:E

126). This conceptualisation literally insists that there is no time in which one experiences the maternal figure's absence. In making creation take place in the space-time where the mother nurtures, Blake also suggests that creativity depends on the maternal environment. Blake amplifies his description of Beulah's loving responsiveness: 'Beulah to its Inhabitants appears within each district / As the beloved infant in his mothers bosom' (M 30:10–11:E 129). In his fiction of males resting in Beulah, Blake gratifies the wish for nurture while simultaneously denying infantile dependence. Beulah's women are correspondingly weak and fearful of the creative and inspired males. The female world of obedience, where they are taught how to die smiling each winter, is carefully separated from the male world of creation – a second realm Blake names 'Eden'. Man drops into Beulah only temporarily for a rest cure before continuing his virile forward progress: 'thro' / The Bosom of the Father' (M 31:4–5: E 130). Beulah is not only the world of self-abnegating nurture – that of Thel's Lily – but also the world of sexual gratification. In Beulah, the female ransacks sea and land for gratifications to the male genius who in return will clothe her in gems. Blake lectures the recalcitrant bride of the Divine Voice in Milton, urging her to 'give / Her maidens to her husband: delighting in his delight / ... As it is done in Beulah' (M 33:17–20:E 133). This is the fantasy of the sexually generous mother-wife we saw in Visions. But Blake has become much more righteous, using biblical language and thought to bolster his ideas. He continues, '& thou O Virgin Babylon Mother of Whoredoms / Shalt bring Jerusalem ... / Shalt give her into the arms of God your Lord & Husband' (M 33:20–4:E 133).

All in all, Blake's concept of Beulah, which isolates and weakens women, doesn't really solve anything. It seems impossible for Blake to imagine real men and women coexisting in a state of peace. Outside of Beulah, Blake's portrayals of women's murderousness go on. His evil women characters increasingly split off, doubling and tripling as though he can't control their rampant proliferation. Their acts too are increasingly horrible. In Jerusalem, for example, he has them dancing in the flayed skins of their victims waving the men's severed organs.

From this it is clear that though Blake valiantly tries to control the fantasy of the destructive mother and give it redemptive meaning, woman's independent presence is still threatening. In his prophecies Milton and Jerusalem, he moves toward what might be called his final solution to the woman problem. At the end of

Milton he suggests for the first time that if the conflict between men is to cease, woman must stop existing. Sexual organisation, which, using a phrase from Ezekiel, he now calls 'the Abomination of Desolation', must disappear 'Till Generation is swallowd up in Regeneration' (*M* 41:25–8:E 142–3). But although Blake announces the end of sexual organisation, male sexuality continues to stand as a model for the human, while the female is either incorporated or isolated restrictively in Beulah. In *Jerusalem* he repeats his ideas about the Beulians as gratifiers of male genius. It is clear the female has no independent existence except as gratifier and she must accept the male's 'Fibres of dominion' (*J* 88:13:E 246).

Finally, during the writing of *Jerusalem*, Blake begins to feel that female sexuality can be dispensed with altogether. He considers female sexuality inferior to the total body sensuality of the child, for the loss of which he holds women responsible. Blake makes Christ sanction his views by reinstating this total body sensuality. When Christ does this, he effectively breaks the female's power over the male.

Sexual organisation is permitted in order for Christ to be born, but once born, his Maternal Humanity must be put off lest the sexual generation swallow up regeneration. At *Jerusalem*'s climactic moment, Enitharmon, who has been resisting giving up her independence, suddenly caves in under the weight of Blake's rhetoric and announces her disappearance: 'My Looms will be no more & I annihilate vanish for ever' (*J* 92:11:E 252). Her husband and brother Los reaches the final insight that 'Sexes must vanish & cease / To be' (*J* 92:13–14:E 252).

Blake's view of male–female relationships hasn't been clear to readers partly because it is at first to be contradicted by his enormous sensitivity to feminine traits such as tenderness and maternal care. Blake views these traits in two ways. On the one hand, they belong to the ideal Female and help her to care for the Male Genius; on the other hand, the poet can incorporate and use them in creation and in drawing close to other men. In this latter view Blake anticipates the modern recognition of bisexuality and its importance for creativity, which arises as a dialogue between the male and female parts of the self. But Blake did not extend the right to express traits of the opposite sex to his females. When they do express them, they become threatening Female Wills and, as we have seen, must be destroyed.

Jerusalem makes it clear that Blake's obsession with sex and women is stronger in his late prophecies than in the early ones. But his emphasis and the structure of his defences have changed. Sexual liberation has been replaced by forgiveness of sins. In the early work, when he fights on the side of impulse, he is fairly conscious of his incestuous and other wishes. (This is a positive fact. His dramatisations of the conflict between impulse and guilt or conscience have an immediacy and power lacking in the late work.) In his middle and late work, he fights his impulses with all his power. He repudiates the incestuous act at the heart of his concept of liberated sex and describes it as the original sin and cause of the Fall. This seems at first a plausible solution – certainly it is a traditional one – to the problem of what to do with one's forbidden impulses, but it doesn't succeed artistically or humanly. Blake can't really transcend his incestuous wishes though he sincerely wants to. He just splits them off from his consciousness. He has to fight very hard to keep them from his awareness though they come out in various ways in the poems. This not only weakens the poetry where the avowed Christian purpose is opposed by subterranean fantasies but it is an additional reason for his misogyny. Women are now the temptresses and whores who pander to his suppressed wishes.

From *Critical Paths: Blake and the Argument of Method*, ed. Dan Miller, Mark Bracher and Donald Ault (Durham and London, 1987), pp. 204–24.

NOTES

[Brenda Webster's essay begins from a critique of masculinist approaches to Blake, and also of some feminist ones, and advances a strong argument for the importance of psychoanalytic categories in viewing the gender content and form of Blake's texts. Considerable attention is given to *Tiriel*, following which *Visions of the Daughters of Albion* is revisited (see George Quasha's and Laura Haigwood's essays above). The argument is taken further into the major Prophetic Books, thus engaging with Jean Hagstrum's essay, and culminates in a discussion of the complex ambivalences underlying Blake's textual dealings with women and sexuality. Ed.]

1. Robert Southey, cited in S. Foster Damon, *William Blake: His Philosophy and Symbols* (Gloucester, MA, 1958), p. 246.

2. Ibid., p. 99.

3. For example, H.M. Margoliouth in his edition of *William Blake's 'Vala'* (Oxford, 1946), p. 144; or John E. Grant, 'Visions in *Vala*: A Consideration of Some Pictures in the Manuscript', in *Blake's Sublime*

Allegory: Essays on 'The Four Zoas', 'Milton' and 'Jerusalem', ed. Stuart Curran and Joseph A. Wittreich, Jr (Madison, WI, 1973), p. 184.

4. Damon, *A Blake Dictionary: The Ideas and Symbols of William Blake* (New York, 1971), p. 196. Though Damon progresses from seeing Blake as a mystic to accepting his sexuality, in both cases he idealises him.

5. Diana Hume George, *Blake and Freud* (Ithaca, NY, 1980), p. 144.

6. See the quotation from Bernard Blackstone, *English Blake* (Hamden, CT, 1966), p. 294, cited in George, *Blake and Freud*, p. 245.

7. Jean Hagstrum, 'Babylon Revisited, or The Story of Luvah and Vala' [see pp. 36–53 above – Ed.] Any doubts about the meaning of the line are cleared up by the variant in *Milton* where the female, repenting of her previous jealousy, begins 'to give/Her maidens to her husband: delighting in his delight' (*M* 33:17–18:E 132).

8. [This passage is omitted, at the author's request, from the version in the present volume. See the original version in *Blake's Sublime Allegory,* ed. Curran and Wittreich, p. 118. Ed.]

9. During the time I was writing the book on which this paper is based (from 1972 to 1979), critics like Carolyn Heilbrun and Irene Tayler praised Blake's freedom from the prison of gender while Sandra Gilbert, Susan Gubar and Diana Hume George compared him favourably to Milton. See Heilbrun in *Far Western Forum*, 1 (1974), 284; Tayler, 'The Woman Scaly', *Midwestern Modern Language Association Bulletin*, 6 (1973), 87; Gilbert and Gubar, *The Madwoman in the Attic: The Woman Writer and the Nineteenth Century Literary Imagination* (New Haven, CT, 1979), p. 200; and George, 'Is She Also the Divine Image? Feminine Form in the Art of William Blake', *Centennial Review*, 23 (1979), 129–40, 137. Susan Fox is a notable exception. She points out that the difference between Blake's (seemingly benign) concepts and his consistently negative images of women must connote at least some uneasiness in the author's mind. See 'The Female as Metaphor in William Blake's Poetry', *Critical Inquiry*, 3 (1977), 519. Since my book was accepted by Macmillan in 1981 several new articles have appeared that point to Blake's anti-feminism: Alicia Ostriker, 'Desire Gratified and Ungratified: William Blake and Sexuality', *Blake*, 16 (1982–3); Anne K. Mellor, 'Blake's Portrayal of Women', *Blake*, 16 (1982–3); and Margaret Storch, whose psychoanalytic approach resembles mine, 'Blake and Women: Nature's Cruel Holiness', *American Imago* (1981).

10. James Reiger, 'The Hem of Their Garments: The Bard's Song in *Milton*', in *Blake's Sublime Allegory*, ed. Curran and Wittreich, p. 260.

11. Paul Ricoeur, *Freud and Philosophy: An Essay on Interpretation*, trans. Denis Savage (New Haven, CT, 1970).

12. See Meredith Anne Skura, *The Literary Use of the Psychoanalytic Process* (New Haven, CT, 1981), p. 216, for a description of the ways the psychoanalytic process may be seen as a model for the literary text.

13. Frederick Crews, *Out of My System: Psychoanalysis, Ideology and Critical Method* (New York, 1975), p. 145.

14. David V. Erdman, *Blake: Prophet against Empire* (New York, 1969), p. 228.

15. Melanie Klein, *Love, Guilt and Reparation and Other Works 1921–1945* (New York, 1975), pp. 114, 126.

Further Reading

In some cases, essays listed below are available in more than one place; I have listed only the most recent or accessible publication.

CLASSIC CRITICISM

These books, all but two published before 1970, are classics of criticism in their own right, and are essential general reading on Blake:

Gerald E. Bentley, Jr (ed.), *William Blake: The Critical Heritage* (London: Routledge, 1975). A collection of short criticism on Blake, from his times to our own.

Harold Bloom, *Blake's Apocalypse: A Study in Poetic Argument* (Garden City, NY: Doubleday, 1963).

S. Foster Damon, *A Blake Dictionary: The Ideas and Symbols of William Blake* (Providence, RI: Brown University Press, 1965). An essential reference text.

S. Foster Damon, *William Blake: his Philosophy and Symbols* (London: Constable, 1924).

David V. Erdman, *Blake: Prophet Against Empire* (2nd edn, Princeton, NJ: Princeton University Press, 1969). The most wide-ranging account of Blake's historical context and political references.

Northrop Frye (ed.), *Blake: A Collection of Critical Essays* (Englewood Cliffs, NJ: Prentice-Hall, 1966).

Northrop Frye, *Fearful Symmetry: A Study of William Blake* (Princeton, NJ: Princeton University Press, 1947). A magnificent reading of Blake from a largely mythic perspective.

A.L. Morton, *The Everlasting Gospel: A Study in the Sources of William Blake* (London: Lawrence & Wishart, 1958). The most important early account of Blake's debt to radical Dissenting sources.

Morton D. Paley, *Energy and the Imagination: A Study of the Development of Blake's Thought* (Oxford: Clarendon Press, 1970). A watershed book which can be seen as inaugurating modern Blake criticism.

MODERN ESSAY COLLECTIONS

The period 1970–90 has seen the publication of eight major essay collections, many arising from conferences. All contain important essays, some of which are also listed individually in later sections:

Stuart Curran and Joseph A. Wittreich (eds), *Blake's Sublime Allegory: Essays on 'The Four Zoas', 'Milton', 'Jerusalem'* (Madison, WI: University of Wisconsin Press, 1973).

David V. Erdman and John E. Grant (eds), *Blake's Visionary Forms Dramatic* (Princeton, NJ: Princeton University Press, 1970).

Robert N. Essick and Donald Pearce (eds), *Blake in His Time* (Bloomington, IN: Indiana University Press, 1978).

Nelson Hilton (ed.), *Essential Articles for the Study of William Blake 1970–1984* (Hamden, CT: Archon, 1986). The most important precursor to the present volume; see Introduction above.

Nelson Hilton and Thomas A. Vogler (eds), *Unnam'd Forms: Blake and Textuality* (Berkeley, CA: University of California Press, 1986).

Dan Miller, Mark Bracher and Donald Ault (eds), *Critical Paths: Blake and the Argument of Method* (Durham and London: Duke University Press, 1987).

Morton D. Paley and Michael Phillips (eds), *William Blake: Essays in Honour of Sir Geoffrey Keynes* (Oxford: Clarendon Press, 1973).

Michael Phillips (ed.), *Interpreting Blake* (Cambridge: Cambridge University Press, 1978).

HISTORICAL AND POLITICAL APPROACHES

These books and essays range from Marxist to New Historicist readings; all have useful things to say about the situation of Blake's texts in his own times and about his perception of the social and political world:

David Aers, Jonathan Cook and David Punter, *Romanticism and Ideology: Studies in English Writing 1765–1830* (London: Routledge, 1981).

Jacob Bronowski, *William Blake and the Age of Revolution* (London: Routledge, 1972). A revised version of Bronowski's earlier *William Blake 1757–1827: A Man without a Mask*, this book is a simple but trenchant account of Blake's politics.

Marilyn Butler, *Romantics, Rebels and Reactionaries* (London: Oxford University Press, 1980). A very important general account of the ideologies of the period.

Stewart Crehan, 'Blake's "Tyger" and the "Tygerish Multitude"', *Literature and History*, 6 (1980).

Minna Doskow, 'The Humanised Universe of Blake and Marx', in *William Blake and the Moderns*, ed. Robert Bertholf and Annette Levitt (Albany, NY: State University of New York Press, 1982). One of several attempts to relate Blake and Marx in terms of labour and alienation.

Gavin Edwards, 'Mind-Forg'd Manacles: A Contribution to the Discussion of Blake's "London"', *Literature and History*, 5 (1979). One of a group of recent essays which focuses on 'London' as a crucial exemplar of Blake's understanding of the world around him.

David V. Erdman, '*America*: New Expanses', in *Blake's Visionary Forms Dramatic*, ed. David V. Erdman and John E. Grant (Princeton, NJ: Princeton University Press, 1970). Erdman's revised view of *America*.

Michael Ferber, *The Social Vision of William Blake* (Princeton, NJ: Princeton University Press, 1985). A highly readable synthesis of Blake as London craftsman, religious Dissenter and political thinker.

Heather Glen, 'The Poet in Society: Blake and Wordsworth on London', *Literature and History*, 3 (March 1976).

Heather Glen, *Vision and Disenchantment: Blake's 'Songs' and Wordsworth's 'Lyrical Ballads'* (Cambridge: Cambridge University Press,

1983). A highly detailed textual reading which places Blake firmly within a complex cultural history.

Kenneth A. Johnston, 'Blake's Cities: Romantic Forms of Urban Renewal', in *Blake's Visionary Forms Dramatic*, ed. David V. Erdman and John E. Grant (Princeton, NJ: Princeton University Press, 1970). This essay and the one below approach Blake as a poet responding to and structurally influenced by the modern city.

David Punter, 'Blake and the Shapes of London', *Criticism*, 23 (1981).

David Punter, 'Blake: Creative and Uncreative Labour', *Studies in Romanticism*, 16 (1977).

David Punter, 'Blake, Marxism and Dialectic', *Literature and History*, 6 (Autumn 1977).

Mark Schorer, *William Blake: The Politics of Vision* (New York: Henry Holt, 1946). This much earlier book is less detailed than Erdman but is highly approachable.

E.P. Thompson, 'London', in *Interpreting Blake*, ed. Michael Phillips (Cambridge: Cambridge University Press, 1978). Perhaps the most challenging and historically informed of recent studies of 'London'.

E.P. Thompson, *The Making of the English Working Class* (London: Gollancz, 1963). This is, obviously, not a book about Blake; but it is very much about the milieu in which Blake lived and worked.

STRUCTURALISM, POSTSTRUCTURALISM, DECONSTRUCTION

These texts range across a variety of approaches, reflecting the trajectory from structuralism to various kinds of poststructuralism over the last twenty years:

Harold Bloom, *Poetry and Repression: Revisionism from Blake to Stevens* (New Haven, CT: Yale University Press, 1976). A classic account of 'the anxiety of influence'.

Stephen Leo Carr, 'Illuminated Printing: Toward a Logic of Difference', in *Unnam'd Forms: Blake and Textuality*, ed. Nelson Hilton and Thomas A. Vogler (Berkeley, CA: University of California Press, 1986). Like several other items in this list, an attempt to think in structuralist and poststructuralist terms about Blake's visual and verbal texts.

Vincent A. De Luca, 'Proper Names in the Structural Design of Blake's Myth-Making', in *Essential Articles for the Study of William Blake 1970–1984*, ed. Nelson Hilton (Hamden, CT: Archon, 1986). The main stance here is structuralist.

Vincent A. De Luca, 'A Wall of Words: The Sublime as Text', in *Unnam'd Forms: Blake and Textuality*, ed. Nelson Hilton and Thomas A. Vogler (Berkeley, CA: University of California Press, 1986). Points a way towards the important connections between contemporary criticism and the sublime.

Robert N. Essick, 'How Blake's Body Means', in *Unnam'd Forms: Blake and Textuality*, ed. Nelson Hilton and Thomas A. Vogler (Berkeley, CA: University of California Press, 1986). On 'the material body of the manufactured objects [Blake] had a role in producing'.

Aaron Fogel, 'Pictures of Speech: On Blake's Poetic', *Studies in Romanticism*, 21 (Summer 1982).

Nelson Hilton, 'Blakean Zen', *Studies in Romanticism*, 24 (1985). One of Hilton's many sparkling essays on Blake, some of which are adapted and collected in the volume below.

Nelson Hilton, *Literal Imagination: Blake's Vision of Words* (Berkeley, CA: University of California Press, 1983).

David E. James, *Written Within and Without: A Study of Blake's 'Milton'* (Bern: Peter Lang, 1977).

Jenijoy La Belle, 'Blake's Visions and Re-visions of Michelangelo', in *Blake in his Time*, ed. Robert Essick and Donald Pearce (Bloomington, IN: Indiana University Press, 1978).

Paul Mann, '*The Book of Urizen* and the Horizon of the Book', in *Unnam'd Forms: Blake and Textuality*, ed. Nelson Hilton and Thomas A. Vogler (Berkeley, CA: University of California Press, 1986). A splendid account of a text somewhat ignored in Blake's canon.

W.J.T. Mitchell, *Blake's Composite Art: A Study of the Illuminated Poetry* (Princeton, NJ: Princeton University Press, 1978). Perhaps the most impressive contemporary approach to the complex interweavings of the various art-forms in Blake.

W.J.T. Mitchell, 'Style as Epistemology: Blake and the Movement towards Abstraction in Romantic Art', *Studies in Romanticism*, 16 (1977).

Karen Shabetai, 'Blake's Antifoundationist Poetics', *Studies in English Literature*, 27 (1987). An unusual approach to the 'modernity' of Blake.

Steven Shaviro, '"Striving with Systems": Blake and the Politics of Difference', in *Essential Articles for the Study of William Blake 1970–1984*, ed. Nelson Hilton (Hamden, CT: Archon, 1986). Contains a fascinatingly eclectic set of readings of 'The Tyger' from contemporary critical positions.

Peggy Meyer Sherry, 'The "Predicament" of the Autograph: "William Blake"', *Glyph*, 4 (1978).

Daniel Stempel, 'Blake, Foucault and the Classical Episteme', *PMLA*, 96 (1981). A rare example of thinking Blake in Foucauldian terms, bridging a gap between deconstructive and historicist thinking.

Thomas A. Vogler, 'Intertextual Signifiers and the Blake of That Already', *Romanticism Past and Present*, 9 (1985). Vogler, in this essay and the two listed below, proves himself one of the most inventive and engaged of deconstructive critics of Blake.

Thomas A. Vogler, '"in vain the Eloquent tongue": An Un-Reading of VISIONS of the Daughters of Albion', in *Critical Paths: Blake and the Argument of Method*, ed. Dan Miller, Mark Bracher and Donald Ault (Durham and London: Duke University Press, 1987).

Thomas A. Vogler, 'Re: Naming MIL/TON', in *Unnam'd Forms: Blake and Textuality*, ed. Nelson Hilton and Thomas A. Vogler (Berkeley, CA: University of California Press, 1986).

Janet Warner, 'Blake's Use of Gesture', in *Blake's Visionary Forms Dramatic*, ed. David V. Erdman and John E. Grant (Princeton, NJ: Princeton University Press, 1970).

PSYCHOLOGICAL AND PSYCHOANALYTIC READINGS

Although from very early years critics have recognised the psychological dimension of Blake's work, there have not been many successful approaches. The texts below range from Jung through Freud to Lacan:

Mark Bracher, 'Rousing the Faculties: Lacanian Psychoanalysis and the Marriage of Heaven and Hell in the Reader', in *Critical Paths: Blake and the Argument of Method*, ed. Dan Miller, Mark Bracher and Donald Ault (Durham and London: Duke University Press, 1987). The most interesting of the very few readings of Blake influenced by Lacan.

Barbara Frieling, 'Blake at the Rim of the World: A Jungian Consideration of *Jerusalem*', *Journal of Evolutionary Psychology*, 8 (1987). There were various early Jungian readings of Blake; this one is very brief but suggestive.

Thomas R. Frosch, *The Awakening of Albion: the Renovation of the Body in the Poetry of William Blake* (Ithaca, NY: Cornell University Press, 1974). Perhaps as much political as psychological.

Christine Gallant, *Blake and the Assimilation of Chaos* (Princeton, NJ: Princeton University Press, 1978). A full-scale Jungian reading, which nevertheless does not eschew other dimensions to the work.

Diana Hume George, *Blake and Freud* (Ithaca, NY: Cornell University Press, 1980). '[A] new kind of psychoanalytic literary criticism, as distinct from a contribution to psychoanalytic theory.'

Diana Hume George, 'Malignant Fires and the Chain of Jealousy: Blake's Treatment of the Oedipal Conflict', *Hartford Studies in Literature*, 11 (1979). A short and approachable essay.

William Dennis Horn, 'William Blake and the Problematic of the Self', in *William Blake and the Moderns*, ed. Robert Bertholf and Annette Levitt (Albany, NY: State University of New York Press, 1982). Kant, Freud, Lacan, Bloom and De Man ... a stimulating mixture.

Elaine M. Kauvar, 'Blake's Interpretation of Dreams: "Mental Forms Creating"', *American Imago*, 41 (1984). An essential piece of psychological exploration.

Brenda S. Webster, *Blake's Prophetic Psychology* (London: Macmillan, 1983). Challenging and thought-provoking.

SEXUAL POLITICS

There is a very complicated debate around the role of sexuality in Blake, which has engaged writers from very different ends of the political spectrum, and some of which is represented in the present volume. The question of what is and what is not a feminist reading continues to be a strenuously contested site, as the texts listed below also evidence:

David Aers, 'William Blake and the Dialectics of Sex', *ELH*, 44 (1977).

Susan Fox, 'The Female as Metaphor in William Blake's Poetry', in *Essential Articles for the Study of William Blake 1970–1984*, ed. Nelson Hilton (Hamden, CT: Archon, 1986). An extremely clear and helpful contribution to the debate, revealing 'a serious self-contradiction in [Blake's] vision of the universe'.

Norma A. Greco, 'Blake's "The Little Girl Lost": An Initiation Into Womanhood', *Colby Library Quarterly*, 19 (1983). As with others in this list, this is naturally a psychological reading as well as being one which looks closely at issues of sexuality.

Norma A. Greco, 'Mother Figures in Blake's *Songs of Innocence* and the Female Will', *Romanticism Past and Present*, 10 (1986).

Anne K. Mellor, 'Blake's *Songs of Innocence and of Experience*: A Feminist Perspective', *Nineteenth-Century Studies*, 2 (1988). A strong essay by one of the leading feminist critics.

Alicia Ostriker, 'Desire Gratified and Ungratified: William Blake and Sexuality', in *Essential Articles for the Study of William Blake 1970–1984*, ed. Nelson Hilton (Hamden, CT: Archon, 1986).

David Punter, 'Blake, Trauma and the Female', *New Literary History*, 15 (Spring 1984).

Margaret Storch, 'Blake and Women: "Nature's Cruel Holiness"', *American Imago*, 38 (1981). In Blake, 'women are benevolent only if they are under male domination'.

FURTHER SUGGESTIONS

Modern criticism of Blake is, above all things, diverse. The books and essays listed below all repay close reading and raise a variety of issues in the contemporary critical context:

Hazard Adams, 'Blake and the Philosophy of Literary Form', *New Literary History*, 5 (1973).

Hazard Adams, 'Synecdoche and Method', in *Critical Paths: Blake and the Argument of Method*, ed. Dan Miller, Mark Bracher and Donald Ault (Durham and London: Duke University Press, 1987). Adams claims here to be developing a 'neo-Blakean critical method'.

Arthur Adamson, 'Structure and Meaning in Blake's "The Mental Traveller"', *Mosaic*, 7 (1974). On the poem's theory of history.

Donald Ault, *Visionary Physics: Blake's Response to Newton* (Chicago: University of Chicago Press, 1974).

Leslie Brisman, *Romantic Origins* (Ithaca, NY: Cornell University Press, 1978). Contains an intricately worked chapter, 'Re: Generation in Blake', on the problem of origins and narrative.

Leopold Damrosch, Jr, *Symbol and Truth in Blake's Myth* (Princeton, NJ: Princeton University Press, 1980). 'No art could be further than Blake's from the familiar maxim that poetry should exhibit organic form'; this is the starting-point for a wide-ranging and judicious book.

Robert N. Essick, *Blake and the Language of Adam* (Oxford: Clarendon Press, 1989). Extremely close reading of the roles and fates of language in Blake's texts.

Zachary Leader, *Reading Blake's 'Songs'* (London: Routledge, 1981).

F.R. Leavis, 'Justifying One's Valuation of Blake', in *William Blake: Essays in Honour of Sir Geoffrey Keynes*, ed. Morton D. Paley and Michael Phillips (Oxford: Clarendon Press, 1973).

David Punter, *Blake, Hegel and Dialectic* (Amsterdam: Rodopi, 1982).

David Punter, 'Blake: Social Relations of Poetic Form', *Literature and History*, 8 (1982).

David Punter, 'The Sign of Blake', *Criticism*, 26 (Autumn 1985). An attempt to engage with the meaning of the critical investment in Blake.

Robert E. Simmons, '*Urizen*: The Symmetry of Fear', in *Blake's Visionary Forms Dramatic*, ed. David V. Erdman and John E. Grant (Princeton, NJ: Princeton University Press, 1970).

Tadeusz Sławek, *The Outline Shadow: Phenomenology, Grammatology, Blake* (Katowice: University of Silesia Press, 1985). This book owes a great deal to deconstruction; but it also uniquely engages with the different tradition of phenomenological criticism.

Ronald Clayton Taylor, 'Semantic Structure and the Temporal Modes of Blake's Prophetic Verse', *Language and Style*, 12 (1979).

Notes on Contributors

David Aers is Professor of Literature in the English Department of Duke University. His publications range from studies of late medieval culture to ones on romanticism; they include *Chaucer, Langland and the Creative Imagination* (London, 1980); *Community, Gender and Individual Identity 1360–1430* (London, 1988) and (ed.) *Culture and History 1350–1600* (Brighton, 1992).

Gavin Edwards has taught at the Universities of Sydney and Gothenburg and at St David's University College, Lampeter. His publications include *George Crabbe's Poetry on Border Land* (1990) and (ed.) *George Crabbe: Selected Poems* (1991).

Jean Hagstrum is Professor Emeritus at Northwestern University, Illinois. He was a Senior Mellon Fellow at the National Humanities Centre in North Carolina from 1985 to 1987, and subsequently Fellow of the Rockefeller centre on Lake Como. His publications include *Esteem Enlivened by Desire: The Couple from Homer to Shakespeare* (Chicago, 1992).

Laura Haigwood is Assistant Professor of English at Saint Mary's College, Notre Dame, Indiana. Her recent publications include 'Gender-to-Gender Anxiety and Influence in Robert Browning's *Men and Women*' and 'Oedipal Revolution in the *Lyrical Ballads*'.

Nelson Hilton teaches at the University of Georgia. He is a founding member of the Santa Cruz Blake Study Group and long-time review editor for *Blake: An Illustrated Quarterly*. His most recent publication is *Lexis Complexes: Literary Interventions*.

W.J.T. Mitchell is Gaylord Distinguished Service Professor of Art and Literature at the University of Chicago, and editor of *Critical Inquiry*. His publications include *Blake's Composite Art*, *Iconology* and *Picture Theory* (forthcoming).

David Simpson is Chair of the English Department at the University of Colorado at Boulder. His publications include *Irony and Authority in Romantic Poetry* (1989), *Wordsworth and the Figurings of the Real* (1982), *Fetishism and Imagination: Dickens, Melville, Conrad* (1982), *The Politics of American English* (1985), *Wordsworth's Historical Imagination* (1987) and *Romanticism, Nationalism and the Revolt Against Theory*.

Brenda Webster is a freelance writer, critic and translator, and President of PEN West. She has written two critical books, *Yeats: A Psychoanalytic Study* (Stanford, 1972) and *Blake's Prophetic Psychology* (London, 1983). In 1994 she published an edition of her artist mother's journal, *Hungry for Light: The Journal of Ethel Schwabacher* (Indiana) and a first novel, *Sins of the Mothers*.

Index

215